Paying the Tab

Paying the Tab

THE ECONOMICS OF ALCOHOL POLICY

Philip J. Cook

PRINCETON UNIVERSITY PRESS

PRINCETON AND OXFORD

Published by Princeton University Press, 41 William Street, Princeton, New Jersey 08540
In the United Kingdom: Princeton University Press, 3 Market Place, Woodstock,
Oxfordshire OX20 1SY

Library of Congress Cataloging-in-Publication Data

Cook, Philip J., 1946–
Paying the tab : the economics of alcohol policy / Philip J. Cook.
p.   cm.
Includes bibliographical references and index.
ISBN-13: 978-0-691-12520-6 (hardcover : alk. paper)
1. Alcoholism—Government policy—United States. 2. Alcoholism—United States—
Prevention. 3. Alcoholic beverages—Taxation—United States. I. Title.
HV5292.C615   2007
363.4'10973—dc22   2006036836

British Library Cataloging-in-Publication Data is available

This book has been composed in Sabon

Printed on acid-free paper.

press.princeton.edu

Printed in the United States of America

10 9 8 7 6 5 4 3 2

To Judy

Contents

viii • Contents

List of Illustrations

Preface

IN MY LIFETIME no president has thought to declare a "war on alcohol." There is no perception of an alcohol-abuse crisis. Indeed, it's hard to imagine the anti-drinking fervor that my grandparents experienced in the early decades of the twentieth century. In Western culture today, drinking is intrinsic to the good life, especially for the more youthful, prosperous, and better educated among us. In the academic community, for example, it's unusual to find someone between the ages of twenty and seventy who abstains except for a specific medical reason, and wine is held in far higher regard than, say, sugary sodas.

But of course the problematic nature of alcohol remains, even if it is not widely condemned. Alcohol abuse is all too prevalent, and an endemic source of harm in the form of injuries, early death, unfulfilled potential, family strife, crime, and violence. Like most everyone else, I have colleagues, relatives, and friends whose lives have been cut short or severely diminished as a result of alcohol abuse—their own, or someone else's. These sad stories add up across the population to a considerable sum, whether accounted in terms of the public health or economic losses—in effect a large "bar tab" that is broadly shared and reduces our standard of living. The cumulative effect is much greater than the toll from illicit drugs. A "war" is not called for, but alcohol surely deserves our serious attention.

What I've learned after years of researching these matters is that the "tab" is much larger than it needs to be or should be. An important remedy has been neglected—the systematic regulation and taxation of the industry. As a result, beer and liquor have become too cheap and readily available, a big change from the 1950s and 1960s that facilitates excess consumption. My aspiration for this book is to make the case for reviving alcohol-control policy to help right the balance between the two sides of this problematic commodity, conveying as it does such harm and such pleasure.

My focus throughout is on the United States. Alcohol abuse is a worldwide problem, and the control of alcohol has engendered an extensive international literature, particularly in Britain, Ontario, and the Nordic countries, as well as the World Health Organization and other international agencies. I draw on that literature in developing the intellectual framework, but my data and the specifics of the policy discussions are more narrowly cast.

My understanding of alcohol policy owes a great deal to an exceptional opportunity I had early in my career. In 1978, I was invited to join an expert panel of the National Academy of Sciences, which was charged by Congress with assessing alternative strategies for reducing the burden of alcohol abuse. At the time my only knowledge of alcohol was personal— I had no systematic knowledge of the alcohol-abuse problem or the policy response to this problem, or of what the scholarly literature had to offer. I was invited to join the panel in the hope that an outsider might bring a fresh perspective. As a result, I was fortunate enough to receive an informal tutorial from some of the giants of the field—Wolfgang Schmidt, Robin Room, Dan Beauchamp, Tom Schelling, and others. The chair of the panel, Mark Moore, encouraged me to conduct original research on the effects of alcohol taxes on drinking and consequences, a project which became my first publication in the area, and indeed the first analysis of a type that has now become commonplace. The research that has accumulated since then, mine and many others', provides the evidence base for the policy conclusions in this book. The intellectual framework owes a good deal to those discussions we had three decades ago under Mark Moore's inspired leadership.

Since the publication of the panel report in 1981, much of my continuing research in this area has been with colleagues. George Tauchen and I collaborated on two papers in the early 1980s that introduced panel-regression methods to evaluate policy changes in the health-behavior field. Michael Moore and I worked together for a dozen years in a fruitful and enjoyable collaboration that began in 1990 when I spent a semester at Duke's Fuqua School of Business. (We've also shared some bottles of good wine—usually his—along the way.) My doctoral student, Bethany Peters, wrote her dissertation on the effects of drinking on productivity, and chapter 8 of this volume borrows from our joint work, first distributed as a National Bureau of Economic Research working paper.

Writing this book has been on my agenda for quite a few years, and I thank Princeton University Press's Peter Dougherty for his patience and encouragement during that long latency. The opportunity to actually write it finally came as the result of my good fortune in winning an Investigator Award from the Robert Wood Johnson Foundation.

In doing the research, I've relied to a considerable extent on assistance from Duke students. First and foremost has been Rebecca Hutchinson, who did the statistical programming on NESARC (National Epidemiologist Survey on Alcohol and Related Conditions) data and helped in myriad other ways. Her can-do attitude carried us through many a challenge. Others who helped along the way include Samantha Abzug, Ellen Goodwin, Michelle Madeley, Robert Malme, Chinmay Shah, Paul Stahle, and Swee San Tan.

I am also grateful to those who provided me with data and source materials, including Janice Brown, Charlie Clotfelter, Gerhard Gmel, Mike Grossman, Laurel Hourani, Sara Markowitz, Inas Rashad, and Robin Room.

Kristin Goss read through an early draft and in her diplomatic fashion helped me bring it into focus. Dan Beauchamp provided helpful comments on chapter 9. I also thank my editor, Tim Sullivan, for his valuable guidance on structuring the argument. Various friends and family members have weighed in on the question of the best title, and I hasten to say that there were many good ideas but inevitably only one slot, which was filled by Matthew Leeberg's suggestion with an assist from Jens Ludwig.

Making the case for a stronger alcohol-control policy faces a real marketing challenge. Unlike treatment, where the success stories always have a face, those individuals whose lives or livelihoods would be saved by alcohol control will never be identified. There are no heartwarming stories about the girl next door who was not raped, or the classmate who was not paralyzed by a drunken driver, or the uncle who did not become alcohol dependent. The individual stories must be imagined. But it is my hope that the big picture emerges from the history, theory, and statistics presented here.

Paying the Tab

CHAPTER 1

Introduction

We all pay the tab for cheap drinks.[1]

EXCESS DRINKING IS A problem for millions of Americans and their families. It is also a problem for the communities in which they live, degrading public health and safety and ultimately lowering our standard of living. The public response to this problem has varied over time, but always with some mix of two general approaches. On the one hand are efforts, both public and private, to reduce excess drinking directly—education, persuasion, counseling, treatment, sanctions of various sorts. On the other hand are measures to reduce excess drinking by restricting availability or raising the price—licensing, product and sales regulation, liability rules, taxes, partial or complete bans. Both approaches can be effective. Yet during the last half century the public policy "mix" has largely neglected the second approach.

In fact, the post–World War II history has seen a long downward drift in prices (adjusted for inflation) together with a general weakening of other restrictions on availability, all without much discussion of what is being lost. To the extent that alcohol has had any prominence on the policy agenda, it has been primarily in connection with drunk driving. A grassroots movement led by Mothers Against Drunk Driving (MADD) and other such groups has succeeded in promoting tougher laws and stronger enforcement. As one consequence of this movement, Congress adopted a national minimum drinking age of twenty-one in 1984 primarily in the hope of reducing the fatal accident rate for teen drivers. These efforts have been quite successful in reducing drunk driving for both teens and adults. However, the "alcohol problem" is by no means limited to the highways. Our policy portfolio should respond to the full array of harms. The regulation of price and availability—alcohol-control measures—has great albeit neglected potential in that role.

Fortunately there has been enough interest in alcohol-control measures to support a research program by economists, epidemiologists, and other scientists. We now have a quarter century of research results on the causal effects of alcohol-control measures on drinking, abuse, and a wide array of consequences. This research has helped develop the case that the price and availability (both commercial and social) of alcohol affect the amount of alcohol-related harm to society. Although researchers in this area are often labeled "neo-prohibitionists" by industry spokespersons, in fact our work is more closely aligned with the alcohol-beverage-control movement of the 1930s that was the successor to Prohibition. The evidence suggests that higher excise taxes and some additional restrictions on marketing would save lives and pass the cost-benefit test. The goal is not prohibition, but moderation.

A Brief History

What is the problem to which alcohol policy is responding? The predominant answer has changed over the course of American history, and policy choices have followed. The first Congress met at a time (the 1790s) when heavy drinking was the norm. Alexander Hamilton, our first Secretary of the Treasury, advocated a domestic whiskey tax to raise revenue, noting that if it also promoted moderation in drinking, that would be all to the good. During the nineteenth century, alcohol became the matter for a broad moral crusade, which waxed and waned and waxed again. By the 1880s, the Women's Christian Temperance Union was denouncing alcohol itself (rather than the abuse of alcohol) as the problem, and actually persuaded most of the state legislatures to mandate WCTU-approved textbooks that labeled alcohol a poison and described at length its various deleterious effects on the body. Advocacy groups of that day also denounced the industry that supplied alcohol, saying that it lured working men into spending money on drinking and other vices, depriving their families of desperately needed necessities. The Anti-Saloon League eventually led the way to adoption of the prohibition amendment, implemented in 1920. But this Great Experiment proved a considerable disappointment. After a dozen years of ambivalent enforcement by federal and state governments, coupled with corruption and gang violence, most of the public and particularly the business community became disillusioned. The new voice of reason, led by business tycoon John D. Rockefeller Jr. and other plutocrats, favored repeal of national prohibition, to be replaced by state alcoholic-beverage-control systems and taxes that would, they believed, create an orderly legal market that was conducive to moderate drinking.

Along with repeal, the 1930s also saw the beginnings of an entirely different conception of the alcohol problem (Moore 1990). The founding and great success of Alcoholics Anonymous, coupled with well-publicized research by Yale scientist Edward Jellinek and the efforts of the National Council of Alcoholism, engendered a new "scientific" understanding. The locus of the problem was shifted from alcohol itself to that small fraction of the population who were vulnerable to alcoholism. Most people, it was thought, could drink safely and moderately—for them alcohol was not a problem—but for those relative few who were vulnerable, drinking posed a great risk. Given this new definition of the alcohol problem, the logical policy solution was not to control supply of the substance, but rather to help the unlucky ones who couldn't handle it. Alcoholism was the problem, alcoholism was a disease, and the right response was to encourage abstinence by those so afflicted. The liquor industry gladly bought into this perspective, since it exonerated their product from blame. Alcoholism research and treatment were established as national health priorities with the creation of the National Institute on Alcoholism and Alcohol Abuse (NIAAA) in 1970.

The alcoholism agenda is worthy but narrow. Programs to identify and treat individuals who have become dependent on alcohol inevitably miss a large portion of youthful abuse, drunk driving, alcohol-fueled domestic violence, and other problems, and bypass important opportunities for the prevention of alcohol dependence and abuse. Even Dr. Jellinek, the godfather of the alcoholism movement, recognized the importance of the social context; he suggested that whether someone with an innate propensity for alcoholism would actually develop the disease depends in part on whether he was living in a wet or dry environment. Thus, an effective prevention program must address the community's involvement in alcohol, not just the involvement of those members who have become dependent. In support of this perspective, an international group of researchers began writing about alcohol as a public health problem during the 1960s. The leaders included Milton Terris and Robin Room in the United States, Griffith Edwards in Britain, Wolfgang Schmidt and Robert Popham in Ontario, Kettil Bruun and Ole-Jørgen Skog in Scandinavia, and others. A number of these pioneers published a brief, elegant book in 1975 with sponsorship from the World Health Organization, making the case for a population-based, evidence-driven, multifaceted, pragmatic approach (Bruun et al. 1975). In the United States, a similar case was made in the report *Alcohol and Public Policy* by an expert panel assembled by the National Academy of Sciences under the leadership of Harvard public policy professor Mark H. Moore. The report was subtitled *Beyond the Shadow of Prohibition* (Moore and Gerstein 1981), but it could just as well have been subtitled *Beyond the Shadow of Alcoholism*.

A comprehensive community-oriented approach continues to be touted by the public health community, but perhaps with more success in Ontario and northern Europe than in the United States. Here public attention came to focus more narrowly on the particular concern of drunk driving. During the 1980s, MADD emerged as a force to be reckoned with by judges and legislatures, advocating effectively for the sensible position that DUI (driving under the influence) was a crime that should be taken more seriously by law enforcement and the courts. One important sidebar to this effort was a law establishing a national minimum drinking age of twenty-one, which Congress, moved by evidence on drunk driving fatalities caused by teenagers, accomplished in 1984. Since then the alcohol "problem" has been equated in most public discourse with drunk driving and underage drinking; whatever political energy exists behind alcohol control has focused on these issues. The fate of alcohol control contrasts markedly with the recent success of advocates promoting tobacco control and taxation.

Tobacco Control

In an era where the public is generally hostile to tax increases, the tobacco tax has become fair game for legislatures around the country. In 2002, for instance, New York State raised its tax to $1.50 per pack, and New York City added another $1.50, up from just 8 cents. Since then, the New York street vendors who import their packs (illegally) from lower-tax areas are known as the "$5 men," in reference to the price they charge; remarkably, it is a multiple of the *legal* price just a few years earlier. Other jurisdictions have joined in the tax-raising jamboree. Between 2000 and 2005, forty-two states and the District of Columbia enacted sixty-three cigarette-tax increases, with nineteen states exceeding $1 per pack.[2] Besides the obvious attraction of bringing in revenue, these taxes are touted as improving the public health by encouraging confirmed smokers to quit or cut back, and by discouraging youths from developing the habit in the first place. These claims do encounter some skepticism. Indeed, it wasn't so long ago that most savvy commentators insisted that smokers' addiction would survive any sort of price increase, and adolescents would always find a way to experiment. But the evidence that price matters when it comes to smoking, accumulated over many years of careful study, is compelling. Death and taxes are both inevitable, but in this case there is a trade-off (Phelps 1988).

Meanwhile, alcohol taxes have received much less attention from state legislatures. State legislatures raised alcohol excise taxes just eight times during the period 2002 to 2005, and all of these increases were modest in magnitude.[3] Why the difference with tobacco? True, fewer people die from drinking than smoking each year, but the alcohol-related death count is still considerable, on the order of 75,000 to 100,000, as compared with 435,000 deaths due to tobacco (Mokdad, et al. 2004; Midanik et al. 2004).[4] Most of these drinking deaths are the result of injury, taking a heavy toll on children and young adults. And unlike most smoking deaths, a sizable share of the drinking deaths involve innocent bystanders—victims of drunk drivers, victims of arguments transformed into deadly assaults due to intoxication, victims who are children abused or neglected by alcoholic parents.

Furthermore, the evidence supporting the public health benefits of increased alcohol taxes is every bit as strong as for cigarette taxes. An increase in the average prices of beer or liquor induced by a tax increase would reduce per capita alcohol consumption, the incidence of alcohol abuse by youths and adults, and the rate of accidents and crimes resulting from abuse. Over the long run, higher alcohol prices would reduce the prevalence of alcoholism and organ damage associated with chronic excess consumption. As in the case of tobacco, a small increase in tax would have a small effect on the public health, a large increase in tax a larger effect. These conclusions are solidly grounded in the evidence compiled by economists and public health researchers.

The divergence between alcohol and tobacco policy is not just for excise taxes, but for other regulations as well. In the late 1990s, at the insistence of the state attorneys general, the tobacco industry agreed to eliminate vending machines and restrict marketing practices in a number of ways. The National Association for Stock Car Auto Racing (NASCAR) Winston Cup series has changed its name and tobacco companies no longer are allowed to sponsor cars and drivers; meanwhile, NASCAR allowed liquor companies to serve as sponsors for the first time in 2004.

Why, then, have legislators pushed up tobacco taxes and tightened controls while neglecting alcohol policy? It is no doubt relevant politically that over twice as many Americans drink as smoke, and the drinkers are as a group more influential politically—they tend to be better educated, richer, and less ambivalent. (Most smokers say that they want to quit. Most drinkers express no such aspiration.) Beyond that political reality, the public health argument for seeking a reduction in drinking has been confused in recent years by evidence that drinking is not all bad. Alcohol appears to be a potent anticholesterol drug that, "taken" in moderation in middle age, may actually extend life. On the other hand, smoking in any amount at any age is harmful. And finally, the public and the legislators they elect are not necessarily reading the latest research on alcohol price effects. Ordinary people (not including economists) may remember that we tried national Prohibition a while back and it proved disastrous. Does it make sense that an increase in taxes and tighter regulations would succeed where a total ban failed?

The Evidence

In what follows, I make an effort to explain the nature of this research evidence in some detail, and in a number of instances provide new results. Because it is not possible to run experiments with alcohol-control measures, making reliable causal inferences is a challenge. Much of the evidence that is most persuasive comes from analyzing the "quasi-experiment" generated by states' changing their policies. For example, the effect of the minimum drinking age law on highway fatality rates can be estimated by comparing changes in youthful highway fatalities in states that changed their minimum with states that didn't; between 1970 and 1988 there were scores of such changes, which together provide the basis for reliable inferences about what difference minimum age laws can make.

The goal here is to get beyond intuition. There is a powerful tendency to assess social-science research findings on the basis of prior beliefs, since in a sense everyone's an expert. If we are already inclined to believe a new research result, then we welcome it as support for our views. If it contradicts our prior beliefs, then we feel free to ignore it; after all, it may be based on faulty methods or poor data, and in any event it will probably be contradicted by another social scientist in the near future. In my experience most people's intuition tells them that prices and regulations simply don't matter, or don't matter much, when it comes to drinking—that drinkers decide whether and how much and in what circumstances to drink for reasons that are scarcely affected by prices and availability. A summary of research results is not going to persuade most people to abandon this intuition, since that would require that they do the hard work of reinterpreting their personal observations. For that reason I aspire to provide enough detail about data and research methods that it cannot be dismissed too easily.

The evidence provides one key argument for putting alcohol control and taxation back on the policy agenda. But the evidence on what works in reducing alcohol-related problems is not a sufficient guide. Policy choices do and should reflect multiple objectives. Improving health and safety are surely on the list, but so are other concerns; our Declaration of Independence sums it up as "life, liberty, and the pursuit of happiness," rather than as just "life." America's history is full of struggle over finding the right balance among conflicting principles when it comes to alcohol policy as in much else. The policy assessment here is explicit about the important values at stake. For adults, the principle that deserves considerable weight in assessments of alcohol control is consumer sovereignty, which is to say respect for individual preferences. Using government powers to compel adults to change their behavior requires strong justification, and usually an adequate justification requires reason to believe that the behavior harms others. Liberty from government interference is also desirable for adolescents, but for that age group it is easier to make the case that they need protection from self-destructive choices. Reasonable perspectives range from the libertarian's to the public health advocate's, a spectrum of increasing value placed on life as opposed to liberty. These and other fundamental differences of opinion are not going to be resolved by any amount of research, but it is informative to lay out the arguments. By most definitions of the public interest, alcohol-control measures have an important role to play.

A ROAD MAP

Understanding modern policy debates over alcohol regulation requires some understanding of how those debates have played out in American history. I begin with a chapter on the history of the federal excises and alcohol regulation through Prohibition and Repeal. That whiskey tax promoted by Alexander Hamilton was the first inland revenue measure of our republic, and it was even more contentious then than now, leading to armed rebellion against federal "tyranny." A failure the first time around, it was reinstated later and was an important source of funding for the Union during the Civil War and even more so thereafter. It was only replaced as the dominant source of domestic revenue when the Sixteenth Amendment established the constitutionality of the federal income tax, making it possible not only to finance World War I but to continue financing the federal government during national Prohibition—which of course ended all tax collections from alcohol. Thus, the Sixteenth Amendment made the Eighteenth (Prohibition) feasible. Prohibition of course did not end drinking, but it did lead to a substantial reduction, especially in the consumption of beer. Although Prohibition was in that sense a success, it was surely a failure politically. There was little enthusiasm for enforcing it, and after a dozen years it was repealed through yet another amendment. What followed was the invention of the modern-day state alcohol-control apparatus, much influenced by the efforts of John D. Rockefeller Jr. to develop a rational policy that would moderate drinking without the corruption and violence of the Prohibition era.

In fact there was little increase in drinking through the 1930s, so the alcohol-control effort appears to have been successful—although the Great Depression of that era gets much of the credit. But with the founding of Alcoholics Anonymous and its development into perhaps the most successful voluntary organization of our time, attention shifted to the science of alcoholism. Instead of the broad population-based prevention approach of taxes and controls, the new focus was identifying and treating alcoholics. Although AA has remained the predominant "treatment" for alcoholism, federal funding for research and medical treatment expanded and became institutionalized with the creation of NIAAA. The research is now producing payoffs in the form of drugs that reduce craving and help people who are inclined to go on the wagon. But no matter how effective, alcoholism treatment now and in the future will have limited scope relative to the full array of alcohol problems. The reason is the "preventive paradox"—that while problems are concentrated among long-time heavy drinkers who are in enough trouble that they might be persuaded (or coerced) into seeking treatment, the bulk of alcohol-related problems are diffused among the much larger group.

Part II begins with a primer on alcohol and drinking, and then goes on to review the evidence on alcohol control. Chapter 4 describes trends and patterns in drinking in America, with some attention to just how those trends and patterns are estimated. Among the possibly surprising facts: a majority of adults either don't drink at all or drink less than once per month, while the heavy drinkers at the top 10 percent of the distribution account for the bulk of sales and consumption. Greatly over-represented among those heavy drinkers are young adults under age thirty, and especially those of the male persuasion. What the American public is drinking these days is beer—that's the form in which over half the ethanol is imbibed—while liquor is far less popular than it was a generation ago.

The health and social consequences of drinking are what make it worthy of special attention. Alcohol is a complex drug that produces a variety of effects on the body. The most alluring effect is intoxication, but that can and does engender serious lapses of judgment and coordination which in turn lead to injury, crime, violence, unprotected and unplanned sex, embarrassment—not to mention a hangover the next morning. Over the long term a routine of heavy drinking can produce dependence, organ damage, loss of friends and family, and poverty. On the other hand, there is considerable evidence now (still controversial) that light or moderate drinking in middle age actually improves health and extends life expectancy, due to its anticholesterol effect.

The core findings on the effects of alcohol control are presented in chapters 5 through 8. Alcohol sales, drinking, and abuse respond to prices and other controls. Whereas for most people the decision whether to drink is not much affected by cost or availability—there are a number of other influences—for some individuals prices influence the decision of whether to drink. For a larger group, the decision of *how much* to drink is influenced by price and availability. Contrary to conventional wisdom, prices even matter for chronic heavy drinkers with a well-developed habit.

The "bottom line" question is whether alcohol-control measures affect the safety and health consequences of drinking. Researchers have extracted compelling evidence from the frequent changes in state laws to establish the importance of minimum drinking age, taxes, vendor liability, and other regulations. The outcomes of interest here include highway safety, sexually transmitted diseases, liver cirrhosis mortality, and violent crime. Also important is worker productivity, a topic that has proven exceptionally difficult to research. But new results presented here indicate that higher alcohol prices increase the earnings of workers, a finding that John D. Rockefeller Jr. would have had no trouble believing.

Part III turns to an assessment of alcohol-control options in light of some important normative considerations. Higher alcohol taxes would improve health and safety and save lives. But they also impinge on the legitimate enjoyment of alcoholic beverages. John Stuart Mill's "harm principle" provides an important distinction between self-harm and harm to others; his view is that the risks to the drinkers themselves are not sufficient to justify restricting freedom. This argument underpins a focus on "negative externalities," such as the risks posed by a drunk driver to others who share the road with that driver. But many commentators believe that focus is too narrow—that adults and especially youths are prone to ignore the more remote consequences of their actions, and as a result may benefit from a somewhat restrictive government policy. Modern research on "behavioral economics" offers some support for this perspective.

Mill's case for limited government appears to have carried the day. There has been a progressive easing of 1930s-era restrictions on alcohol commerce, most obviously as local jurisdictions that took advantage of local-option laws to stay dry in the early years have now elected to become "wet" for the most part. In addition, the eighteen states that chose to institute a state monopoly over part of the alcohol business have tended toward liberalization. There have also been pronounced trends in industry structure that have influenced production and prices. Most notable is the increasing concentration in production—over half of all beer sold in this country, for example, is now manufactured by a single company. The private industry structure to some extent has been influenced by the concern from the saloon era about preventing too close a connection between manufacturer and outlet. The resulting three-tier system of manufacturer, distributor, and retailer remains in place, although it is being challenged in the courts.

The great variety of government regulations could in principle be evaluated one by one, but it seems clear that the most important and comprehensive possibility is raising taxes on alcoholic beverages. Given the social cost of drinking, higher taxes are readily justified. Critics of this approach point out that taxation is a crude measure that does not distinguish between harmless and harmful consumption. While true, the fact is that more refined interventions leave much of the problem untouched; even if we do adopt (and pay for) tougher measures against drunk driving and domestic violence and so forth, there will remain a worthwhile opportunity to do still more through a general reduction in drinking. The fact that some of the reduction will come out of heart-healthy consumption by middle-aged drinkers is of some concern, but is balanced by other effects on health.

Youths present a special sort of challenge for alcohol regulation. The minimum drinking age has beneficial effects but also unintended consequences, beginning with the fact that it turns millions of our youths into criminals. Enforcing this prohibition has become a priority for colleges, the military, and other authorities, with some success. But it is an uphill battle to effectively limit youthful drinking in an environment that accommodates adult drinking so freely. This is further reason to embrace a more comprehensive strategy.

Alcohol is the source of great enjoyment and also great harm. In the face of this complex challenge, we should take advantage of the full array of cost-effective policy options. The neglect of alcohol-control measures by policymakers during the last few decades is a wasted opportunity to reduce that harm while preserving much of the enjoyment, and thereby improve our collective standard of living.

PART I

Rise and Fall of Alcohol Control

CHAPTER 2

A Brief History of the Supply Side

> This "dreadful example" is now so firmly established that
> it has become a maxim of popular culture, a paradigm of bad
> social policy, and a ritual invocation of opponents of a
> variety of sumptuary laws.
> —Paul Aaron and David Musto,
> *"Temperance and Prohibition in America"*

NATIONAL PROHIBITION, the Noble Experiment of the 1920s, is the most remarkable feature in the long history of American policy toward alcoholic beverages. It involved two amendments to the U.S. Constitution—the Eighteenth, which mandated national prohibition, and the Twenty-first, which repealed it—both ratified quickly and with broad support. The experience with prohibition has had a powerful influence on public discourse. That it failed, and was destined to fail because it sought to "legislate morality," are lessons that have become part of the conventional wisdom. People who now seek to reduce alcohol abuse by advocating controls on supply and higher taxes are vulnerable to the "neoprohibitionist" label, suggesting that they are both moralistic and naïve. Yet those lessons appear to be an overgeneralization from faulty claims about what actually transpired. Getting the history right is an important first step in making progress on regulation of the alcohol beverage industry.

That history has a little-told chapter of the decade following Repeal, when the states adopted a new role of regulating commerce in alcoholic beverages, attempting to find a compromise that would allow the public access to alcoholic beverages without opening the door to excess. Several versions of that compromise were instituted and are still in place today, although the high hopes of 1930s reformers have given way to widespread cynicism about what can be accomplished. The post-War period has seen increasing deregulation in most respects.

Alcohol taxation has a less dramatic history (at least since the Whiskey Insurrection of 1794) than Prohibition but is nonetheless relevant in understanding the context in which tax issues are debated today. Although alcohol taxes may logically serve in place of direct prohibition to reduce consumption and abuse, that sumptuary role has never been prominent.

Rather, alcohol taxes have been imposed in the past, as they are today, for the obvious reason of generating revenue, and in that regard they played a remarkably important role for much of U.S. history.

ALCOHOL EXCISE TAXATION

A tax on liquor was the first internal revenue measure imposed by the first Congress of the United States. The excise tax on distilled spirits was approved in March 1791, and became effective that July.[1] Secretary of Treasury Alexander Hamilton was a strong advocate; he believed that customs duties on imports were not adequate to the task of funding the $2.2 million per year needed to service the national debt (accumulated during the Revolution) and the $600,000 per year required for current government services (Hu 1950, 11). He argued for the liquor tax in particular on the grounds that the demand for liquor tended to be inelastic: "Experience has shown [that luxuries of this kind] lay the strongest hold on the attachment of mankind, which, especially when confirmed by habit, are not easily alienated from them" (11). He also noted that if people did drink less as a result of the tax, the effect would be desirable from the point of view of health and morals. But it was clear that revenue rather than morality was the primary goal.

The tax was controversial from the beginning. Farmers west of the Appalachians were particularly antagonistic, since it fell on their only export to the outside world. Transport via the Mississippi was barred by Spain, so export goods had to travel the costly overland route to the cities of the eastern seaboard. The only economical way for farmers to get their crop to market was in concentrated form, distilled into whiskey (Tachau 1985, 99). Furthermore, the tax collectors had to be paid in cash, and cash was very scarce—indeed, whiskey was the common medium of exchange in remote areas, but whiskey could not be used to pay the whiskey tax (Hu 1950, 19).

Congress soon reduced the tax rate and made other concessions, but widespread evasion and overt resistance continued to be the norm—reminiscent of the American colonists' response to the British Stamp Act. In the four westernmost counties of Pennsylvania, attacks on collectors and compliant farmers became flagrant enough to pose a serious challenge to the untested authority of the national government. Hamilton and Washington mustered 15,000 militia to march on Pittsburgh, where they met no resistance and, ironically, spent enough money to ease the currency shortage (Hu 1950, 29). The show of force helped establish the principle of national government authority. But in fact the tax was not productive. It continued to be expensive to collect, widely evaded, and often lost to embezzlement by collectors (Hu 1950; Boyd 1985). The tax was revoked in 1802 by the Jefferson administration.[2]

After a brief re-imposition during the War of 1812 (repealed in 1817), there was no further recourse to liquor excises or any other internal federal taxes until the Civil War. By that time, spirits production was big business and prices were so low that liquor was used for many purposes besides drinking—a fluid for lamps, bathing, industrial products (Hu 1950, 36). With the war under way, Congress sought new sources of revenue. In 1862, it imposed a tax of 20 cents per proof gallon, raised to 60 cents in 1864 and then to a near-confiscatory $2.00.[3] Following the war, Congress adopted a more considered approach; the rate was lowered to 50 cents in 1868, low enough that there was little incentive for moonshining, and required an adhesive stamp to indicate payment. A large increase in revenue resulted (Hu 1950, 38). The federal licensing system for breweries and distilleries (with an accompanying requirement of detailed recordkeeping) that was established in 1862 was maintained until national prohibition (U.S. Congress 1931, 4).

Corruption flourished following the Civil War, and a particularly innovative form of corruption drove the federal liquor tax upward. Speculators who bought existing whiskey stocks could profit from an increase in the tax if the increase only applied to new production—the resulting increase in retail price would give them a windfall gain. Congress acceded to these investors' interests, raising the tax in 1872 and again in 1875, in both cases with an exemption for existing stocks. The infamous Whiskey Ring was finally broken in 1875, and since then it seems safe to say that investors in the liquor business have not lobbied for higher liquor taxes.

Remarkable from our current perspective is just how important liquor and other alcoholic-beverage taxes were as revenue sources during the period from the Civil War through World War I. The revenue numbers are small by modern standards—$51 million in 1869, up to $247 million in 1916. But the scope of the federal government was such that this revenue constituted a large portion of the total (see fig. 2.1). Every year from 1890 to 1916, alcohol tax revenues exceeded 30 percent of all federal tax revenues and as much as 80 percent of tax revenue from internal sources (Hu 1950, appendix 1). With U.S. entry into World War I, escalating revenue needs led to sharp increases in alcohol tax rates and collections, but caused a still greater increase in other taxes—most notably the new federal income tax, made possible by the Sixteenth Amendment.[4] By fiscal year 1919, just before the imposition of national Prohibition, alcohol tax collections reached an all-time high of $483 million, but that was just 12 percent of total revenues in that year. In a sense, the income tax made Prohibition feasible—the Sixteenth Amendment cleared the way for the Eighteenth.

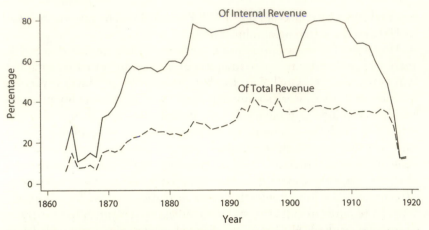

Figure 2.1. Federal Alcohol Exercise Tax as a Percentage of Internal and Total Tax Revenues (1863–1919).
Source: Hu (1950, table x).

NATIONAL PROHIBITION

Prohibition became law in 1920, the culmination of a social movement that had waxed and waned for over a century. In fact, there had been an active temperance movement as far back as 1813 (Warburton 1934). National Prohibition was the culmination of what historians identify as the third wave of this ongoing crusade. The first wave brought some form of prohibition in thirteen states (most of the North) by 1855, but these laws were soon repealed. A second wave of state-level prohibitions came in the 1880s, but only three states were still dry as of 1904. The third wave, starting mostly in the South and West, began a few years later, and ended up engulfing the nation.

The Anti-Saloon League proved the most politically effective organization working for prohibition. It was a nonpartisan, single-issue activist group, with support coming primarily from Protestant evangelical churches and the business community (Aaron and Musto 1981, 156). Its initial successes were persuading state legislatures to adopt a local option, whereby each community had the right to ban saloons by majority vote. By 1906, 40 percent of the population lived in no-license territory (Warburton 1934, 502). State-level prohibition was also placed on the political agenda, and by 1913, nine states had adopted some degree of prohibition, though generally with laws that allowed the continued sale of beer and wine (Kyvig 2000). In November of that year, the Anti-Saloon League first publicly declared its support for a prohibition amendment. Congress endorsed the amendment in December 1917, which was sent on to the state legislatures for ratification. In just thirteen months, forty-four states had approved, and the Eighteenth Amendment was added to the Constitution (Kyvig 2000, chap 1).[5]

Historians have provided a number of different accounts of how prohibition engendered such broad support (Gusfield 1963; Clark 1976; Morone 2002). It was a moral crusade for many who viewed drinking and the saloons that sold the drinks as the source of a variety of evils. The temperance movement, most notably the Woman's Christian Temperance Union (founded in 1874), had laid the groundwork. It and other such organizations worked to deliver temperance instruction through the churches, and lobbied successfully for laws and regulations requiring the public schools to include the dangers of drinking in their curriculum. "By 1910 a large proportion of the voters had been taught during their early years that alcohol in any form was a poison, that not only spirituous liquors but also beer and wine were dangerous drinks and that their use led to poverty, disease and crime" (Warburton 1934, 502).

Much of the crusade was animated by the public perception of the degrading effects of the saloon on family life, and of the political corruption sponsored by the liquor trade. At a time when most drinking was on-premise, saloons were omnipresent in the cities, located conveniently near the factories so that the working men could spend their pay before going home. Their enticements were not necessarily limited to beer and spirits, but sometimes included prostitution and gambling as well. Carrie Nation's well-publicized ten-year career of "hatcheting" saloons gave vivid representation to the women and children who were viewed as the ultimate victims of these dens of iniquity. (Nation, who got her start in Kansas in 1900, once described herself as "a bulldog running along at the feet of Jesus, barking at what he doesn't like.")[6] Most often saloons were "tied houses" that served only the products of the brewer or distiller that owned them, and at the behest of the owner engaged in promotion to encourage heavy drinking. The industry routinely sought to circumvent or change local regulations by playing an active role in politics and corrupting local officials. Prohibition was embraced by many middle-class activists who viewed it as another of the reforms needed to make government more honest and democratic, and to improve the lives of poor families; by that account, it was an integral part of the Progressive movement (Timberlake 1963).[7]

Although support for temperance and prohibition was strongest in rural areas, it received vital help from prominent members of the business community, many of whom believed that "a sober, temperate worker was more productive, stable, and happier" (Burnham 1968, 54). Indeed, businesses sometimes made abstention a requirement of employment for the sake of reducing industrial and transportation accidents. As late as 1915, with prohibition in clear sight, the liquor industry tried to blacklist forty-nine American firms, including railroads and manufacturing concerns, which had barred employees from drinking while on duty (Fosdick and Scott 1933, 148). Yale economist Irving Fisher, a prominent academic supporter of prohibition, noted years later that "All of us know that industrial efficiency was one of the chief reasons for Prohibition. Frederick W. Taylor, the chief apostle of Scientific Management, favored Prohibition and predicted its coming on just these grounds" (Fisher 1927, 158).

National Prohibition was imposed in stages. As more and more states adopted some version of prohibition, Congress moved to protect them from interstate shipments of alcohol with the Webb-Kenyon Act of 1913, and then the tougher Reed "bone-dry" Amendment of 1917. (By that time, twenty-six states, including a majority of the U.S. population, had adopted prohibition; U.S. Congress 1931, 5). With the U.S. entry into World War I in that year, Congress adopted the Food Control Law, forbidding the manufacture of distilled spirits. It closed breweries in September 1918, and then imposed prohibition of any sale of liquor, which went into effect on July 1, 1919 (Dills and Miron 2003). Such measures were viewed as necessities of wartime mobilization, but the war also engendered support for sacrifice and a rejection of all things German, not the least of which was beer (Kyvig 2000, 10). Congress finally enacted the National Prohibition Act, popularly known as the Volstead Act, to implement the Eighteenth Amendment (over President Wilson's veto), with the effective date of January 16, 2000.

The Amendment stated that "the manufacture, sale, or transportation of intoxicating liquors within, the importation thereof into, or the exportation thereof from the United States and all territory subject to the jurisdiction thereof for beverage purposes is hereby prohibited." The term "intoxicating liquors" was a matter of some debate, with the particular question of whether beer and even wine might be excluded from the ban. But the Volstead Act, which was drafted by the Anti-Saloon League, banned all beverages containing more than one-half of 1 percent alcohol, which is to say all alcoholic beverages (Kyvig 2000). Section 3 of Title II of the Volstead Act stated that "all of the provisions of this Act shall be liberally construed to the end that the use of intoxicating liquor as a beverage may be prevented" (U.S. Congress 1931, 8–9).

True to the wording of the Eighteenth Amendment, though, the Volstead Act banned only manufacture and sale, while permitting purchase, possession, and consumption of legally acquired alcohol.[8] Any drinker with foresight and resources could have filled his liquor cabinet in, say, 1916, and continued to drink legally thereafter from his own stock. Also permitted was home production of wine and hard cider for personal use.[9]

Unsurprisingly, sales of grape juice and concentrates soared in the 1920s; apparently buyers were undeterred by the warning labels on some containers stating: "After dissolving the brick [of grape juice concentrate] in a gallon of water, do not place the liquid in the jug away in the cupboard for twenty days, because then it would turn into wine" (Binkley 1930, 108). Physicians could prescribe alcohol for medicinal purposes, although in 1921 Congress limited the amount to one pint of spirits every ten days, despite the testimony of physicians and pharmacists concerning the medical benefits of drinking (Burnham 1968, 31).[10]

In practice these legal sources supplied only a small portion of the drinking during the Prohibition era of the 1920s. Far more important were several illegal sources: diversions from production of alcohol for industrial use, international smuggling, and illegal production. By 1930, illegal distilleries were the main source of liquor, generally a high-quality product. The bulk of this was not the Appalachian moonshine that had been produced since 1791. Some of the Prohibition-era distilleries were comparable in scale to the legal distilleries of the pre-Volstead era, and were located in or near cities (U.S. Congress 1931, 29). The best liquor available was that smuggled in from Canada and from ships anchored on "Rum Row" in the Atlantic, beyond the twelve-mile limit of U.S. jurisdiction. By the late 1920s, one million gallons of Canadian liquor per year, 80 percent of that nation's greatly expanded output, made its way into the United States (Kyvig 2000, 21). Al Capone, the most famous of the bootleggers, explained that "Prohibition is a business. All I do is supply a public demand" (Burnham 1968, 26).

The flow of liquor was facilitated by the lack of interest on the part of the Harding and Coolidge administrations in enforcing the Volstead Act. Enforcement responsibility was given to the Treasury Department, with expenditures divided about evenly between the Prohibition Unit of the Bureau of Internal Revenue and the Coast Guard. Over half a million persons were convicted of federal law violations, but the typical penalty was just a small fine (Warburton 1934, 506). The states, which were provided by the Eighteenth Amendment with concurrent jurisdiction in enforcement, were for the most part missing in action (Burnham 1968, 57). At least until congressional reforms of 1927, the federal enforcement effort was staffed through the spoils system, poorly organized, and prone to corruption and malfeasance (U.S. Congress 1931, 14; Aaron and Musto 1981, 158).

The reformers and moralists, who had high hopes for national Prohibition, were disappointed. It did not succeed in converting America to a nation of teetotalers. What's more, the illicit liquor trade engendered considerable corruption and violence. John D. Rockefeller Jr., who had been a supporter of the Anti-Saloon League, switched sides, lamenting the failure of Prohibition to win over public opinion: "That this had not been the result, but rather that drinking has generally increased; that the speakeasy has replaced the saloon, not only unit for unit, but probably twofold if not three-fold; that a vast array of lawbreakers has been recruited and financed on a colossal scale" (Kyvig 2000, 152).

The most effective organization working to ease prohibition, and, beginning in 1927, for outright repeal, was the Association Against the Prohibition Amendment. It was led by Pierre S. du Pont, retired chairman of General Motors, who, like Rockefeller, saw prohibition as a costly failure. Du Pont solicited other millionaires to the cause on the basis that an end to Prohibition would restore alcohol-excise revenues and save them huge amounts in corporate and personal income taxes (Aaron and Musto 1981, 166). The Women's Organization for National Prohibition Reform also formed to campaign for an end to prohibition, at least in its hardline Volstead form. The Women's Organization convened in 1930 and produced a unanimous declaration, which said in part:

> We are convinced that National Prohibition, wrong in principle, has been equally disastrous in consequences in the hypocrisy, the corruption, the tragic loss of life and the appalling increase of crime which have attended the abortive attempt to enforce it; in the shocking effect it has had upon the youth of the nation; in the impairment of constitutional guarantees of individual rights; in the weakening of the sense of solidarity between the citizen and the government which is the only sure basis of a country's strength. (Kyvig 2000, 123).

This list of unfortunate consequences was the usual matter for advocates of repeal, but the introductory phrase "wrong in principle" is an intriguing addition.

Herbert Hoover created the National Commission on Law Observance and Enforcement, commonly known as the Wickersham Commission after its chair, former Attorney General George Wickersham. It issued a report in January 1931 that carefully documented the corruption, crime, widespread drinking, and lack of state effort in enforcing prohibition (U.S. Congress 1931). Most of the Commission members, including Harvard Law School Dean Roscoe Pound, filed individual opinions calling for reform. But Hoover, who had campaigned as a "dry," was inclined to step up enforcement rather than liberalize the law.

Repeal gained support as the economy slid into depression following the stock market crash of October 1929. Restoring the legal alcoholic-beverage industry was widely viewed as an opportunity to generate much-needed jobs and tax revenues. The Democratic National Convention of 1932 came out with a ringing endorsement of repeal, persuading Franklin D. Roosevelt to convert to the cause (Kyvig 2000, 158). Congress adopted a repeal amendment shortly after his election—before he even took office. The amendment specified a ratification procedure which required each state to organize a special convention just for that purpose. The usual procedure of ratification by vote of the state legislatures might have encountered more difficulties, since the legislatures did not fully reflect the growing popular sentiment in support of repeal. In the event, the popular vote to select convention delegates ran heavily in favor in most states—more than 70 percent voted for repeal in half the thirty-nine states that elected a convention in 1933, and a majority in all but two,[11] with the aggregate vote going 3 to 1 in favor—and the amendment was quickly ratified (Harrison and Laine 1936, 230). In anticipation of ratification, Congress modified the Volstead Act to legalize 3.2 beer, resulting in a nationwide celebration of historic dimensions. Something like thirty states had prohibition laws on the books (or in their state constitutions), most of which were soon repealed. The experiment was over.

Lessons of Prohibition

Was Prohibition a failure? Obviously it was a political failure—popular support had largely evaporated by 1932. And it was a failure relative to the unreasonable expectations of temperance-movement advocates. But for our day, the key question is simply whether it succeeded in causing a substantial reduction in drinking and the harms associated with excess drinking. If not, then Prohibition stands as an object lesson in the futility of attempting to change drinking habits by restricting the supply of alcohol. On the other hand, if Prohibition *did* reduce drinking and abuse, then the lesson for our time becomes something like this: Restricting supply is a potentially effective approach to reducing consumption and abuse, but beware of the unintended side effects!

That the actual effects of Prohibition on drinking continue to be debated reflects the fact that while it is known as the noble experiment, it was not a *controlled* experiment. Among the difficulties in doing an evaluation are these:

- National Prohibition was imposed in stages, rather than all at once. The right baseline for any comparison of before and after this experimental intervention is not clear.

- This experiment had the effect of eliminating the best measure normally available of alcohol consumption—tax-paid sales. All sales during Prohibition were off-the-books.

Table 2.1
Trends Possibly Affecting Demand for Alcohol

	1910	1920	1930
Percent of population living in urban areas	45.8	51.4	56.2
Number of college students	332,696	521,754	971,584
Number of registered vehicles	468,000	9,232,000	26,545,000
Number of telephones	7,635,400	13,329,400	20,201,000

Source: U. S. Department of Commerce 1934.

- The intervention was of uncertain strength. Enforcement efforts varied over the period, and differed among states. There were no consistent measures available of the proximate effects of enforcement, as indicated by prices and availability.

- The right specification of the *alternative* to Prohibition is not obvious, and must be spelled out for the sake of the evaluation. For example, an interesting comparison might be to an alternative scenario in which Congress voted down the Prohibition Amendment and reversed the wartime run-up in alcohol excise tax rates, allowing the 1920s to be a time of "normalcy" with respect to alcohol markets. Since our modern-day interest is in the effects of prohibition with a small "p," the alternative scenario might also specify that the states had rescinded their prohibition laws.

- Most important, other factors that influence drinking and the consequences of abuse were not constant during the 1920s. It is easy to identify underlying trends that would have promoted increased drinking in the absence of prohibition. The 1920s was, after all, the Jazz Age, the Flapper Era, the time of relaxed social mores, when popular culture spread quickly through the new media of radio, film, and automobile. It was also a time of rising incomes and demographic change toward greater urbanization. Table 2.1 summarizes some of these trends. In any event, the baseline period (whatever is chosen) does not serve as an adequate control group for the Prohibition experiment.

Despite these various difficulties, there were reputable scholars who took seriously the task of evaluating Prohibition at the time and produced several systematic studies of remarkable quality. Yale economist Irving Fisher authored a series of books that assembled data and arguments, generally in support of the view that Prohibition was benefiting the nation on balance (Fisher 1927, 1928, 1930). But the most persuasive and thorough

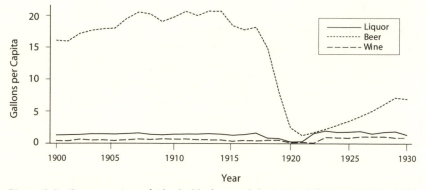

Figure 2.2. Consumption of Alcohol before and during Prohibition (1900–1930). *Source*: Warburton 1932.

account was written by Brookings Institution economist Clark Warburton, who published *The Economic Effects of Prohibition* in 1932.

Warburton and the others analyzed indicators of drinking and its consequences, finding strong evidence that there was less drinking and abuse during the 1920s, and especially the early 1920s, than there had been prior to World War I. Warburton took as his preferred baseline 1911–1914, just prior to the advent of federal War-related tax increases, production bans, and restrictions on exports to dry states. If we accept his estimates of drinking trends, then the notion (popular then and ever since) that there was somehow more drinking during Prohibition than before can be decisively rejected. Of course, that does not answer the question of the extent to which drinking was reduced relative to what it would have been otherwise, given the underlying cultural, social, and economic trends of the 1920s. Rising incomes and the more permissive culture of the 1920s would likely engender increased per capita consumption in the absence of Prohibition, so the actual decline in consumption speaks still more strongly to the effectiveness of Prohibition.

Table 2.2 provides per capita alcohol-consumption estimates during four periods before and during Prohibition, while figure 2.2 depicts the trends in consumption. The data are taken from Warburton, who triangulated estimates for the Prohibition years (when all sales and consumption were off-the-books) from imputations based on agricultural sources of production, death rates from alcohol-related causes, and arrests for drunkenness. A relatively recent effort generated very similar results based on imputations from death rates, drunkenness arrests, and hospital admissions for alcoholic psychosis (Miron and Zwiebel 1991).

The general picture here is of a sharp drop in alcohol consumption during the War, a low point during the first few years of the Volstead Act,

TABLE 2.2
Alcohol Consumption before and during Prohibition

	1911–1914 Local Prohibitions	1918–1919 Wartime Restrictions	1921–1922 Early Years of National Prohibition	1927–1930 Later Years
Ethanol (gallons per capita)	1.69	0.97	0.73	1.14
Index	100	57	43	67
Beer (gallons per capita)	20.53	11.44	1.49	6.27
Index	100	56	7	31
Liquor (gallons per capita)	1.47	0.80	0.92	1.62
Index	100	54	63	110
Wine (gallons per capita)	0.59	0.50	0.51	0.98
Index	100	85	86	166

Source: Warburton 1932, table 47, 107; Warburton 1934, 12: 507.
Note: All indexes are relative to 1911–1914.

and an increase through the 1920s. It is also interesting to note that by far the greatest reduction was in the consumption of beer; liquor consumption actually surpassed the pre-War level by the end of the 1920s. So Prohibition was associated with a reduction in overall consumption of ethanol, coupled with a substitution of liquor for beer. That makes sense given the economic logic of the black market, which favors the more concentrated product that has greater value per unit of volume. The costs of concealing manufacture and transport from law enforcement (and protecting the product from rival gangs) is mostly a function of the volume of beverage; if a gallon of beer and a gallon of liquor have the same costs of concealment, then the proportionate effect on the cost of liquor would be less than of beer. The same logic applies to possession by drinkers—carrying a hip flask of beer would provide less of the desired buzz than a hip flask of whiskey.

Death rates from alcohol-related causes are useful as proxies for per capita consumption, and even more directly as proxies for the prevalence of excess consumption. The most common indicator for this purpose has been the cirrhosis mortality rate, used by Warburton and many other authors in the context of judging the effects of Prohibition (Warburton 1932; Terris 1967; Bruun et al. 1975; Gerstein 1981; Dills and Miron 2003). Warburton also analyzed the death rate due to alcoholism. Table

TABLE 2.3
Alcohol-Related Death Rates before and during Prohibition

	1911–1914 Local Prohibitions	1918–1919 Wartime Restrictions	1921–1922 Early Years of National Prohibition	1927–1929 Later Years
Cirrhosis mortality per 100,000 residents	13.9	9.3	8.0	8.2
Index (relative to 1911–1914)	100	66	58	59
Alcoholism mortality per 100,000 residents	5.8	2.4	2.6	5.3
Index (relative to 1911–1914)	100	41	45	50

Source: Warburton 1932, 213.
Note: All figures are for the Vital Statistics registration states of 1900.

2.3 presents these results. The cirrhosis mortality rate dropped sharply from 1916 to 1920 and then plateaued through the end of the 1920s. The alcoholism mortality rate dropped at the same time, and then trended slowly upward during the 1920s. In any event, these patterns suggest that the prevalence of chronic heavy drinking followed the same pattern as per capita consumption of ethanol.[12]

Warburton was able to disaggregate the national trends in alcohol-related disease to some extent. Vital Statistics data indicate that death rates due to alcoholism fell proportionately more in rural areas than in cities between his baseline period (1911–1914) and the late 1920s, although there was little rural-urban difference in the declines in cirrhosis mortality (Warburton 1932, 239). More interesting is his comparison across different economic classes of workers. He notes that in 1927, 55 percent of the labor force were wage earners outside of agriculture (237); the industrial policyholders with Metropolitan Life Insurance Company experienced larger declines in death rates from alcohol-related causes than for the population at large, suggesting disproportionate cutbacks in heavy drinking. Warburton argues that the "business, professional and salaried class," which made up 26 percent of the workforce by 1927, sustained their average consumption levels:

> It is reasonable to conclude that the per capita consumption of alcoholic beverages by the business, professional and salaried class is fully as great in recent years as it was prior to prohibition. It appears probable that this class consumes the major portion of the alcohol sold illegally under prohibition. (1932, 240)

They were purchasing most of their alcoholic beverages from speakeasies and bootleggers at average prices from three to four times as high as before the War, and perhaps two or two and a half times the price that would have prevailed in the absence of Prohibition. Thus, in Warburton's judgment, this high-status, high-income group drank as much on average in the late 1920s as prior to the War despite a doubling of the price, while wage earners cut back considerably.

This differential impact across social class helps explain the origin of the oft-repeated claim that Prohibition had no effect on drinking, or actually was associated with an increase in drinking. Drinking was an important feature of the revolution in manners and morals of the 1920s. "Liquor became a luxury item, a symbol of affluence and eventually status. Where before men of good families tended not to drink and women certainly did not, during the 1920s it was precisely the sons and daughters of the 'nice' people who were patronizing the bootleggers and speakeasies" (Burnham 1968, 63). The magazines and newspapers of that day, like our own, focused on the lifestyles of the rich and famous. As historian John C. Burnham points out, "The journalists and other observers did indeed report honestly that they saw 'everyone' drinking. They seldom saw the lower classes and almost never knew about the previous drinking habits of the masses" (Burnham 1968, 63).

In contrast, when social worker Martha Bensley Bruere conducted a survey of other social workers across the country for the National Federation of Settlements in the mid-1920s, she received reports suggesting that although the law was widely flouted in the large cities of the North and East, and New Orleans appeared to be America's wettest city, most of the South and West was quite dry. Throughout the nation, the middle and upper classes were much more likely to be drinking than were working-class folks (Bruere 1927; Kyvig 2000, 25).

So what are the lessons of the Prohibition "experiment"? Despite the lack of effective enforcement, it appears that the Volstead Act was successful in raising retail prices of alcoholic beverages by a factor of two or more, even as late as 1930. And the Prohibition period was associated with a substantial reduction in per capita alcohol consumption as compared with the pre-War baseline period 1911–1914. Mortality rates from alcohol-related diseases were also lower, indicating that the prevalence of chronic heavy drinking was way down during the 1920s. These reductions were not uniform across the socioeconomic spectrum, but rather were largest among those groups least able to afford the higher prices; on the other hand, the evidence suggests that the professional and upper classes were drinking as much on average in 1930 as in 1912. If we make the reasonable assumption that the increased incomes and relaxed morals of the 1920s would have resulted in *increased* consumption in the absence of national Prohibition, then it is possible to conclude that the Prohibition experiment demonstrated that drinking habits of all income groups proved susceptible to alcohol-control measures.

What remains unclear is just what aspects of wartime controls and Prohibition were most important. Increased prices were doubtless part of the story, but it is difficult to sort out the price effect from the potential effects on demand of three other factors (MacCoun and Reuter 2001): (1) uncertainty about the quality of alcohol available on the black market, with a real possibility that a bottle of "whiskey" might actually contain toxic denatured industrial alcohol; (2) reduced availability, and in particular the necessity of either dealing with suppliers who were by definition criminals, or else going to the effort of home production; (3) moral scruples about violating at least the spirit of the law (a concern that was surely undercut by the allure of sampling the "forbidden fruit"). If the price effect was indeed the dominant factor, then the sad conclusion is that Prohibition was a success, but just as effective would have been the imposition of taxes high enough to double the pre-War price.

Alcohol Control Following Repeal

The best hope for Repeal was that it would end the lawlessness and corruption associated with Prohibition without opening the door for the return of the saloon. The leaders of the repeal movement gave this matter a good deal of study. The AARP had sponsored inquiries into foreign regulatory systems as possible models for the states during the late 1920s, and on the verge of Repeal, John D. Rockefeller Jr. funded a broad inquiry headed by Raymond B. Fosdick and Albert L. Scott (Fosdick and Scott 1933). They conducted a field investigation of alcohol-control measures in England, France, Germany, Italy, Russia, Poland, Finland, Sweden, Norway, Denmark, and all the Canadian provinces, as well as studying the American experience, and produced an impressive report titled *Toward Liquor Control*. In his introduction, Rockefeller notes: "If carefully laid plans of control are not made, the old evils against which prohibition was invoked can easily return" (Fosdick and Scott 1933, viii). The Fosdick-Scott report helped show the way to avoid reverting to the bad old days.

The challenge facing the states should not be underestimated. Prior to Repeal, the states had had little experience with regulating the alcohol-beverage industry, as opposed to suppressing it. Traditionally, regulation of drinking and alcohol sales had been left to local governments (Harrison and Laine 1936, 6), while the federal government imposed excise taxes and maintained the licensing and recordkeeping systems necessary to collect those taxes. With the Twenty-first Amendment, each of the state governments had to create a regulatory system *de novo*.

Fosdick and Scott present their ideas in the rhetoric of a rational policy analysis, in contrast to the illogic of the temperance movement: "American liquor legislation in the past has . . . been guided more by emotion than by reason or experience" (28). Reason and experience are the basis for their fundamental conclusion that distilled spirits should be regulated more closely than the more-dilute fermented beverages, beer and wine. "Such a system directs its spear-head against alcohol in the forms most liable to abuse by man, and, by permitting relative freedom in the use of the weaker drinks, tends to promote temperance" (29–30). They note that "The argument for treating the two classes of beverages alike in the past has been that the beer drinker of today becomes the whiskey sot of tomorrow" (30), but conclude that in fact beer and wine can serve as a substitute for whiskey, so that the weaker beverages should be made more readily available.

Their boldest recommendation (seconded by Rockefeller) was in support of establishing a state monopoly for distribution and retail package sales of stronger forms of alcohol. This approach, modeled in part on the systems then in place in the Canadian provinces, had the virtue of limiting the scope of the private-profit motive, and with it the motive for stimulating sales and encouraging intemperance. "Foreign experience and our own analysis of the problem here and abroad indicate that such a system makes it possible adequately to meet an unstimulated demand within the limits of conditions established solely in the interests of society" (64). The authors proposed as a second-best alternative the development of a statewide licensing system for distributors and retailers, with severe restrictions on advertising and "all sales practices which encourage consumption" (49). In either system the state was to institute a system for licensing and regulating outlets for on-premise consumption.

As it turned out, a majority of states adopted a license system, but seventeen states did institute some version of a monopoly system. Kansas, Mississippi, and Oklahoma remained dry, although even they allowed the sale of beer (Prendergast 1987, 46). The division of "wet" states between monopoly and licensing systems is tabulated in table 2.4. It is interesting to note that nine of the twelve states with a Canadian border adopted the monopoly approach, while only five of the remaining thirty-one states did so. There were some notable differences among the monopoly states: first, some limited the monopoly to distilled spirits, while others included wine (see table 2.4). Second, while all these states created a monopoly in wholesale distribution, a handful allowed some private licensees to sell package goods at retail, and Wyoming privatized all retailing. Looking back, it is remarkable how durable the initial choices made by those inexperienced state legislatures have proven (Wagenaar and Holder 1991). None of the states have switched from license to monopoly distribution, although Oklahoma was added to the list of monopoly states when it repealed statewide prohibition in 1959. And although a number of monopoly states have privatized wine distribution since World War II, only two of the monopoly states have chosen to end their retail monopolies in liquor distribution—Iowa, in 1987, and West Virginia, in 1991.

The simple division of state systems between monopoly and license conceals the complexity and variation of the alcohol beverage control (ABC) systems that were initiated during the 1930s. Years later, a study by the nonprofit group Medicine in the Public Interest sought to characterize the state systems along twenty-two dimensions (Medicine in the Public Interest 1979, 3), which covered the "who, when, where, what, and how" of alcohol sales (24). The ABC laws established a minimum age for purchase, an array of licenses for different types of sales, and fees and rules regulating each type. To prevent the return of the tied house, states banned ownership of retail outlets by distillers or brewers. To prevent the return of the saloon, a number of states banned or sharply limited sales of liquor by the drink, and when it was permitted, restricted the kinds of promotion. Most states allowed for local option to ban sales. License states differed with respect to whether package sales of spirits were limited to specialized liquor stores, or could be included with a broader retail operation (see table 2.4).

Although under the Twenty-first Amendment the states took the lead in regulating distribution and sales, the federal government wasted no time in re-imposing excise taxes and a system for ensuring collection. In January 1934, Congress enacted a liquor tax of $2 per proof gallon, and an additional duty on imports (Hu 1950, 74). More comprehensive legislation was enacted the following year: The Federal Alcohol Administration Act of 1935, which still defines the legal framework for federal regulation today, required that importers, manufacturers, wholesalers, and warehousers obtain federal permits, prohibited sales of illicit alcohol, and imposed regulations on labeling and advertising (Medicine in the Public Interest 1979, 20). Federal administration and enforcement of this law was given to the Treasury Department, signaling the priority on tax collection (Harrison and Laine 1936, 16).

The debate over the appropriate structure of federal tax rates reflected at least three concerns. First, the "voluntary self-control" brought about by high taxation was declared by the Rockefeller report to be "an indispensable and desirable measure" (Fosdick and Scott 1933), and that pro-temperance view had its advocates. A related issue was whether to keep the beer tax low in order to encourage consumption of this milder beverage. More influential, however, was the traditional interest in bringing in revenue, tempered by the belief that if the excise taxes were set too high, the result would be to sustain bootlegging and illicit production. "Nothing will so quickly demobilize the moonshiner and the bootlegger, and

TABLE 2.4
Prohibition and Repeal, State by State

States	Date State Adopted Prohibition	% Popular Vote for Twenty-first Amendment	Monopoly (M) or License (L)[#] January 1949	% Population in Dry Areas January 1949	Did Not Ratify Eighteenth or Twenty-first Amendment
Alabama	1915	58.7	M–SW	58.7	
Arizona	1915	76.9	L–B	0	
Arkansas	1916	59.5	L–B	33.3	
California	—	76.2	L–B	0.0	
Colorado	1916	68.0	L–B	4.4	
Connecticut	—	87.2	L–B	2.1	18th
Delaware	—	77.2	L–N	—	
Florida	1919	80.1	L–N	18.1	
Georgia	1908	n.a	L–B	62.2	21st
Idaho	1916	58.0	M–SW	0	
Illinois	—	78.2	L–B	13.3	
Indiana	1918	64.4	L–B	0	
Iowa	1916	60.1	M–SW	0	
Kansas	1881	n.a.	Prohibition		21st
Kentucky	—	62.3	L–N	56.2	
Louisiana	—	n.a.	L–B	19.6	21st
Maine	1851	68.4	M–SW	30.2	
Maryland	—	81.8	L–B	10	
Massachusetts	—	81.7	L–B	5.1	
Michigan	1918	74.8	M–SW	—	
Minnesota	—	65.8	L–B	18.2	
Mississippi	1909	n.a.	Prohibition		21st
Missouri	—	76.2	L–M	0	
Montana	1918	n.a.	M–SW	—	
Nebraska	1917	n.a.	L–B	0.2	21st
Nevada	1918	n.a.	L–B	0	
New Hampshire	1918	71.4	M–SW	12.5	

throw into chaos the corrupt system they have created, as reasonable liquor taxes and low liquor prices" (Fosdick and Scott 1933, 111).

In fact, the "gangsterism" of the Prohibition era had not ended on the day of Repeal. Initial liquor tax collections were disappointingly low, in part because the bootleggers continued to supply something like 45 million gallons per year (66 percent of the tax paid amount) (Hu 1950, 86).

TABLE 2.4 (cont'd)
Prohibition and Repeal, State by State

States	Date State Adopted Prohibition	% Popular Vote for Twenty-first Amendment	Monopoly (M) or License (L)[#] January 1949	% Population in Dry Areas January 1949	Did Not Ratify Eighteenth or Twenty-first Amendment
New Jersey	—	86.3	L–N	2.5	
New Mexico	1918	77.5	L–B	6.2	
New York	—	88.7	L–N	0.5	
North Carolina	1909	29.0	M–SW	74.1	21st
North Dakota	1889	n.a.	L–B	0	21st
Ohio	1919	71.2	M–SW	8.4	
Oklahoma	1907		L–N		21st
Oregon	1916	65.2	M–SW	50.0	
Pennsylvania	—	76.0	M–SW	0	
Rhode Island	—	87.8	L–B	0.9	18th
South Carolina	1916	48.0	L–N	0	21st
South Dakota	1917	n.a.	L–B	0	21st
Tennessee	1909	51.4	L–N	68	
Texas	1918	61.4	L–B	52.7	
Utah	1917	60.8	M–SW	0	
Vermont	—	66.7	M–SW	35.7	
Virginia	1916	63.0	M–S	11.1	
West Virginia	1914	61.6	M–SW	8.8	
Washington	1916	70.7	M–S	0.7	
Wisconsin	—	82.1	L–B	5.8	
Wyoming	1919	85.4	M–Wholesale	0	

[#] S = Spirits; W = Wine; B = Broad; N = Narrow (liquor store only).
† Delegates to convention were not selected until 1934, following ratification (Kyvig 2000, 179).
* Delegates chosen in precinct meetings and county conventions (Kyvig 2000, 178).

To combat this problem, the Alcohol Tax Unit of the Bureau of Internal Revenue was organized in 1934. It launched a large law enforcement effort, with over 1,000 investigators deployed against the bootlegging gangs of the Northern metropolitan areas and elsewhere (Hu 1950). That effort, plus new regulations to facilitate enforcement, resulted in a considerable shrinkage of the black market by 1937. As a result, excise tax collections on distilled spirits nearly doubled, from $164 million in 1934, to $298 million in 1937. It seems reasonable to conclude that the federal government was more motivated and far more successful in enforcing the tax law, which pays for itself, than the prohibition laws. Over the subsequent years the tax rates were increased a number of times to fund the war effort, just as with the First World War; in 1944, the excise tax on a proof gallon was set at $9, and tax collections approached $2 billion. Certainly there remained a profitable niche for small bootlegging operations, but the large-scale criminal organizations had been defeated.

The states also began taxing alcoholic beverages, and for them, unlike the federal government, it was a new venture. The typical pattern in the license states was to tax spirits more heavily than beer or wine; in the monopoly states, the same pattern was achieved through designated markups of the prices paid distillers (Kansas State Government 1949). State excise tax rates were typically much lower than federal rates, but still of noticeable importance in state finances.

CONCLUDING THOUGHTS

The vision of the alcohol-control advocates was of a happy medium between laissez-faire and prohibition, of an orderly, crime-free market structured by rational regulations that promoted temperance. Fosdick and Scott offer a wonderful image: "the forty-eight states will constitute a social science laboratory in which different ideas and methods can be tested, and the exchange of experience will be infinitely valuable for the future" (Fosdick and Scott 1933, 150). But the enthusiasm for supply regulations in support of temperance did not last long enough to benefit from this new noble experiment. By 1950, a study commission representing the state governments concluded that "any attempt at establishing a relationship between consumption and systems of control would involve the untenable assumption that restriction on consumption as such is an objective of control" (Joint Committee of the States to Study Alcoholic Beverage Laws 1950, 7; Prendergast 1987, 46). After just fifteen years, the regulators and the public had lost faith in the virtues of regulating consumption, defining the mission instead as maintaining an orderly market and collecting taxes. What went wrong had less to do with actual experience in the "laboratory," and more to do with the ascendance of the alcoholism movement—a topic for the next chapter.

The possibility of using taxes to promote temperance had been part of the public dialog as far back as Alexander Hamilton, but that notion always seemed to lose out to the allure of revenue. In 1950, Tun Yuan Hu observed that "it has been urged in early post-repeal discussions that sumptuary control in the interest of temperance rather than revenue should, at least in the long run, govern federal spirits taxation. But so far, the idea does not seem to have gained ground" (146).

Nonetheless, *something* was holding down consumption during the decades following Repeal. As best one can judge from available indicators, there was not much more drinking in the 1930s than during the 1920s, no doubt in part because of the greatly reduced Depression-era incomes and perhaps also because of continuing restrictions on availability. Per capita consumption of ethanol did begin increasing after World War II, and finally returned to the 1914 level by 1970 (Nephew et al. 2003). By that time the conventional wisdom was that Prohibition had failed and that any regulations on availability were a useless distraction in the quest for moderation.

CHAPTER 3

The Alcoholism Movement

> One martini is all right. Two is too many, three is
> not enough.
> —James Thurber

THE TEMPERANCE MOVEMENT was grounded in the belief that alcohol is a dangerous drug—a poison—that threatens all who imbibe with physical, social, and moral harms. Hence it made sense to institute broad limits on the availability of alcohol. National Prohibition was the ultimate realization of this approach, and although it was eventually deemed a costly failure by the vast majority of Americans, temperance thinking continued to be influential following Repeal, animating the push for state alcohol-control systems during the 1930s. But an alternative perspective gained great traction during the 1940s and 1950s, namely that the "problem" is alcoholism, to which only a fraction of the population is vulnerable, and that the right "solution" is not general alcohol control (which in any event would—in this view—have little effect on drinking by alcoholics) but rather special assistance for the unlucky few who contract this "disease." In other words, the problem is with the person rather than with the substance, and the solution is in helping those individuals rather than in restricting supply to everyone.

THE ASCENT OF ALCOHOLISM

It was soon after Repeal that alcoholic Bill W. (New Yorker William G. Wilson) was inspired by a conversation with an alcoholic friend who had found the strength to stop drinking through a religious conversion. Shortly thereafter Wilson, now sober, found himself in Akron, Ohio, tempted to get drunk after the failure of a business deal. Instead, he sought out another alcoholic, a surgeon named Bob Smith. Their conversation not only helped Wilson remain sober, but proved to be the beginning of a close association with Dr. Smith. On June 10, 1935, Smith had his last drink, and the two of them decided to begin helping others as well (Kurtz 1980, 33). From these humble origins in Akron, Alcoholics Anonymous (AA) grew into the most successful self-help organization of our time.

The national organization now claims over a million members in 50,000 groups, with another million members abroad (www.aa.org).

AA's core ideas were taken from the founders' own experience but also from other sources with which they had some acquaintance, including psychologist Carl Jung and philosopher/psychologist William James. Alcoholics were helpless on their own, but when they finally "hit bottom" then, through faith in God and the help of others with similar experience, they might find their way to sobriety. The AA's Twelve Steps begin with a statement of surrender—"We admitted we were powerless over alcohol"—and of acceptance of a "power greater than ourselves." Steps 4 through 10 then provide for confession, contrition, and restitution. The final two steps concern the development of a greater spirituality and commitment to help other alcoholics. Twelve "Traditions" of AA were also codified, defining the nature and mission of the local group: Its only purpose is to help alcoholics and the only requirement for membership is a desire to stop drinking. Groups are to preserve the anonymity of members and avoid any sort of controversy or entanglement in politics.

In the early years, AA got a boost from the alcohol research program at Yale University under the leadership of biostatistician E. Morton Jellinek. He published two landmark articles in 1946 and 1952 offering a science-based understanding of alcoholism, one that was congruent with the AA perspective. His subsequent book, *The Disease Concept of Alcoholism* (1960), further developed his ideas and became the "canonical scientific text for the classical disease concept" (Fingarette 1988, 20). In that book he identified five varieties of alcoholism, designated by the Greek letters alpha through epsilon, of which two—gamma and delta—had sufficient indication of alcohol dependence or addiction to constitute a disease.[1] He identified as Gamma alcoholics those that exhibit dependence through tolerance and loss of control in their drinking, and as Delta alcoholics those who were unable to abstain but were able to limit their drinking on any one occasion. Jellinek noted that the gamma type fit the stereotype that AA propounded "to the exclusion of all other species" (Jellinek 1960, 38), although in his own research on over two thousand AA members, he had identified a subgroup who had never suffered loss of control. His earlier research did document a definite progression from psychological to physical dependence and marked behavior changes (1952), similar to the AA view of the "downward spiral."

Jellinek's designation of alcoholism as a "disease" was not a new idea. In fact, many physicians had embraced this view during the nineteenth century. The Association for the Study of Inebriety, which promoted a disease concept of alcoholism and advocated the establishment of specialized hospitals for inebriates, was established in 1870 (Babor et al. 1996, 7). One contemporary observer noted somewhat cynically that "The prevalent opinion at the present day is, that drunkenness is a disease. Medical authorities are divided on the subject. Many physicians, especially specialists who make the treatment of drunkenness a business and source of profit, are positive that it is a disease" (Todd 1882). Temperance writers often adopted the language of mental illness, using terms like compulsion, loss of control, and addiction in talking about alcohol problems (1980, 30). But whereas the temperance-era advocates believed that everyone was at risk, the alcoholism movement insisted that it was just a small minority who were vulnerable. Dan Beauchamp makes the point by use of public-health vocabulary, that the focus was shifted from the *agent* (alcohol), to the *host* (the drinker) (Beauchamp 1980, 32). Alcoholics, the hosts, are viewed as intrinsically different from social drinkers—the AA tenet is that alcoholics are "allergic" to alcohol, though Jellinek viewed the "allergy" notion as at best a metaphor.

The "disease" message was promoted by the National Committee for Education on Alcoholism (later called the National Council on Alcoholism), founded under the sponsorship and financing of the Yale Group in 1944. The founder was Mrs. Marty Mann, the first woman to achieve sobriety with AA. Her specific goals were to eliminate the stigma surrounding alcoholism, to educate the public that alcoholism was a disease and alcoholics were "sick," and to promote public support for helping alcoholics (National Council on Alcoholism 1984). By 1949, the NCA had opened fifty field offices ("affiliated local committees") to carry the effort forward at a grassroots level. National public advocacy by NCA and others who advanced a "scientific concept of alcoholism" was finally rewarded in 1970 with the passage of federal legislation to create the National Institute of Alcohol Abuse and Alcoholism, which in turn led to a vast expansion in federal financing for alcoholism treatment and research.

ALTERNATIVE PERSPECTIVES ON ALCOHOLISM AS A DISEASE

The characterization of alcoholism touted by AA and others has been challenged by researchers, philosophers, and advocates for alternative perspectives. The debate begins with the question of whether alcoholism is properly labeled a disease, and goes on to contend the specifics: loss of control, the possibility of returning to controlled drinking (with or without intervention), and whether and in what ways alcoholics are different. Perhaps the most important issue for the purposes of policy design has been the extent to which alcoholism is "the problem"—that is, the extent to which alcoholics are responsible for alcohol-related problems in the society.

The obvious symptom of alcoholism is chronic heavy drinking—that is, drinking enough to cause or put the drinker at risk of organ damage and social and financial problems. But in most accounts, heavy drinking is not enough to make the diagnosis of an illness. The *defining* characteristic is dependence on alcohol, as evidenced by a repeated tendency for the individual to drink more than he intends or, in some sense, wants. Jellinek reserved the "disease" label for those alcoholics who evidenced dependence either by an inability to stop drinking once started (gamma) or an inability to refrain from starting in the first place (delta); in both cases Jellinek believed that the anomalous behavior was the result of "physiopathological processes" (1960, 40) associated with the effect of long-term drinking.

Other scholars have not viewed the identification of some physiological component to the disease as essential. A leading proponent of the "disease" conception in recent years, the psychiatrist George Vaillant, suggested that "uncontrolled, maladaptive ingestion of alcohol is not a disease in the sense of biological disorder; rather, alcoholism is a disorder of behavior" (1983, 19). He goes on to say, "I willingly concede . . . that alcohol dependence lies on a continuum and that in scientific terms behavior disorder will often be a happier semantic choice than disease" (20). And to a large extent the question does seem to be one of semantics, albeit one with high stakes. Valliant says that "calling alcoholism a disease, rather than a behavior disorder, is a useful device both to persuade the alcoholic to admit his alcoholism and to provide a ticket for admission into the health care system" (20). The "disease" label may help remove the stigma from alcoholism, since it suggests that the alcoholic has lost volition and hence is no longer blameworthy for all the damage he does to his family and community. The National Council on Alcoholism has long made the case that treatment rather than blame is what the public owes alcoholics.

One problem with making "loss of control" and "craving" the defining characteristic of the disease is the evidence suggesting that alcoholics are not necessarily helpless in the face of the temptation to drink, and in fact are, under some circumstances, able to exercise control. A series of studies and experiments provided new evidence on the "control" issue beginning in the 1960s. The research, some of which was conducted in in-patient alcoholism clinics, included experiments in which patients were given the opportunity to "buy" drinks in exchange for "work" in a token economy, or were allowed to drink but lost privileges if they drank too much (Mello 1972; Pattison et al. 1977). This research demonstrated that many alcoholics can and do control their drinking in response to short-term contingencies that they care about. And those experimental results fit with more extensive observations on the natural histories of alcoholics, which often include instances or long periods of controlled drinking.

Curiously, "the natural history of alcoholism" was best documented by George Vaillant, a proponent of the "disease" designation. Vaillant utilized longitudinal data from Harvard Medical School's Study of Adult Development, which included 660 men followed from 1940 to 1980, from adolescence into late middle life. The great advantage of this sample for documenting the natural histories is that it is "prospective," selected early in the subjects' lives and without regard to how much they drank. (This is in contrast with Jellinek's data, which are retrospective accounts by AA members, ensuring that every story ends in a similar way.) Of course, over the years many members of the sample came to drink heavily and develop alcohol-related problems. Vaillant was able to document the large variety of drinking trajectories based on interview data, finding in particular that it was common to observe transitions from harmful drinking to more moderate drinking. He concluded that alcoholism is a chronic disorder, though recovery is common with or without treatment (1983, 309). But in support of the AA perspective, he found that the further along the continuum of alcohol-related problems individuals find themselves, the more they resemble other alcoholics (309). One marker for being far along on that continuum is having undergone detoxification, a procedure reserved for those who required medical help to mitigate severe withdrawal symptoms. It was rare, he found, for this group to return to asymptomatic drinking—a few years later, they were abstinent, continuing to abuse, or dead.

One prominent critic of the "disease" label for alcoholism is the sociologist Herbert Fingarette, whose book *Heavy Drinking: The Myth of Alcoholism as a Disease* pointed out that experts had long rejected the simplistic, unitary construct of alcoholism promulgated by AA, and indeed that alcoholics do not constitute a distinct group within the population of people that have problems with alcohol. "Depending on the definitions and statistical techniques used, the estimated number of 'alcoholics' in the U.S. can range from near zero to as many as 10 million or more" (1988, 5). He advocates an alternative term of "heavy drinking" to capture the great variety of patterns of chronic alcohol abuse that create a substantial risk of alcohol-related problems, suggesting that at any given time about 20 percent of the population drinks enough to be in that category" (5–6). In his view, that relatively large group is the proper target of public concern, rather than the narrower focus on those who are deemed to be addicted.

The belief that alcoholism *is* in some important sense a disease spawns the hope that medical research can discover its causes, identify those who are most susceptible, and develop effective treatments. This enterprise has been complicated by the realization that alcoholism (whether disease or not) has multiple causes, both individual and environmental. Jellinek, the scientific godfather of the "disease" concept, asserted as much. He offered this "working hypothesis," which would receive broad support from researchers today:

> In societies which have a low degree of acceptance of large daily amounts of alcohol, mainly those will be exposed to the risk of addiction who on account of high psychological vulnerability have an inducement to go against the social standards. But in societies which have an extremely high degree of acceptance of large daily alcohol consumption, the presence of any small vulnerability, whether psychological or physical, will suffice for exposure to the risk of addiction. (Jellinek 1960, 28–9)

In his view, it is the interaction of individual susceptibility and the "wetness" of the environment that determine the likelihood of an individual succumbing to alcoholism. Thus, alcoholics may be different than others, but they are *more* different (and fewer) in a dry environment than a wet one. Logically, then, interventions intended to reduce general consumption may reduce the prevalence of alcoholism—an observation that the old temperance advocates would passionately endorse!

The investigation of innate susceptibility has long been an active area of research. The evidence that there are biological differences in how the body processes alcohol is as clear as the "flushing" response common among some Asian populations (the result of a genetic variation in how alcohol is metabolized). To investigate the possibility of a genetic basis for alcohol-related problems, epidemiologists have studied patterns of occurrence within families. Particularly telling is evidence from comparisons of identical twins and fraternal twins. Any pair of twins share the same family and community environment, but identical twins also have the same genetic makeup, which is not true of fraternal twins. The case of a genetic basis to alcoholism is strengthened by the observation, based on large epidemiological studies, that identical twins are more alike with respect to presence or absence of alcoholism than are fraternal twins. Further confirmation comes from studies of children raised by foster parents: the likelihood of an adopted child becoming alcoholic is statistically related to whether the biological parents were alcoholic. These and other findings have demonstrated conclusively that familial transmission of alcoholism risk is at least in part genetic, and that many genes appear to play some role in shaping alcoholism risk, probably through several different biological mechanisms (National Institute on Alcohol Abuse and Alcoholism 2003b). Biology is not destiny in this area, but it is surely relevant.

Although alcoholism is the result of both individual and environmental determinants, medical interventions necessarily treat individuals. Whether alcoholism is best thought of as a disease, a behavior disorder, or a myth is less important for practical people than ascertaining what (if anything) the medical community can do to help those who are afflicted.

Alcoholism Treatment

Professional treatment for alcohol-related problems is a large enterprise in the United States. In 2001 there were over 750,000 admissions to substance-abuse treatment services with an alcohol problem as the primary diagnosis. Given the conflicting views of whether alcoholism is a "disease," it is interesting to see how the matter has been resolved in clinical practice, and with what effect.

The American Psychiatric Association has published a series of reference books under the title *Diagnostic and Statistical Manual of Mental Disorders* beginning in 1952, which since then have served as a standard reference for researchers. The third edition (DSM-III) was published in 1980, and for the first time included specific diagnostic criteria for the major disorders as an aid to clinical practice. It also provided the first classification system that distinguished between two alcohol use disorders—abuse and dependence (Hasin 2003, 6). The fourth edition, published in 1994 (DSM-IV), refined these criteria.

In DSM-IV, alcohol dependence is "a maladaptive pattern of drinking, leading to clinically significant impairment or distress," as manifested by meeting *three* or more of a list of seven criteria at any time in the previous year: increase in tolerance, withdrawal symptoms (or drinking to avoid withdrawal), neglect of important activities due to drinking, a great deal of time spent drinking, continued use despite physical or psychological problems related to drinking, persistent desire or unsuccessful attempts to cut down or stop, and impaired control over drinking. Note that this multidimensional diagnosis is flexible enough to accommodate a wide variety of heavy-drinking patterns and associated problems.

"Alcohol abuse" is a separate diagnostic category in DSM-III and DSM-IV, reserved for those who do not meet the standard of "dependence" but do have a pattern of drinking in a risky or harmful fashion. By definition "dependence" is a more serious condition, and has a poorer prognosis (Hasin 2003). Alcohol "abuse" is typical of youths, while dependence often emerges later in life.

Although participation in AA or other twelve-step programs is the dominant approach to alcoholism treatment in the United States (U.S. Department of Health and Human Services 2000, 445), a remarkable variety of other treatments are available. A 1995 review (Miller et al. 1995) mentioned twenty-five psychological therapeutic approaches in current use, including social skills training, motivational enhancement, behavior contracting, cognitive therapy, marital and family therapy, aversion therapy, and relaxation training (U.S. Department of Health and Human Services 2000, 444). Alcoholism treatment approaches also differ greatly with respect to intensity. Most costly are the inpatient rehabilitation programs that traditionally last twenty-eight days and provide highly structured treatment services, including group therapy, individual therapy, and education (Fuller and Hiller-Sturmhofel 1999, 70). Outpatient treatment programs range in intensity from daily sessions in a hospital, to counseling sessions offered once or twice a week. Many clients are admitted for detox, either in a hospital or, more commonly, a freestanding facility, and then are referred to treatment.

The overall volume of treatment activity is not measured on a routine basis. But the unique Alcohol and Drug Service Study does provide a snapshot for October 1, 1996: on that day, about 1 million individuals were actually in substance-abuse treatment provided by any of 12,387 facilities. Most of these individuals (81 percent) were being treated for alcohol abuse, but in most of these cases there were other drugs involved as well. For the clients for whom alcohol was the *primary* or only drug of abuse (47 percent of all cases), most were being treated in an outpatient setting, such as a community mental health facility or a private (usually nonprofit) facility. But 44,000 of the alcohol abusers were being treated as inpatients in a hospital or other residential facility (Substance Abuse and Mental Health Administration 2003).

Additional information is available on an annual basis from the Treatment Episode Data Set (TEDS), a federal compilation of state administrative data on admissions. In 2001, a total of 1.7 million admissions were included in TEDS.[2] Of these, alcohol is the primary drug of abuse in 44 percent of all cases.[3] The primary sources of referral include the criminal justice system (37 percent), self-referral (31 percent), and medical providers (21 percent). One-quarter of alcohol-related admissions begin (and sometimes end) with detox (Substance Abuse and Mental Health Services Administration 2003).

The variety of treatment approaches (for those clients who are receiving something more than detox) reflects considerable uncertainty and disagreement among professionals about what works. Systematic evaluation has been rare, and evaluations based on the behavior or impressions of alcoholics who have been through these programs are not a reliable guide. The evaluation challenge is that in any cohort of alcoholics that reach the sort of crisis that might lead them to treatment, there are some who improve on their own even if they do not ultimately receive any treatment.

For that reason, a good evaluation requires a control group with which to compare the subsequent behavior of the treated population. As of 1980, the most rigorous evaluation study concluded that commonsense advice plus the natural history of the disorder may accomplish just as much as hospitalization, family therapy, referral to AA, or Antabuse (Orford and Edwards 1977; Vaillant 1983, 10); in other words, whether and what sort of help an alcohol abuser sought was pretty much irrelevant to whether he improved. And it continues to be the case that most people who go through a period of problematic drinking do not seek professional help (Room 1989) and many nonetheless are able to resolve their problems (Sobell et al. 1996).

Most of the evaluation research in recent years has compared alternative treatment approaches with each other and lacked a "no treatment" control group. For example, Diana Walsh and her colleagues structured an experiment with 227 alcohol-abusing participants whose employers had referred them to an employee assistance program. This group was randomly assigned to either (a) compulsory three-week inpatient treatment, with one year of AA attendance thereafter; (b) compulsory AA attendance by itself; or (c) the opportunity to choose whether or not to enter the inpatient treatment program. A two-year follow-up found that the first group (with required hospitalization) did the best on drinking measures, but that work-related outcomes were not significantly different among the groups. Other evaluation research has concluded that inpatient treatment is not warranted except perhaps for clients with serious co-occurring medical or psychiatric conditions or few social resources (Finney, Hahn, and Moos 1996).

One of the largest high-quality evaluation studies, Project MATCH, randomly assigned 1,726 patients to one of three approaches, each of which involved a twelve-week period of individual outpatient counseling sessions. The approaches included cognitive-behavioral therapy, which seeks to develop the patient's skill in coping with various situations in which he might be tempted to drink; motivational enhancement therapy, which seeks to strengthen the patient's intrinsic motivation to change; and twelve-step facilitation therapy, which provides professional guidance through the first steps of AA. The experimental sample included 774 who were beginning outpatient aftercare following a period of inpatient treatment; the remainder were initiating treatment as outpatients. In the aftercare sample, no differences were found in drinking outcomes during the first year, and the differences for the outpatient sample were small or nil, depending on which measure was used. It is true that the twelve-step facilitation treatment had an edge by one measure—the percentage who achieved the treatment goal of continuous abstinence for one year—but even there the numbers were distressingly small. Just one in four of that relatively successful group were able to achieve that goal (Fuller and Hiller-Sturmhofel 1999, 74). The original purpose of Project MATCH was to determine whether the effectiveness of treatment differed with the individual characteristics of the client, but there were few notable results on that score. And since MATCH did not include a no-treatment control group, it is not known whether any of the treatments outperformed "natural history."

Although there is real doubt about the efficacy of psychotherapy alone in helping alcoholics to give up drinking, the evaluation research on several new medications is more promising. The only drug approved for this use prior to the 1990s was disulfiram (Antabuse), which has proven a disappointment. When taking disulfiram, the patient knows that any relapse to drinking will have intensely unpleasant consequences, including nausea and flushing. Of course the patient who decides to start drinking again can simply opt out of taking the drug, and that has proven to be so common in practice that the drug appears to be of little therapeutic benefit. On the other hand, the new "anti-craving" medications naltrexone and acomprosate have done well in clinical trials, and the combination of the two drugs may be particularly effective (Kiefer et al. 2003). These drugs appear to work by blocking some of the pleasant, reinforcing effects of alcohol. Development of additional medications that target the mechanisms of addiction is a likely consequence of the vast research effort in the biochemistry of brain function. Of course the utility of any such medication is limited by the simple fact that the patient must be motivated to quit drinking.

Medical interventions actually can be helpful in providing some abusers with the motivation to cut down on drinking. In what is perhaps the most surprising set of findings from the evaluation literature, brief counseling delivered by a family physician or other member of the medical team has been shown to be effective in family-medicine settings (U.S. Department of Health and Human Services 2000, 433). The typical protocol involves the use of a screening instrument such as CAGE, a very abbreviated diagnostic instrument for identifying problems with alcohol (Ewing 1984.:)

1. Have you ever felt you should Cut down on your drinking?
2. Have people Annoyed you by criticizing your drinking?
3. Have you ever felt bad or Guilty about your drinking?
4. Have you ever had a drink first thing in the morning to steady your nerves or to get rid of a hangover (Eye opener)?

When it appears warranted, the physician or another member of the medical team is to initiate one or more brief (15 minutes) counseling sessions, with some sort of follow-up. The evidence from a number of randomized clinical trials indicates that months or even years later, patients are somewhat more likely to be drinking at moderate levels (Whitlock et al. 2004). The efficacy of this approach is not limited to family-practice settings. A large experiment with screening and brief intervention in emergency care found that at six months, patients in the intervention group had 47 percent fewer new injuries than control patients. The difference was most pronounced for those in the mild to moderate range of alcohol problems (U.S. Deptartment of Health and Human Services 2000, 433).

This approach has the potential to make some difference with the large portion of the population that drinks too much, at least on occasion, but would not ordinarily consider seeking treatment. That group, it turns out, accounts for the bulk of alcohol-related problems.

Concluding Thoughts

Experience with Prohibition called into question the temperance movement's emphasis on supply-side controls. The alcoholism movement provided an alternative perspective—that alcohol was not a problem for the great majority of people, but rather only for a distinct and relatively small group who were unfortunate enough to be susceptible to alcohol's addictive qualities. As a *New York Times* article celebrating the fifteenth anniversary of Repeal put it, "the doctors, the psychiatrists and some lay groups are [now] doing what should have been done long before—attempting to remove the causes of alcoholism rather than punish the happy or unhappy soul who feels that he needs a drink or two or a great many drinks."[4]

The alcoholism movement engendered a research program that continues to this day, seeking to identify individual characteristics that create susceptibility to alcohol problems, and to develop effective treatments for those who succumb. This medical approach is vital and has made some progress. But it has intrinsic limitations. First, it is not just alcoholics (by any definition) who cause and suffer harm as a result of their drinking—in fact the problem is more diffuse. For example, consider the percentage of drunk drivers who are alcohol dependent. Based on a large national survey, 3.4 percent of the adult public is currently dependent by DSM-V definition, and an additional 14.0 percent have ever been dependent. Together these two groups accounted for less than half of all respondents who admitted driving a vehicle after 3 or more drinks in the past year.[5] This is an example of the preventive paradox, that the population subgroup with the highest concentration of the problem (the alcoholics) accounts for only a fraction of the overall problem, much of which is diffused through the larger subgroup of nondependent drinkers (Kreitman 1986). Second, treatments ranging from AA participation to the latest anti-craving drugs are necessarily of limited effectiveness because they all require voluntary compliance by the drinker; the great challenge is to motivate alcoholics to quit or at least seek help in quitting. Thus, alcoholism is not the sum total of the alcohol "problem," and alcoholism treatment is not the "solution" even potentially. It remains important to seek methods for preventing the development of alcoholism and more generally the development of harmful drinking patterns. That reality brings us back to supply controls. As Jellinek recognized long ago, the prevalence of alcoholism is closely linked to the wetness of the drinking environment. The management of the terms on which alcohol is available to the public is in that sense a relevant aspect of the policy portfolio.

By 1980, a new consensus had emerged among experts, emphasizing the diversity of drinking patterns that could be considered problematic, and encouraging a broad multifaceted policy response that included both primary prevention and development and delivery of effective treatment modalities. This eclectic, pragmatic, evidence-based approach is that of public health (Beauchamp 1980).

PART II

Evidence of Effectiveness

CHAPTER 4

Drinking: A Primer

> Then there is the man who drowned crossing a stream with
> an average depth of six inches.
> —W.I.E. Gates

QUANTIFICATION IS ESSENTIAL to assessing the scope, pattern, and trend of drinking, and to evaluating particular interventions intended to reduce problematic drinking. But not just any data will do—what we need depends on how the "problem" is defined. As we have seen, the temperance reformers of the early twentieth century saw alcohol itself as the problem, and ultimately adopted abstinence as the goal. For them, "success" would be equated with an increasing prevalence of teetotalers and falling sales figures. On the other hand, for advocates in the alcoholism movement, data on overall sales are essentially irrelevant—what's needed are data on the prevalence of the "disease," regardless of how much those so afflicted were actually drinking. Finally, for those taking a population-health perspective, data on the entire distribution of consumption are of interest. Both abstinence and heavy drinking have implications for health and other consequences, and average (per capita) drinking is relevant to the extent that that average is closely linked to the prevalence of heavy, problematic drinking. This third perspective guides the discussion that follows here.

What will become clear is that there are a variety of pitfalls in using available data on sales and consumption patterns, and that what we most want to know is the hardest to measure reliably. But measure we must. The alternatives—anecdotes, casual observation—tend to be even less reliable.

THE ACTIVE INGREDIENT

Alcoholic beverages include wines, beers, and spirits. Wines are fermented from the sugars in fruits or berries (most commonly grapes) or other sources (Keller 1978). Beers are fermented from grains after the starch in them is first converted to sugar. Spirits are distilled from wines or beers. The distinctive ingredient in all these beverages is ethyl alcohol, also known as ethanol. For most beers, the alcohol content ranges from 2 percent to 8 percent by volume;[1] unfortified wines contain between 8 percent and 14 percent (with 14 percent being the upper limit from the fermentation process). Fortified wines, including vermouth, sherry, and port, contain about 20 percent, which is achieved by the addition of brandy (distilled wine) or pure alcohol. Spirits usually contain between 40 and 50 percent alcohol; the alcohol content is referred to in terms of the "proof," a number that is simply twice the percentage of alcohol content by volume. Thus, 80 proof whiskey is 40 percent alcohol.

Alcoholic beverages are consumed in the form of drinks. A typical drink of beer includes 12 ounces, which is the amount in a standard can or bottle. A standard drink of wine is about 5 ounces, while a drink of spirits may include 1.5 ounces—often diluted with water or some mixer. The amount of ethanol included in each of these drinks will depend on the actual strength of the beverage, but for the typical strengths of each type as sold in the United States, each type of drink will include approximately 0.6 ounces:

12 ounces of beer	×	5% alcohol	=	0.6 ounces
5 ounces of wine	×	12% alcohol	=	0.6 ounces
1.5 ounces of spirits	×	40% alcohol	=	0.6 ounces

That a standard drink of beer, wine, or spirits provides the same dose of alcohol is surely more than a coincidence, and very convenient for those who are studying alcohol consumption. An individual's ethanol intake can be estimated by asking how many "drinks" he or she had on a given occasion.

MEASUREMENT

Measuring *individual* alcohol consumption is an essential aspect of an epidemiological study of the health and behavior consequences of drinking. Research on *population-level* trends and patterns of alcohol consumption requires some basis for estimating aggregate consumption. How should we go about making estimates of individual or aggregate consumption? The answer is: with boldness tempered with humility. Quantification is essential, but precise quantification is rarely possible.

Generally it is easier to estimate aggregate consumption (at the state or national level) with some degree of accuracy than to develop accurate estimates of individual drinking, or of the distribution of drinking patterns within a population. The aggregate data are usually derived from tax records, on the assumption that tax-paid sales of alcoholic beverages are approximately equal to consumption. On the other hand, patterns of drinking across population subgroups and individuals must usually be estimated through surveys, where the quality of the data is limited by respondents' willingness and ability to report just how much they drink. Under exceptional circumstances, including a handful of national road-side surveys, these self-report data may be supplemented by a breath or blood test, which provides some indication of whether the individual had any drinks within a few hours of the test, and how many.

Tax Records

Both federal and state governments impose excise taxes on alcoholic bev-erages. The federal excise taxes, and most state taxes as well, are legislated to be proportional to the volume of beverage sold, rather than to the value of that beverage. So, unlike a typical sales tax, which is a percentage of price, the excise taxes on alcoholic beverages are usually quoted as so many dollars per unit of liquid. In particular, the federal excise tax on beer as of 2006 is $18 per barrel (31 gallons); still wine is taxed at $1.07 per gallon. Spirits are taxed in proportion to ethanol content—$13.50 per "proof gallon" defined as the amount of liquid that contains a half-gallon of ethanol.

Tax records are a basis for calculating the volume of beer and wine sold at wholesale, and the volume of ethanol sold in the form of spirits.[2] These data are by no means perfect as a basis for estimating alcohol consumption. Among the problems:

- The presumption that consumption is equal to wholesale shipments takes no account of wastage, illicit production for sale (moonshining), or production at home.

- Consumption lags wholesale shipments. Adjustments in retail and home inventories may affect wholesale shipments without a corresponding change in consumption.

- Purchase and consumption are not confined to residents of the jurisdiction in which the tax is paid. For jurisdictions in which tourists represent a large part of the market for alcoholic beverages, the sales-per-resident figures are hence misleadingly high.

- Computing the aggregate ethanol content of tax-paid shipments requires an estimate of the average ethanol content for beer and wine. Translating "drinks" into ethanol intake is a rough-and-ready process at best. For example, while regular beer has about 5 percent ethanol, light beer is about 4.2 percent, ice beer 5.5 percent, and malt liquor 6.5 percent (Dawson 2003,

21)—and even those numbers are averages over the variety of products available in the category. In recent years, NIAAA has used 4.5 percent as the conversion factor for beer, although there has been some fluctuation in the true average (Kerr and Greenfield 2003).

Despite these potential problems, the tax data are generally accepted as the best available basis for estimating aggregate consumption of ethanol. The various sources of error will balance out to some extent, and in any event probably don't amount to much on a percentage basis. But in analyzing estimates from tax records, it pays to remember that the data are just an approximation of the real thing. Certainly when we attempt to trace consumption over several decades, apparent trends are somewhat misleading given that the role of illicit production was greater in the 1950s than it is today, while wastage was probably less (given that average prices were much higher). And in comparing sales across states, the tax-based data need to be adjusted for the fact that some states—New Hampshire, Nevada—sell a large percentage of alcoholic beverages to visitors from out of state.

Figure 4.1 depicts the national trend in sales of ethanol, based on wholesale shipments of alcoholic beverages multiplied by their average ethanol content and divided by the population age fourteen and over (a standard if somewhat arbitrary age cutoff). The per capita consumption of ethanol peaked in 1980 and 1981 at 2.76 gallons[3]—the equivalent of over eleven drinks per week for every man, woman, and adolescent. Since then the annual average dropped about 22 percent to 2.14 gallons per capita in 1997–1998, with an upward trend since then. Also of interest are the trends in the relative importance of beer, spirits, and wine. Spirits and beer were of similar importance as sources of ethanol until the mid–1970s.[4] However, since then ethanol consumption from spirits has plummeted. In 2003, beer accounted for 55 percent of all ethanol, compared to 30 percent for spirits and 15 percent for wine.

Broadly speaking, the consumption trends observed in the United States are similar to those in most other economically advanced countries. Between the Second World War and the 1970s, consumption increased in almost all countries that were able to offer reasonably accurate statistics, with the largest growth rates recorded by countries that started from a relatively low level. Consequently, the trend was toward narrowing of international differences in ethanol consumption (Sulkunen 1983). Consumption per capita fell in most OECD countries during the 1980s (Edwards et al. 1994, 35). In recent years, apparent per capita alcohol consumption in the United States is about the same as Canada and the United Kingdom and lower than in Western Europe with the exception of several Nordic countries. At the very top of the world-drinking list are Luxembourg, Ireland, Portugal, France, and Germany

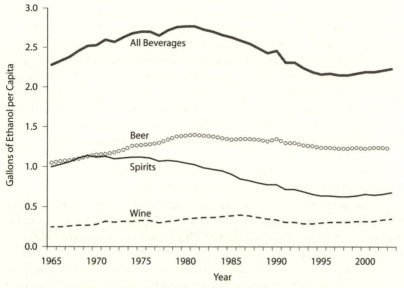

Figure 4.1. Per Capita Consumption of Ethanol (1965–2003).
Source: Annual tax-paid sales data (http://pubs.niaaa.nih.gov/publications/surveillance73/tab1_03.htm)
Note: Population data for those age 14 and over (15 and over prior to 1970).

where consumption is half again as high as in the United States (Commodity Board for the Distilled Spirits Industry 1999). The Japanese average about the same alcohol intake as North Americans, while estimates indicate that the Chinese and residents of other Asian countries drink a good deal less, as do Latin Americans.

The geography of drinking within the United States can be ascertained up to a point from tax data. Per capita sales of alcoholic beverages range from 2.89 gallons in Delaware to 1.27 gallons in Utah (Nephew et al. 2003).[5] There is a regional pattern, with New England states at the high end and the East South Central region (Alabama and its neighbors) at the low end. Interestingly, the differences among states are less now than a couple of decades ago: The interstate standard deviation, with state per capita sales weighted by population, declined from 0.55 gallons per capita in 1980 to 0.32 gallons per capita in 2000.

Survey Data

Needless to say, the per capita average ethanol consumption conceals a great deal of variation across individuals and groups. According to one national survey, for example, 35 percent of the U.S. adult population did not have even a single drink of alcohol in 2000.[6] Average consumption for those who drink is half again as high as the average consumption when the abstainers are included in the denominator. And even that average conceals the great variety of drinking practices.

The only practical means of obtaining information on individual consumption, and on drinking patterns within a group, is by self-report. The report may be requested in a questionnaire on medical issues distributed by a primary care physician to her patients, or by a researcher conducting an epidemiological study of the health consequences of drinking, or in interviews with a population sample that is representative of a state or the nation. Although a vast number of surveys that include some items on drinking have been fielded (Sindelar 1993), only a handful provide consistent information over time for the U.S. population.[7]

A comprehensive survey of alcohol use may include items about whether the respondent has ever drunk, and if so whether he drank in the last year, and the last month (Rehm 1998). Sometimes there are also items about the preceding week or two weeks. To determine the quantity of consumption, surveys tend to adopt one of two approaches. The quantity-frequency (QF) approach asks those who admit to drinking on just how many occasions they have had a drink in the previous year or month, and then how many drinks they "usually" had per occasion. This approach works well for respondents who tend to drink the same amount per occasion, but will be misleading for others: for example, a person who has a beer with dinner on weekdays and then drinks a six-pack on Saturday nights could honestly report "six occasions per week" and "one" as the number of drinks usually consumed, but the result would be to capture only half of his weekly consumption. As a partial solution to this problem, the QF approach is sometimes enhanced to include an item on the frequency of heavy drinking, usually defined as five or more drinks.

An alternative approach seeks to obtain more detailed information by asking how many days in a given period the respondent consumed one or two drinks, how many days he consumed three or four drinks, and so forth. Although this approach provides a logical basis for estimating total consumption, it imposes greater demands on the respondent's patience and recall ability.

The fact is that no matter what sequence of questions is included, surveys tend to underestimate overall alcohol consumption by a wide margin. If tax data on sales are used as the standard, then survey-based estimates of national consumption only captured 40–60 percent as a rule during the 1970s (Midanik 1982). This rule still applies in the case of some more recent surveys. For example, the 2001–2002 National Epidemiologic Survey on Alcohol and Related Conditions (NESARC), conducted by NIAAA, provides an estimate of per capita consumption that is about half of recorded per capita sales.[8]

The rather large shortfall in survey-based estimates may be the result of samples that are unrepresentative of the drinking public in important ways. Some heavy-drinking groups are underrepresented either because they are not in the sampling frame (homeless people and those in institutions) or because it is difficult to contact them and gain their cooperation (e.g., people with transitory lifestyles) (Polich and Orvis 1979, 56). But probably more important than bias from unrepresentative samples is the tendency of respondents to understate their true consumption. That bias in self-reporting is not surprising. People who are embarrassed about their drinking habit, or who are concerned that the survey interviewer may think less of them if they tell the truth, or are worried that the promised anonymity of the survey will be violated, will be inclined to understate their drinking. Of course it is also true that respondents may have a selective memory when it comes to recalling how much they drink. As the old joke has it, denial is not just a river in Egypt.

With surveys, the details matter. Results are sensitive to the specific methods used: the precise wording of questions, the sequence in which questions are asked, the means of administering the questions (by phone, in person, in writing), and of course the sampling procedure. For example, a comparison of two sets of survey results for high school seniors showed that Monitoring the Future (MTF) data indicated a much higher prevalence of drinking and bingeing than the National Longitudinal Survey of Youth (NLSY) (Cook, Moore, and Pacula 1993). One likely explanation is that MTF questionnaires were administered in the classroom, while NLSY respondents were interviewed at home.[9]

Similarly, three different national surveys using somewhat different items and sampling methods, but all of high quality, produced estimates of the annual prevalence of current drinking ranging from 44 percent to 65 percent—a far larger difference than would result from random sampling variability (Dawson 2003, 24).[10] On the other hand, the results from the National Alcohol Survey, fielded every five years using a consistent design, tend to be quite similar from one wave to the next, with estimates for the prevalence of current drinking of 69 percent (1984), 65 percent (1990), and 65 percent (1995).

Given these problems, should we pay any attention to survey results on drinking patterns? Fortunately, accurate reports from respondents are not necessary for learning something about drinking patterns across the population. What is needed are reports that bear a systematic relationship to the truth. For example, the true patterns would be preserved if all respondents reported a fraction of their true consumption, so long as that fraction were the same for everyone. In fact, even if the fraction reported differs among individuals, we could accurately compare relative consumption levels across groups as long as the fraction was the same *on average* for each of the groups. And the per capita consumption levels of different groups are not the only statistic for which surveys are used: some characteristics of the consumption distribution, such as the percentage who drink, may be more accurately assessed from surveys than other statistics, such as the percentage who drink heavily. But there is little direct evidence on this matter.[11]

Certainly any prudent user of survey data would proceed with great caution, checking to the extent possible with other surveys, with sales data, and with other benchmarks. Some patterns come through so consistently as to be entirely credible, while others are more questionable. It is entirely credible that men drink more than women, since that is a universal finding from surveys and because it comports with data from alcohol involvement in traffic accidents and other administrative sources—not to mention casual observation. On the other hand, the consistent finding from surveys that blacks drink less than whites is called into question (although not flatly contradicted) by data on alcohol involvement in traffic accidents and some other measures. In any event, President Reagan's approach to nuclear disarmament treaties may apply to use of survey data: "trust, but verify."[12]

THE DISTRIBUTION OF ALCOHOL CONSUMPTION IN THE POPULATION

Within most any group, alcohol consumption will differ widely among individuals. A well-known rule of thumb in marketing science, known as the Pareto Law or the Law of the Heavy Half or the 80–20 Rule, is that the top 20 percent of buyers for most any consumer product account for fully 80 percent of the sales. Alcoholic beverages are no exception. The heaviest drinkers account for the bulk of all ethanol consumption. The distribution is highly skewed to the right, with median less than the mean: in other words, most drinkers consume less than the per capita average. This pattern is apparent in every national survey, and is illustrated here using one of the best, the National Epidemiologic Survey on Alcohol and Related Conditions (NESARC).[13]

Suppose we divide American adults into deciles according to how much they drink, and personify each decile by a single individual (Gerstein 1981, 193). The average consumption of these ten individuals is the national average (in 2000) of 2.2 gallons of ethanol or 556 drinks each year.[14] Imagine them lined up in order of their alcohol consumption, from low to high. The first three individuals drank nothing at all in the past month. The fourth and fifth individuals had less than one drink in the past month. At the end of the line with the highest consumption, the tenth person consumed 316.5 drinks during the past month (see figure 4.2).

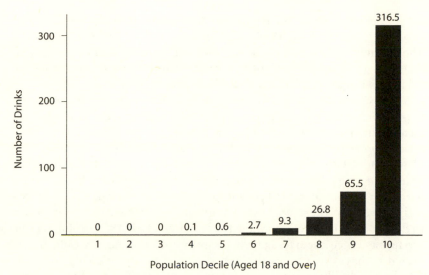

Figure 4.2. Number of Drinks Per Capita Consumed in the Past Month by Decile. *Source*: 2001–2002 NESARC.

Thus, the top decile consumes well over half the alcohol in any one year; people in this group are drinking an average of seventy-four standard drinks per week. On the other hand, the median adult drinks only rarely, and the median among those who do drink—excluding the abstainers—is just over three drinks per week. In short, most adults in America abstain or drink very lightly, whereas those who drink heavily consume most drinks. The general shape of the distribution, while based on survey data, has been documented in many times and places, and is widely accepted as a stylized fact by scholars in the field.[15] One consequence is that the heaviest drinkers are of greatly disproportionate importance to the sales and profitability of the alcoholic-beverage industry: if the top decile somehow could be induced to cut their consumption level to that of the next lower group (the ninth decile), then total ethanol sales would fall by 60 percent.

Actually it is unlikely that any available intervention (short of rigorously enforced rationing) would truncate the distribution in this fashion. International comparative studies of drinking distributions have found remarkable consistency in their shape. This phenomenon was first documented by the Frenchman, Sully Ledermann, in the 1950s: he asserted, making a rather bold inferential leap from the evidence available to him, that the size distribution of alcohol consumption among *any* naturally occurring population group has the same general shape, namely that of a lognormal distribution (Ledermann 1956). That specific claim has been investigated quite thoroughly by alcohol researchers, with mixed results, but it does appear that the lognormal distribution provides a reasonably good fit (Edwards et al. 1994; Schmidt and Popham 1978; Skog 1980). The distribution has a single peak (mode) at a low level of consumption, and a long tail to the right of that mode, with the mean exceeding the median in rough concordance with the lognormal pattern.[16]

As per capita consumption by drinkers increases (over time or across populations), the consumption associated with each quantile tends to increase in proportion (Edwards et al. 1994, 83–90). Hence, as per capita consumption declines, as it did in many Western countries in the 1980s and 1990s, the prevalence of heavy drinking will decline also. Indeed, the prevalence of heavy drinking (defined by any absolute standard with respect to annual consumption) typically declines proportionately *more* than the average consumption, and in fact has been shown to fit a quadratic function (Skog 1985; Bruun et al. 1975). Thus, if one group has twice the average consumption of another, it would be expected to have four times the prevalence of heavy drinking. And the 20 percent decline in average consumption in the United States in the 1980s and 1990s implies a 36 percent decline in the prevalence of heavy drinking.

Patterns among Groups

Survey data indicate certain consistent differences in drinking among population groups. To illustrate, we tabulate results from the NESARC for 2001–2002. Sixty-five percent of adults reported having at least one drink during the previous twelve months. The prevalence of self-reported drinking decreases in middle age and is lower for women than men. For both men and women the prevalence of drinking increases with education and family income, and is lower for blacks than whites or Hispanics. The proportion of drinkers who drank five or more drinks on a single occasion in the previous twelve months follows pretty much the same patterns (see figures 4.3 and 4.4).

To isolate the effects of these and other characteristics, multivariate logit regressions were estimated with demographic and socioeconomic characteristics as covariates. The complete results are displayed in table 4.1. This table provides separate estimates for men and women. The first two columns of numbers report the results on the correlates of the likelihood of drinking (versus abstaining entirely); the last two columns of numbers report the correlates of the likelihood of occasional binge drinking for those who drink. These results, unlike those in the bar charts of figures 4.3 and 4.4, measure the partial effect of a particular characteristic, holding constant other characteristics. Among the more interesting findings are these:

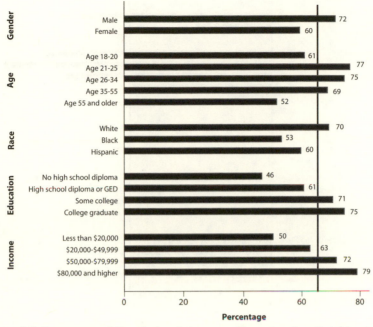

Figure 4.3. Percentage of Population Subgroups Reporting Any Drinking in the Past Twelve Months.
Source: 2001–2002 NESARC.
Note: Vertical bar represents drinking prevalence for entire adult population.

- The prevalence of drinking peaks in the early twenties for both males and females; furthermore, the likelihood that a drinker binges on occasion is highest for this age group.

- Blacks are less likely to report drinking than Hispanics or whites.

- Never-married singles are more likely to drink, and binge if they do drink, than married people.

- Respondents in the two highest income brackets (greater than $50,000 per year) are more likely to drink than the lowest income group (less than $20,000 per year).

- People with a college degree are more likely to drink, but less likely to binge if they drink, than people with less schooling.

- People in "fair" or "poor" health are generally less likely to drink than those in good health.

- For women, working outside the home or attending school are associated with higher rates of drinking.

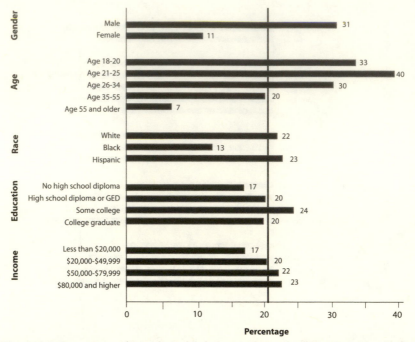

Figure 4.4. Percentage of Population Subgroups Reporting Binge Drinking in the Past Twelve Months.
Source: 2001–2002 NESARC.
Note: Vertical bar represents binge drinking prevalence for entire adult population. "Binge drinkers" are those who report consuming five or more drinks on an occasion.

It is important to note that each of these patterns emerges even after all other characteristics on the list are taken into account. Thus, we cannot "explain" the finding with respect to health status by saying that it just reflects the association between health status and age. The regression results demonstrate that even after adjusting for age, health status is associated with the likelihood of drinking.

EXPENDITURES

The analysis so far has focused on the ethanol content of alcoholic beverages, for obvious reasons. Books are not written about alcohol-free beer and "bloody shame" cocktails. But it should not be forgotten that the ethanol comes in the form of a commodity, or class of commodities, and it is those commodities that are manufactured, imported, shipped, and sold at retail. Drinking choices reflect preferences over beverages, which have a variety of relevant attributes other than ethanol content—some of

TABLE 4.1
Logit Estimates for Any Drinking and Binge Drinking in the Past Twelve Months,
Age 18 and Older

	Any Drinking		Binge Drinking (Drinkers Only)	
	Males	Females	Males	Females
Age				
(Default age 65 and older)				
Age 18 to 20	0.451[a]	0.274[a]	1.873[a]	2.855[a]
	(0.101)	(0.091)	(0.127)	(0.203)
Age 21 to 25	1.056[a]	0.972[a]	2.284[a]	3.073[a]
	(0.091)	(0.071)	(0.113)	(0.187)
Age 26 to 34	0.965[a]	0.880[a]	2.023[a]	2.655[a]
	(0.075)	(0.059)	(0.101)	(0.183)
Age 35 to 49	0.623[a]	0.651[a]	1.548[a]	2.195[a]
	(0.063)	(0.053)	(0.095)	(0.180)
Age 50 to 64	0.328[a]	0.371[a]	1.031[a]	1.387[a]
	(0.059)	(0.051)	(0.094)	(0.183)
Marital Status				
(Default: Single)				
Married	− 0.439[a]	−0.499[a]	−0.499[a]	−0.667[a]
	(0.054)	(.043)	(0.056)	(0.070)
Divorced or Separated	−0.344[a]	−0.027	−0.136[b]	0.067
	(0.062)	(0.049)	(0.064)	(0.070)
Widowed	−0.564[a]	−0.510[a]	−0.238	−0.360[b]
	(0.092)	(0.058)	(0.148)	(0.160)
Race and Ethnicity				
(Default white and other)				
Hispanic	−0.103[b]	−0.621[a]	−0.092[c]	−0.326[a]
	(0.047)	(0.039)	(0.051)	(0.066)
Black	−0.371[a]	−0.723[a]	−0.738[a]	−0.970[a]
	(0.048)	(0.039)	(0.062)	(0.078)
Education (Highest Degree				
Completed)				
(Default: High school dropout)				
High School Diploma or GED	−0.033	0.042	−0.036	−0.074
	(0.041)	(0.034)	(0.049)	(0.061)
College Degree	0.259[a]	0.261[a]	−0.391[a]	−0.299[a]
	(0.045)	(0.037)	(0.049)	(0.060)

Table 4.1 (*cont'd*)
Logit Estimates for Any Drinking and Binge Drinking in the Past Twelve Months, Age 18 and Older

	Any Drinking		Binge Drinking (Drinkers Only)	
	Males	*Females*	*Males*	*Females*
Employment or Student Status (Default: Neither employed nor student)				
Working Full Time	0.076 (0.050)	0.378[a] (0.037)	0.139[b] (0.060)	0.033 (0.062)
Working Part Time	0.140[b] (0.071)	0.358[a] (0.047)	0.145[c] (0.083)	−0.118 (0.076)
Enrolled as a Student Full Time	−0.079 (0.099)	0.279[a] (0.083)	−0.000 (0.106)	0.046 (0.100)
Enrolled as a Student Part-Time	−0.188 (0.129)	0.279[a] (0.083)	−0.153 (0.131)	−0.103 (0.127)
Annual Household Income (Default: under $20,000)				
$20,000–$49,000	0.254[a] (0.046)	0.321[a] (0.036)	−0.066 (0.059)	−0.165[a] (0.064)
$50,000–$79,999	0.537[a] (0.057)	0.619[a] (0.048)	−0.104 (0.067)	−0.133[c] (0.077)
$80,000 and more	0.740[a] (0.067)	0.981[a] (0.058)	−0.062 (0.073)	−0.010 (0.087)
Self-Perceived Health Status (Default: excellent health)				
Very Good Health	0.162[a] (0.046)	0.098[b] (0.039)	0.169[a] (0.047)	0.152[b] (0.059)
Good Health	0.031 (0.049)	−0.033 (0.041)	0.293[a] (0.054)	0.210[a] (0.067)
Fair Health	−0.215[a] (0.061)	−0.342[a] (0.051)	0.298[a] (0.079)	0.265[a] (0.097)
Poor Health	−0.713[a] (0.085)	−0.728[a] (0.073)	0.184 (0.136)	0.524[a] (0.158)
Missing Health	−1.116[a] (0.240)	−1.931[a] (0.261)	−0.451 (0.485)	−1.076 (1.041)

TABLE 4.1 (*cont'd*)
Logit Estimates for Any Drinking and Binge Drinking in the Past Twelve Months,
Age 18 and Older

	Any Drinking		Binge Drinking (Drinkers Only)	
	Males	Females	Males	Females
Body Weight				
Body Weight (in 100 lb)	0.115[b]	−0.019	0.137[a]	0.147[b]
	(0.048)	(0.0400	(0.052)	(0.064)
Missing Body Weight	−0.710[a]	0.734[a]	−0.724[a]	−0.228
	(0.165)	(0.098)	(0.258)	(0.188)
Sample Size	18518	24575	13067	13879
R²	0.081	0.132	0.096	0.118

Source: 2001–2002 NESARC.

Note: Indicator variables for Census divisions were included in these regressions, but the results are omitted from this table.

[a] Significantly different than zero at the 1% level.
[b] Significantly different than zero at the 5% level.
[c] Significantly different than zero at the 10% level.

which (such as whether the beverage is purchased for consumption on premise or at home) affect the socially relevant consequences. The economic characteristics of the markets for alcoholic beverages are thus an important part of the story.

In fact, the alcoholic-beverage industry is not that large, although larger than the other legal vices. Total domestic sales of alcoholic beverages amounted to $129 billion in 2001 (Adams Business Media 2003), less than 2 percent of personal consumption expenditures in that year.[17] In comparison, sales of tobacco products in 2001 accounted for 1 percent of total expenditures, while sales of lottery tickets accounted for less than 1 percent of total consumer expenditures in the same year (U.S. Census Bureau 2003). Since most drinking households spend less than the average, it's safe to say that expenditures on alcoholic beverages do not impose a financial burden for most drinking households.

Beverages are sold both as package goods for home consumption (off-premise) and as drinks at bars and restaurants (on-premise). Expenditures are divided about evenly between on- and off-premise, but most alcohol by volume is consumed off-premise: 79 percent of spirits and wine, and 75 percent of beer, in 2002 (Adams Business Media 2003).[18]

Not all drinks are purchased by consumers. Firms buy alcoholic beverages for office parties, or to entertain clients. Fraternities and clubs may buy alcohol for their members. The proportion of the market accounted for by such purchases is not part of any public database. By one estimate, employers pick up the tab for about 20 percent of sales (Sammartino 1990, 76).

Concluding Thoughts

The most reliable data we have on drinking are a by-product of the tax-collection system. Per capita tax-paid sales provide fairly reliable information about trends and interstate patterns in per capita ethanol consumption. These data are of considerable interest to the alcohol-beverage industry, but only indirectly relevant to understanding the drinking "problem." That requires information on the distribution of drinking across the population, not only with respect to the number of drinks per month, but also the extent to which those drinks (if more than a few) are concentrated on a few days rather than spread more evenly. For that sort of assessment, survey data are needed. But survey results in this area are like many police informants—the information they provide is essential, but should always be treated with skepticism until verified by other sources.

As we have seen, there are certain patterns in drinking that have become well established after decades of study. Some of the demographic and socioeconomic patterns are in this category. Men really do drink more than women, and youths more than the elderly. Among the most intriguing findings is that the population distribution of consumption among those who drink follows a particular shape, akin to the lognormal distribution, with a high concentration of total consumption at the upper tail. Sully Ledermann and his followers concluded that this regularity implied a vital role for *average* consumption in dictating the prevalence of heavy drinking, with the implication that any effort to reduce the prevalence of heavy drinkers would require a reduction in average consumption. That remains an intriguing hypothesis rather than a fact, one that helps motivate the population perspective. If correct, it suggests that the upward trend in average consumption since 1998 portends increased alcohol-related problems.

CHAPTER 5

Prices and Quantities

> Alcoholic beverages seem to behave in consumer markets like
> other commodities.
> —Kettil Bruun and colleagues,
> *Alcohol Control Policies in Public Health Perspective*

THE NOBLE EXPERIMENT of Prohibition was a failure in the sense that it lost popular support. But as we have seen, it was associated with a sharp reduction in alcohol consumption and alcoholism. Although there is some wisdom in the view that "you can't legislate morality," legislation *can* influence prices and availability, and hence the choices people make— regardless of whether those choices are informed by moral considerations as well.

As it turns out, the evidence on how prices and availability affect drinking is not limited to the unusual circumstances of Prohibition. Economists and others have analyzed the response of alcohol sales and consumption to more routine changes in supply that result from taxes and regulations. The clear conclusion is that even modest government efforts to limit supply can reduce alcohol consumption. More surprising, given common notions of addiction, is that supply limitations have a direct effect on the prevalence of alcohol abuse and dependence. Higher prices may help some people retain or regain control over their drinking.

THE PRICE EFFECT

Prices matter. The First Law of Economics is that of "downward sloping demand." If the price of a commodity increases, the quantity demanded by consumers will decline—*not* because they want it any less, but because they have other wants as well, and limited means. Like most laws, this one is violated occasionally, but in unusual circumstances. For example, for commodities in which consumers tend to judge quality by price, as perhaps with a luxury brand of skin moisturizer, it is possible that a higher price will attract greater interest on the part of buyers. But the fascination with such cases outstrips their actual importance in the real world. Economic science offers a strong presumption that alcoholic beverages will obey the First Law. For evidence we need look no further than the politics of alcohol excise taxes—the producers, distributors, and retailers line up to lobby Congress against excise taxes because they know that prices can't be raised to cover the cost of the tax without losing sales.

Still, the First Law does not tell us what we really want to know—whether a price increase will result in a reduction in the average consumption of one ingredient of alcoholic beverages (the alcohol). For example, in response to higher beer prices, consumers may increase their purchases of wine or spirits. A beer-tax increase may also cause substitutions within the "beer" category, such as between on-premise and off-premise consumption, or between beers with higher and lower ethanol content. And it is not clear whether a reduction in overall sales of ethanol, if it does occur, will affect the incidence of risky drinking occasions. To determine the effect of beverage prices on the quantity and patterns of ethanol consumption, then, it is necessary to turn to actual experience—the data.

MULTIPLE DETERMINANTS OF DEMAND

The first thing to note is that for most individuals the prices of alcoholic beverages are not the primary influence on whether they drink and if so, how much. Drinking choices are largely governed by personal circumstances, tastes, and the social environment (Bobo and Husten 2000; Godfrey 1989). Journalist Pete Hamill's paean to the "drinking life" provides a more poetic statement of this truth: "The culture of drink endures because it offers so many rewards: confidence for the shy, clarity for the uncertain, solace to the wounded and lonely, and above all, the elusive promises of friendship and love" (1995).

We saw in chapter 4 that about one-third of the adult public abstains from drinking entirely, and another 15 percent drink less than once per month. For most people the decision to abstain is not an economic one, but rather a choice reflecting such considerations as poor health, pregnancy, religious scruples, or simply a dislike for the taste or the "buzz." Abstention prevalence increases with age, as older people often quit drinking due to poor health or other concerns. Table 5.1 lists the main reason given by nearly 16,000 abstainers in a National Health Interview Survey. Note that a majority simply weren't interested—60 percent said they disliked alcohol or thought there was no need to drink it. One in seven cited medical reasons, and another 5 percent were either recovering alcoholics or had a family member who was an alcoholic. Finally, 16 percent cited religious or moral reasons, or said that they were brought up not to drink. Only 1 percent of these respondent abstainers indicated that cost was

TABLE 5.1
Distribution of Abstainers by Main Reason for Not Drinking

Main Reason for Not Drinking	Percent of Abstrainers
No need/not necessary	18
Don't care for alcohol/dislike it	42
Medical/health reasons	14
Religious/moral reasons, brought up not to drink	16
Cost too much	1
Family member an alcoholic	3
Recovering alcoholic	2
Other	5

Source: 1990 National Health Interview Survey, HPDP Sample, item 1d.

their main reason, although cost presumably played a secondary role for some of the others.

For those who do drink, the choice of how much to drink is also influenced by personal circumstances and tastes. Physiological factors play a role: many people of Asian origin, for example, have an unpleasant flushing response (as a result of difficulty in metabolizing alcohol) if they drink too much. The development of tolerance also has a physiological basis, as the body adapts in a variety of ways through the accumulation of drinking experience. But the taste for alcohol, like the taste for most any commodity, reflects a more general learning process in the context of family, community, and media influences.

For most drinkers, and especially younger drinkers, drinking is a social activity, and drinking choices are shaped by social context. A "swinging single" may transition to a more sedate lifestyle after finding a mate, and hence cut back on drinking, as barhopping gives way to evenings at home or PTA meetings (Miller-Tutzauer, Leonard, and Windle 1991). Work life also plays a role, with certain industries and occupations—the military, construction, sales, "hospitality"—being more conducive to drinking than others (Stinson, DeBakey, and Steffens 1992). The "wetness" of the social environment also has a geographic dimension. The expectation (and reality) of whether drinks will be served at a party, or ordered by a group of friends dining at a restaurant, is different in Salt Lake City than in Boston, as are the likely social sanctions for becoming intoxicated. Even the season of the year has some influence, with, for example, a higher prevalence of drinking occuring in early winter than throughout the rest of the year (Cho, Johnson, and Fendrich 2001; Dexter 1900).

Although personal circumstances, tastes, and social environment go a long way toward explaining drinking patterns and levels, it is also true that for some people some of the time, economic considerations play a role. Prices of alcoholic beverages, as well as personal income and the costs of consumption activities that may serve as substitutes for drinking, are part of the story, as is the availability of alcohol—where and when it can be acquired and consumed. The First Law of downward sloping demand applies more reliably to aggregate drinking in a community than to drinking by any one individual in that community. A price increase will have no effect on teetotalers, and is unlikely to affect choices made by moderate drinkers who are wealthy enough not to notice. But although a price increase affects the decisions of only a fraction of the drinkers, the aggregate result will be a decline in per capita consumption, and the "law" is thereby upheld.

This price effect is amplified somewhat by the fact that people tend to coordinate their drinking on social occasions. If individual drinking decisions are positively linked to the drinking practices of others, then there will be a "social multiplier" in the response of aggregate alcohol consumption with respect to prices and other external influences (Glaeser, Sacerdote, and Scheinkman 2003); social influence will amplify the direct effects of such variables. For example, when two friends have dinner together, if one decides to forego a before-dinner drink due to the price increase (the direct effect), the other may decide to forego the drink because her friend is not drinking (social influence). Estimates of the price effect using aggregate data do not distinguish between the direct and social effect, and there is only limited evidence on the contribution of the multiplier (Norton, Lindrooth, and Ennett 1998; Gaviria and Raphael 2001; Bullers, Cooper, and Russell 2001; Mason and Windle 2001; Baumann and Ennett 1996).

Economists usually report the responsiveness of quantity demanded to price changes in terms of an "elasticity." The price elasticity of demand is simply the percentage change in quantity associated with a 1 percent increase in price. For example, a typical estimate of the price elasticity of demand for beer is −0.3, which is to say that a 1 percent increase in price (an increase from, say, $7.00 to $7.07 in the average price of a six-pack) causes a reduction of three-tenths of 1 percent in quantity. It's hard to believe that anyone would forego a six-pack just because of an extra 7 cents, but notice that an elasticity of −0.3 supports that intuition; that elasticity implies that the 1 percent increase in price will discourage a purchase just three times in a thousand. Casual observation and introspection (the usual sources of such intuition) are not reliable guides concerning such rare events. Perhaps it's more intuitive that a larger increase in price, say from $7.00 to $7.70, will have an effect. With an elasticity of −.3, that 10 percent price increase would reduce quantity sold by 3 percent.

Given the limited role of price in influencing drinking decisions, why is it of particular interest? The answer is that prices, unlike tastes or upbringing or cultural environment, are directly influenced by policies governing the marketing of alcoholic beverages. Liquor prices are set by a state agency in control states. Excise taxes, which apply to all types of beverages in all states, are passed along to buyers as higher prices. Policies influencing the competitive environment in which alcohol is sold also affect prices. The list of such policies is long. It begins with licensing rules and fees, and goes on to include rules limiting on-premise price promotions, advertising, and the direct shipment of alcohol to homes. Although government agencies also attempt to influence drinking through education and public service spots, those efforts are of uncertain and limited effectiveness. Prices matter, and they can be influenced in reliable fashion through taxes and regulation.

EVIDENCE FROM AGGREGATE SALES

Econometric studies of sales data for alcoholic beverages have been conducted in many countries with a wide variety of data sets. One review tabulated results from such studies for 18 nations, including the United States (Edwards et al. 1994). Estimated elasticities for beer, wine, and spirits differ widely over time, place, data set, and estimation method, but one conclusion stands out: In almost every case the estimated price elasticity is negative. In that fundamental respect, at least, it appears that alcoholic beverages are like other commodities (Bruun et al. 1975; Leung and Phelps 1993; Cook and Moore 2000).

Clements and colleagues (1997) report results for their estimates of systems of demand equations for Australia, Canada, Finland, New Zealand, Norway, Sweden, and the United Kingdom, in each case using aggregate data covering about thirty years. Their average price elasticities are −0.35 for beer, −0.68 for wine, and −0.98 for spirits. Beer has a smaller price elasticity than liquor in all seven countries. This pattern is well established though still somewhat mysterious.[1]

Still, the econometric literature on the price elasticity of alcohol sales reveals a distressingly wide range of results. Even when we limit the comparison to estimates for U.S. data, there is nothing like a consensus on the magnitudes. One problem is that the econometricians do not have the benefit of controlled experiments. The effects of the price changes that do occur may well be concealed or confounded by the effects of other

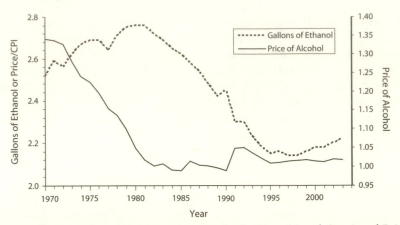

Figure 5.1. U.S. Ethanol Consumption Per Capita (Age 14 and Over) and Price of Alcohol (1970–2003).
Source: NIAAA and Bureau of Labor Statistics.
Note: "Price of alcohol" is the ratio of the "alcohol" component of the CPI to the overall CPI, set equal to 1 in 1983.

changes in the economy or society. Isolating the effect of price changes from all the other changes is difficult in this circumstance, and estimated values are likely to be sensitive to the nature of the data and statistical method—all the more so because the real world rarely offers anything but small year-to-year changes in prices.

These issues can be illustrated by a look at the sales data for the United States from 1970 to 2003. To keep things simple and focused on the consequences of public concern, it is useful to combine sales of beer, wine, and spirits into a single quantity figure based on ethanol content. As seen in figure 5.1, the per capita annual sales of alcoholic beverages dropped from 2.76 gallons (in 1980) to 2.14 gallons per adult (in 1997), with a slight increase in subsequent years. During the period since 1980, there was little change in the average price of alcoholic beverages (adjusted for overall inflation). The large reduction in alcohol sales during this period reflects changes in other factors that influence drinking, such as income, culture, demography, patterns of work and play, or perhaps the increasingly effective campaign against drunk driving by Mothers Against Drunk Driving and other advocacy groups.

The one "bump" on the flat price trend during this period is the 5 percent jump in real (inflation adjusted) alcoholic-beverage prices in 1991, which resulted from a substantial increase in federal excise taxes on beer, wine, and liquor at the beginning of that year.[2] This abrupt change in prices seems like a promising source of evidence on the magnitude of the price effect. Looking at the sales trend around that time, note the small upturn in 1990 followed by a sharp drop in 1991. The upturn was surely the result of a surge in wholesale shipments to beat the increase in the excise tax. By 1992, retail and home inventories had adapted to the new tax level, and sales were a good deal lower than prior to the tax increase, but not noticeably different than what can be projected from the trend line of the 1980s. If other economic factors had been pretty much constant during this brief period, it would hence be a reasonable conclusion that ethanol sales had not been much affected by that tax increase. But as it turns out, the economy was slipping during this period, which would have pushed alcohol sales down even in the absence of the tax increase; median household income, adjusted for inflation, declined by 2.3 percent between 1988 and 1992. Trying to sort out the effects of the price increase and income reduction net of trend is more than eyeballing a simple graph can accomplish!

A standard approach for taking account of several factors simultaneously is multivariate regression. A regression of annual ethanol sales on prices, median household income, and time trend, all (except the trend) in natural-log form, yields strong evidence that price has the expected effect on sales.[3] The estimated price elasticity of demand is −0.40 (with standard error of 0.18).

How accurate are these estimates? It is difficult to say. The regression analysis has a built-in presumption that the combined effects of trends in all variables relevant to determining per capita sales (other than price and income) yielded a constant rate of change in the rate that the demand for ethanol during these three decades was evolving. That assumption fits the data well, but may still be in error—in which case the estimates of price and income elasticities may be substantially biased. An alternative approach is to introduce other covariates to control for trends in culture, lifestyle, demographics, and all the rest of the factors that may influence drinking trends. But that method for "holding other factors constant" isn't satisfactory in this case—there's not enough data to control for each of the potentially relevant effects. Even with a larger data set this approach will never be entirely convincing because there are so many possible candidates for those "other factors."

Another method utilizes data on price and alcohol sales for states. Sales data are available by state as a by-product of the requirement that wholesale shipments be reported for excise-tax purposes (see chapter 4). With state data, instead of having a single time profile of sales and prices, we have fifty. And it is helpful that demographic, cultural, and economic trends in the fifty states tend to have a lot in common, but that the states follow somewhat different pricing policies with respect to alcoholic beverages. In effect the states serve as "controls" for each other, while providing evidence on how different price trajectories influence sales over time. Estimates of price effects utilizing panel data on states were first published by George Tauchen and me (Cook and Tauchen 1982), and this approach has become standard (Ruhm

TABLE 5.2
Effects of Excise Taxes and Income on Alcohol Sales (1971–2000)

Ln State Sales (ounces of ethanol per capita)	Estimated Coefficient on Excise Tax (Standard Error)	Estimated Coefficient on Ln Income (Standard Error)	Estimated Price Elasticity
Beer	−1.66[a] (0.48)	0.144 (0.099)	−0.74
Wine	−1.21[b] (0.58)	0.535[a] (.149)	−0.49
Liquor	−2.44[b] (1.05)	0.346[b] (.152)	−1.47
Combined Ethnol	−1.84[b] (0.85)	.342[b] (.151)	

Source: State panel data, 1971–2000; OLS regression results.

Note: Robust standard errors in parentheses, state clusters. Regression specifications included state and year fixed effects. Sales units are ounces of ethanol while tax units are dollars per ounce of ethanol. For a description of how prices and tax rates were calculated, see the appendix. The number of states in the sample vary with availability of tax information: for the beer regressions, all 50 states and DC are included, for wine, 47 states and DC, for liquor, 32 states and DC. "Combined ethanol" is ounces of ethanol sales from all 3 sources combined; the tax index is the weighted average of tax per ounce for each state, with weights equal to share of ethanol from each beverage type (averaged over 30 years, separately for each state). "Income" is personal disposable income per capita, adjusted for inflation. The price elasticity is computed by multiplying the tax coefficient by the average price, and then dividing by the estimated tax markup.

[a] p<.01; [b] p<.05

1995; Young and Bielinska-Kwapisz 2003). Table 5.2 provides an updated set of results, using annual data for the period 1971 to 2000.

The results summarized in this table are based on panel regressions using thirty years of annual state data. Every regression includes the variables of particular economic interest—the "price" variable together with per capita income, both adjusted for inflation. The price variables are actually the excise tax rates. These are utilized in lieu of a good alcohol-price index at the state level.[4] Fortunately for our (statistical) purposes, the tax rate is a good proxy for average price: as a rule, changes in excise taxes are quickly passed along to the consumer as higher prices, with some markup (Young and Bielinska-Kwapisz 2002, 2003).

To ensure that the estimates of the effects of these variables are not being confounded by other variables, every regression includes a full set of "state" and "year" fixed effects. The "state" fixed effects control for all the ways in which Alabama is different from Utah is different from

Massachusetts, year in and year out, when it comes to influencing per capita alcohol consumption. The "year" fixed effects control for any shared national trend in the noneconomic influences on drinking.

The results confirm once again that prices matter in alcohol sales. In each case the price (tax) effect is negative and estimated quite precisely. The estimated price elasticities are quite high for beer and, true to form, higher still for liquor. The results on the income variable confirm that people tend to drink more as their incomes increase; in particular, a 10 percent increase in average income, other things equal, leads to a 3.4 percent increase in average ethanol sales (with wine and liquor especially responsive). This estimate is more reliable than the much smaller estimate from national trend data, reported above.

It would be interesting to explore the cross-price effects as well. What, for instance, is the effect on beer sales of an increase in the liquor tax, or the effect on liquor sales of an increase in the beer tax? It seems most natural to believe that the different types of alcohol will be substitutes, as people seek to economize in response to an increase in beer prices, say, by switching to wine or liquor. But the data do not provide much evidence one way or the other on this matter.

Note that what is being measured in table 5.2 is the effect of state-level tax and price changes on *sales* rather than on *consumption*. The price elasticity of sales is somewhat larger (in absolute value) than of consumption. A difference between sales and consumption stems from off-the-books home production and moonshining, though that is a small percentage of the total in recent decades when commercial moonshining has not been profitable. Another difference between a state's recorded sales and its average consumption may arise if it is practical for residents to buy their alcohol in another state with lower prices. Cross-border sales can be quite important in small states. New Hampshire's high sales rate (typically the highest in the nation) has much more to do with its success in attracting Massachusetts residents to its state liquor stores than to the Granite State's own drinking habit. But for the most part, trends in sales data are a good guide to trends in consumption data.

PRICES AND DRINKING PATTERNS

Estimates of the price effect for alcohol sales are of interest to alcoholic-beverage marketers and government analysts seeking to project tax revenues. But for those concerned with the health and behavioral consequences of drinking, the change in per capita sales is of less interest than possible changes in drinking patterns: abstention, bingeing, and chronic heavy drinking. It is logically possible that an increase in per capita sales

could occur without a change in the prevalence of drinking or abuse—
if, for example, the only thing that changed was the amount consumed
by moderate drinkers. In practice, however, per capita consumption
tends to be positively correlated with the prevalence of drinking and
heavy drinking.

These relationships can only be documented by analyzing survey data.
The National Epidemiological Survey of Alcohol and Related Conditions (NESARC) is one of the largest and best alcohol-oriented surveys.[5]
Three drinking measures from that survey are the focus here: whether
respondents are current drinkers, how much they drink, and whether
they binge (have five or more drinks on a single occasion). It turns out
that all three of these drinking choices are closely related to per capita
drinking in the respondent's state of residence. For both men and
women, and for each age group, the likelihood of drinking and of
bingeing increase with state per capita consumption, as does the amount
drinkers choose to drink.[6]

The NESARC data also provide an opportunity to analyze the effect
of prices or taxes on drinking patterns. The results are remarkably consistent. Respondents in states with high taxes are less likely to drink and
less likely to binge than otherwise similar respondents in states with low
taxes. On the other hand, the tax rate has little effect on the average
quantity of drinks consumed by those who do drink. Table 5.3 provides
some specific estimates.

In table 5.3, we see that an increase in the state excise-tax index of 10
cents per ounce of ethanol (about a nickel per drink) is associated with a
substantial reduction in the odds of drinking or bingeing, for both men
and women. The reduction is expressed in terms of the odds of being a
drinker. For example, about 70 percent of men drink, and so the odds of
being a drinker are 70/30 = 2.33. As shown in the table, a 10-cent increase
in the tax would reduce the odds by 28 percent, to 1.68—which implies
a drinking prevalence of 63 percent. Similar calculations apply for groups
that begin at other prevalence rates, and for bingeing; there the overall
prevalence is about 20 percent.

In every case the prevalence of drinking and bingeing is also closely
associated with average ethanol consumption in the state, even after accounting for the effect of tax and individual characteristics. Table 5.3
includes the effects of a change in per capita annual consumption of one-
tenth of a gallon of ethanol—from, say, 2.1 gallons (the national mean)
to 2.2 gallons. That increase is associated with an increase of a few percentage points in the odds of drinking and bingeing, and would also have
some effect on average consumption by those who drink.

Similar regressions run for other subsamples defined by age, race, and
income produce consistent results. In particular, the tax index has a significantly negative effect on the likelihood of being a drinker for every

TABLE 5.3
Effect of State Alcohol Taxes and Per Capita Alcohol Sales on Individual
Drinking Patterns

	Percent Change in Odds of Being a Drinker	Percent Change in Odds of Bingeing	Percent Change in Ethanol Consumption (Drinkers Only)
Males			
Increase tax per ounce by 10 cents	−28	−30	+1
Per capita ethanol sales increase by 0.1 gallons	+4.3	+3.0	+3.2
Females			
Increase tax per ounce by 10 cents	−36	−28	+14
Per capita ethanol sales increase by 0.1 gallons	+5.4	+4.8	+3.4

Sources: Individual characteristics and drinking from NESARC. Tax index and p.c. ethanol sales are measured at the state lever for 2000. The tax index is defined in the appendix. Respondents in monopoly states are excluded.

Notes: Each cell is based on the coefficient estimates from a different logit regression (column 2 and 3) or OLS regression (column 4). All regression control for age, employment and/or student status, marital status, income, race, completed schooling, health status, height, and weight. All coefficient estimates are significantly different from zero at the 1% level except for ethanol consumption. The 10 cent increase is in 2003 dollars, equal to 5.41 cents adjusted to the 1982–1984 base for the CPI.

age, race, and income group, and in most cases also has a significantly negative effect on bingeing.

It is intriguing that the state per capita sales variable remains highly influential in these regressions even after controlling for price.[7] A natural interpretation is that individual drinking decisions are being influenced by the "wetness" of the environment. In a state where overall sales and consumption levels are high, individuals are more likely to find themselves in social situations where alcohol is being served and consumed. It is also true that alcohol sales may reflect differences in licensing restrictions and commercial availability.[8]

HABIT FORMATION

One clear message from these empirical results is that ethanol is a commodity, or more precisely a key ingredient in a class of commodities, and some consumers decide how much of this commodity to purchase based partly on their incomes and prices. But of course ethanol is not *just* another commodity—it has several unusual features. It is, after all, a drug that taken in excess leads to a variety of physical and social problems, both in the short run and the long. And it is habit forming, so that current consumption may enhance future appetite. For people who get caught in its snare, drinking may escalate in importance to the point that the urge to drink heavily gains de facto priority over other goals, including the preservation of health, career, and family.

That drinking is habit forming has important economic implications. What is the evidence? Suggestive of habit is the fact that there is a great deal of continuity in drinking behavior—whether someone drinks today is a strong predictor of whether they'll be drinking five or ten years from now (Moore and Gerstein 1981; Cook and Moore 2001). But there are other reasons besides habit for this observed persistence in drinking. For example, there may be innate differences in the taste for alcohol and its effects, or persistent differences in circumstances related to drinking. Since we don't run long-term drinking experiments on people, it is difficult to distinguish between "habit formation" and other possibilities. The ideal experiment would randomly sort youths into two groups, give one of them greater access to alcohol for some period of time, and then check years later to see whether the "wet" group is still drinking more than the "dry" group. As it turns out, there is something similar to this experiment in real life. In the 1970s and 1980s, many states permitted purchase of alcohol at age eighteen, while others held the line at twenty-one. Youths growing up in a state with a younger minimum age had greater opportunity to drink. One study compared adults in their twenties who had grown up in the "18" states with those in the "21" states (Cook and Moore 2001). Sure enough, the former group were still drinking significantly more than the latter. That difference was evident even after controlling for personal characteristics and current state of residence. So not only is drinking habit forming, but the logical implication—that current consumption depends on availability years earlier—is borne out in practice.

Economists have been interested in the implications of the fact that drinking is not only habit forming, but widely *believed* to be habit forming (Becker and Murphy 1988; Becker, Grossman, and Murphy 1991). Looking forward, some people will moderate their drinking or abstain now because of concerns about acquiring a habit. For those who have had alcoholics in the family, that possibility is sometimes particularly salient (see table 5.1). The cost of acquiring a strong taste for drinking and partying will depend in part on plans for the future, and the extent to which the individual is future oriented. For example, an adolescent who hopes to start a family in a few years may avoid drinking now, knowing that she'll have to abstain during pregnancy, whereas a college-bound adolescent may drink now with the thought that it will be easier to get through college if she has acquired some tolerance to alcohol. Those adolescents who live mostly in the present will not be concerned about such thoughts, or, if they do think about it, may underestimate the difficulty of cutting back sometime in the future.[9] In fact, even adults tend to be poor predictors of how difficult it will be to change a habit in the future (Loewenstein 1999; O'Donoghue and Rabin 1999).

For someone who has not only acquired a habit, but has suffered losses in health and social standing from his drinking, it is hard to believe that an increase in the prices of alcoholic beverages or other restrictions on availability would make much difference. It seems too late for those who have become dependent, but that is not necessarily true. For some alcohol-dependent people, higher prices and reduced availability will help shore up a desire to cut back or abstain. The self-control problem is one of timing. People, like other animals, have trouble resisting the impulse for immediate gratification when it is available, even when in a cooler moment they know it is the wrong choice. In the abstract, they may believe that drinking is not worth the likely consequences down the road, but finding themselves in a situation with drinks readily at hand and no *immediate* offsetting consideration, they may well succumb to the temptation.[10]

There is some experimental evidence indicating that when there are immediate costs to obtaining a drink, alcoholics will moderate their intake (Babor 1985). In an early experimental study, Nancy Mello and her associates (Mello, McNamee, and Mendelson, 1968) compared drinking patterns of fourteen male alcoholics as a function of the cost of a drink. Subjects who were required to work twice as hard for their alcohol drank half as much as comparable subjects in an identical situation. Other experiments with inpatient alcoholics found that their drinking could be reduced by contingent loss of privileges and financial incentives for abstinence (Mello 1972; Babor et al. 1978). Another study recruited thirty-four adult males from the community for an experiment comparing the responsiveness of the casual drinkers and heavy drinkers to changes in price. The response of both groups to a "happy hour" in which prices were cut in half was to approximately double the number of drinks they consumed (Babor et al. 1978).

A pioneering study of survey data on alcohol dependence and abuse provides further evidence of the importance of prices in curtailing problematic drinking (Farrell, Manning, and Finch 2003). The survey of 43,000 adults in 1991 and 1992 included a number of items on drinking and abuse, which were the basis for measuring several latent factors of current alcohol dependence and abuse.[11] Controlling for other personal characteristics, the authors found that both alcohol prices and income significantly affected the likelihood of being a drinker, and, among drinkers, the likelihood of having various symptoms of dependence and abuse—bouts of heavy drinking, physical consequences, and increased salience of alcohol. The price elasticities are high enough—typically more than one in absolute value—to suggest that alcohol price increases provide a powerful check on problematic drinking.[12]

DRINKING BY YOUTHS

Much of the econometric research has focused on drinking by youths. Teenagers and young adults are of special concern for several reasons. First, youths exhibit relatively high rates (compared with their elders) of binge drinking and involvement in motor-vehicle accidents and violent crime (Grossman et al. 1994). Second, to the extent that drinking is habit forming, youthful drinking sets the pattern for later consumption. And third, drinking behavior during the transition from adolescence to adulthood may have important consequences for human capital and family formation—the topic of a subsequent chapter (Cook and Moore 1993b).

The sensitivity of youthful drinking to both minimum-legal-drinking-age (MLDA) laws and to beer prices has been well documented.[13] (The focus on beer is dictated by the fact that most ethanol consumed by youths in the United States is in the form of beer.) Studies using five different data sets suggest that whether and how often youths drink and how often they binge are all importantly related to prices and MLDA (Grossman et al. 1994; Cook and Moore 2001).[14] Incidentally, the research on MLDA laws necessarily draws on data from a previous era when each state was free to set its own minimum, and there was a range from eighteen up to twenty-one. In recent years federal pressure has forced every state to establish twenty-one as the minimum age. One study using data from the 1980s found a small but discernible difference in drinking by eighteen-year-old youths who were in low-MLDA states and otherwise similar youths in high-MLDA states; an additional two in every one hundred abstained when it was illegal for them to drink.[15]

Underage drinking typically takes place with peers and too often involves driving. The link is so tight that laws which target driving after drinking have the effect of reducing the overall frequency of binge drinking by youths. This unexpected consequence was documented in connection with the adoption of the zero-tolerance (ZT) laws adopted by every state during the late 1990s. In 1995, Congress, having already established twenty-one as the MLDA, adopted a new mandate requiring states to impose strict penalties on underage youths caught driving after drinking any amount.[16] All the states had come into line by 1998. The resulting natural experiment generated strong evidence that the ZT laws reduced by 13–20 percent binge drinking and total alcohol consumption by males (Carpenter 2004a). Thus, the demand for alcohol was reduced by limiting one unfortunately complementary activity, namely, driving.

DRINKING AND SMOKING

Consumers make choices about whether and how much to drink in the context of other choices about consumption activities. Of particular interest is the link between drinking and smoking. It seems likely that public interventions intended to reduce smoking may also have an effect on drinking. The reverse may also be true—that regulations on alcohol may affect smoking rates. These cross-substance effects could have an important effect on the health consequences of such interventions.

Using the economists' lingo, the question is whether tobacco and alcohol are complements or substitutes in consumption. "Complements" are items that tend to go together, like bread and butter. "Substitutes" are items that tend to be viewed as alternatives for a particular consumption "niche," such as margarine and butter. If dairy-marketing regulations drive up the price of butter, the direct effect will be a reduction in butter consumption, and the collateral effects will likely include a reduction in bread consumption and an increase in margarine consumption.

What about tobacco and alcohol? One clue from survey data is that smoking and drinking go together, as we would expect if they were complements (Anthony and Echeagaray-Wagner 2000). The image that comes to mind is Rick's Bar in the movie *Casablanca*, though in the United States (and other countries) the smoke-filled bar is giving way to indoor smoking prohibitions. Still, smokers are more likely to drink than nonsmokers and are over twice as likely to drink heavily and to binge drink. Figure 5.2 depicts these associations for the adult population as a whole. Regression estimates demonstrate that this association is very strong even after controlling for age, race, education, income, health status, main activity, and marital status.[17]

But the fact that people who smoke are more likely to drink (and drink a lot) does not prove alcohol and tobacco are complements. They are only complements if the use of one of them enhances the utility of using the other (like the bread and butter example). An alternative explanation for the overlap is that the tastes for both smoking and drinking tend to be mediated by common factors, such as religion, upbringing, personality, genetic tendencies, or circumstance (Little 2000). If they are related through a common cause, rather than through a direct interaction, then the observed overlap is compatible with smoking and drinking being substitutes. For example, socially ill-at-ease people may be inclined to both

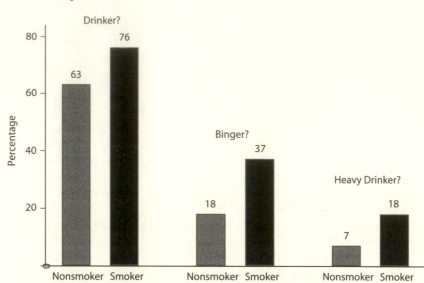

Figure 5.2. Drinking Prevalence among Smokers and Nonsmokers.
Source: 2001–2002 NESARC.
Note: "Drinker" is anyone who drank in previous 12 months. "Binger" is anyone who had five or more drinks on a single occasion. "Heavy drinker" is anyone who consumed an average of two or more drinks per day.

drink and smoke when with friends, but upon finding themselves in a social situation where smoking is prohibited, may compensate by drinking even more than otherwise. Similarly, alcoholics who go on the wagon may increase their smoking to help get through the difficult transition to sobriety.

Of course, both tobacco and alcohol serve a variety of psychic and social purposes, and have correspondingly diverse links with each other in consumer behavior. If tobacco and alcohol tend to be substitutes for some, complements for others, and unrelated for many, what we are seeking is a population average or net effect. And the best evidence concerning that net effect arises from dynamic situations—for example, from observing what happens to drinking when cigarette prices are increased through higher taxes, or stronger restrictions on smoking are imposed (Dee 1999; Picone, Sloan, and Trogdon 2004). On average, do smokers who are induced to cut back on their cigarette use also cut back on drinking?

The large jump in cigarette prices that began in 1998 with the Master Settlement Agreement provides a natural experiment of just this sort (Carpenter and Cook 2006). By 2002, cigarette prices had increased by 67 percent relative to overall inflation. Alcohol prices were flat during this period. Cigarette sales fell, but there is no evident effect on the trend in alcohol sales during this period, which remained essentially unchanged. The likely conclusion is that cigarettes and alcohol are neither complements nor substitutes, but rather quite neutral—at least in the short run. Assuming this effect is symmetric, a large increase in alcohol prices would have little effect on smoking.

Concluding Thoughts

Individual choices about whether and how much to drink are influenced by myriad factors, including, for some people at least, the price of a drink. A wide array of evidence suggests that in response to an increase in prices of beer, wine, or liquor, per capita consumption of ethanol falls. What's more, price increases reduce the prevalence of drinking, heavy drinking, and bingeing, and appear to reduce the prevalence of dependence and abuse as well. The breadth and extent of the response to higher prices depends on just how much higher—small price increases have small effects, large increases, large effects. As we shall see in subsequent chapters, these findings, based on sales and survey data, are supported by the analysis of data on drinking-related consequences.

CHAPTER 6

Alcohol Control as Injury Prevention

> Alcohol is the AIDS virus of injury control. It lowers the
> defenses and immunity to injury, leaving people vulnerable to
> what would otherwise be nonthreatening situations.
> —William H. Foege, *"Highway violence and public policy"*

> A member of the Baker faction in Clay county is said to have
> declared that three drinks of "mountain dew" cause, on the
> average, one fight.
> —S. S. MacClintock,
>   *"The Kentucky mountains and their feuds"*

THE PUBLIC INTEREST in regulating alcohol stems primarily from the consequences of overindulgence, which include the indiscretions and injuries
associated with inebriation, and the long-term effects of heavy drinking
on organ function and volition. The key question is whether regulations
which limit availability and raise the price of alcohol are actually effective
policy instruments. Is highway safety enhanced by the minimum age laws,
excise taxes, and liability rules for bars? Would there be noticeably fewer
gonorrhea cases and unwanted pregnancies if Congress raised the beer
excise tax? Does alcohol availability affect rates of criminal violence and
suicide? The answer to each of these questions is yes. But that answer flies
in the face of conventional wisdom. Many would be skeptical or down-
right disbelieving that so much could be accomplished through alcohol
controls, even if they accepted the fact (argued in the previous chapter)
that prices and availability do influence alcohol consumption. Closing the
gap between the experts and the public on this matter requires not only
a summary of findings, but also an explanation of the research methods
that make those findings credible.

To organize the discussion of the notable consequences of drinking for
individuals and for society, the chapter begins with the effects of ethanol
as a drug acting on the mind and body of the individual drinker, and then
goes on to consider some of the consequences for the public's health,
safety, and general welfare. One theme here is the Manichean nature of
this substance: alcohol consumption does great harm but also much good.
Albeit natural to emphasize the harms, since it is the harmful consequences of drinking that account for the public concern and regulation

of alcoholic beverages, it is also important to acknowledge the benefits (Peele and Brodsky 2000). Some of the potential benefit comes in the same currency as the most notable harm, namely morbidity and mortality: while alcohol abuse accounts for a large share of serious injuries and deaths, especially among youths, moderate drinking appears to improve health and reduce mortality rates among older people (although such benefits are by no means proven). If true it is possible to drink too little as well as too much.

Even though every drinker can say from personal experience what she likes and doesn't like about alcohol, personal experience provides less guidance with respect to these health- and safety-related consequences. Most of the serious consequences are either low-probability events associated with drinking episodes, or the result of the cumulative effects of years of drinking. Sorting out the contribution of drinking to accidents, various sorts of organ damage, or improved blood circulation requires analysis of systematic data on large samples of individuals. A second theme for this chapter is that even for epidemiologists, developing reliable estimates of the extent to which alcohol should be blamed or credited with respect to various outcomes is a challenge—but that that problem is not necessarily an impediment to estimating the effect of alcohol-control measures on these outcomes. Economists and other social scientists have sought to directly estimate the effect of alcohol-control measures on acute consequences such as highway fatality rates. The predominant method involves a quasi-experimental approach, analyzing how state-level outcome measures vary as a function of changes in tax rates, minimum drinking ages, and other control measures, using other states as the "control group."

ALCOHOL AS A DRUG

Alcoholic beverages have value to consumers both as drink and as drug. As drink, beer and wine may serve as an alternative to water or soft drinks, providing a thirst quencher and a tasty complement to a meal. The taste of a fine wine is so highly prized that a single bottle may sell for hundreds of dollars, while a cold beer after working outside on a hot day can seem priceless. Alcoholic drinks also have a more prosaic virtue: Historically and even in modern times and places where the drinking water is contaminated, they have offered a nearly germ-free alternative (Vallee 1998). But it seems safe to say that the current popularity of alcoholic beverages is not so much the result of concerns about the purity of drinking water or even the taste, as it is about the drug effects of ethanol. Ethanol when ingested has effects on the body, especially the central nervous system, that are experienced by drinkers as pleasurable.

Of course it is also tempting to drink too much, with a variety of consequences that are far from pleasant and may be harmful to the drinker and to others as well.

When someone drinks an alcoholic beverage, the ethanol is absorbed into the bloodstream through the lining of the stomach and intestines (Kuhn, Swartzwelder, and Wilson 1998). As it circulates in the bloodstream, the alcohol is soon distributed evenly throughout the body's tissues and fluids. It is absorbed in the fatty material of the brain and affects neurological function in both the central nervous system (brain and spinal cord) and the peripheral nervous system, with a pervasive effect on other organs as well. The alcohol is metabolized, primarily in the liver, with the help of specialized enzymes. The liver metabolizes alcohol at a constant rate of approximately one-half ounce per hour, breaking it down into acetaldehyde (a toxic chemical), and then acetate. These metabolites also circulate and have some effect on the body; for example, they may make the drinker nauseous.

The psychoactive effects of alcohol are varied and complex. A dose of alcohol initially may have a stimulant effect, and cause a feeling of well-being. A neurological basis for this feeling has been identified: a rising concentration of alcohol stimulates the release of the neurotransmitter dopamine in the brain's reward centers, just as do cocaine and amphetamines (Kuhn et al. 1998). But after the initial high, alcohol is a sedative, akin to barbiturates and benzodiazepines like Valium.

As a drinking session continues, blood alcohol concentration (BAC) increases, since absorption into the blood can proceed much faster than the liver can break it down. For example, on average a 170-pound man who has four drinks in an hour on an empty stomach, or a 135-pound woman who has three drinks, may reach a BAC of 0.08 percent, the level at which it is illegal to drive in most states (National Highway Traffic Safety Administration 1992; Hingson and Winter 2003, 66). But the rate of absorption and subsequent metabolism varies depending on circumstances. Most important, alcohol is absorbed much more rapidly on an empty stomach than on a full stomach, and more rapidly in concentrated form (spirits) than dilute (beer). Absorption rates also differ among individuals according to such factors as age, gender, and body fat.

The drinker may experience a variety of effects as he continues to drink and become intoxicated, including dizziness, clumsiness, nausea, and impaired perception and cognition. At a sufficient level of concentration in the blood (BAC greater than 4 parts per thousand or so), the drinker will lapse into unconsciousness. Death can follow, either directly or through related hazards, such as aspirating vomit. Alcohol interacts with other drugs and is particularly potent when taken in conjunction with other sedatives.

Some of the psychological effects are rewarding. Drinking may produce a sense of warmth, numb physical pains and worries, ease social anxieties, and block out the nagging voice of conscience. Attracted by these and other pleasures, an individual may develop a stronger taste for alcohol, with a tendency to increase the amount consumed on any one occasion, and to drink on an increasing number of occasions. As with some other drugs, repeated use leads the body and mind to adapt in certain ways, most notably with an increased tolerance—a lessened effect for any given dose. Tolerance may in turn motivate higher levels of consumption. If heavy drinking continues for an extended period, the drinker may become dependent on alcohol, even to the point of suffering withdrawal symptoms or intense cravings when sober.

DRINKING AND DRIVING

The dominant public health concern related to alcohol is the contribution of drinking to the rates of traumatic injury and death. Drinking is involved in about two of every five injury deaths each year in the United States, and in about one-third of all injury deaths, the victim or other involved party has been drinking enough to be intoxicated by the usual standard (Centers for Disease Control and Prevention 2004b; Smith, Branas, and Miller 1999). It is a natural presumption that when someone who has been drinking heavily gets into a motor vehicle crash, falls off a ladder, or gets into a fight, that the alcohol is the cause—that if he had chosen to drink Coke instead of beer, the crash or the fall or the fight would never have happened.

The statistical basis for estimating the role of drinking in injury begins with descriptive data from various sources that document the circumstances of death or injury. Usually the most comprehensive data are for deaths, since they tend to be better documented by public agencies than nonfatal injuries.

Epidemiologists seek to go beyond the presumption that drinking is to blame for alcohol-involved injury events, and estimate the *proportion* of such cases in which the drinking should in fact get the blame. That turns out to be a statistical challenge, because it requires comparing actual death and injury rates to a hypothetical scenario where less alcohol has been consumed.

Statistics on alcohol involvement provide only a first cut at ascertaining the role of drinking as a cause of injury fatalities. Take the case of motor vehicle crashes. In 41 percent of fatal crashes in 2002, there was a driver (or pedestrian) who had had at least one drink, and 35 percent involved a BAC greater than the legal limit of 0.08 percent (Hingson and Winter

2003, 63). In how many of these cases was it the drinking per se that caused the crash?

This sort of question is familiar to epidemiologists. The term of art is "attributable portion." What portion of motor vehicle deaths is causally *attributable* to drinking? The attributable portion may be understood in this case as the percentage that would have been prevented if all the drivers and pedestrians in question had been sober—usually with the implicit understanding that that hypothetical change in drinking would not have affected their choices about when and where to drive. In fact, interventions designed to reduce drinking and driving, if effective, are likely to change travel patterns as well as the prevalence of DUI. For example, a police crackdown on drunk driving might persuade some people to stay home instead of driving (to a bar), while others might still go out and drink but take a taxi or public transportation. Those adaptations may have an additional effect on traffic accidents by, say, reducing traffic congestion on weekend evenings. But it is still of interest to estimate the portion that would have been prevented if the same people had driven the same trips, only sober.

Before attempting to estimate the attributable portion of highway fatalities to assign to drinking, it is useful to identify the causal mechanisms. The case that drinking impairs driving and increases the chance of a serious accident has been established beyond doubt. Drinking affects a number of physical and mental capacities that are relevant to safe driving. In addition to the impairment of attention and information-processing capacity, drivers under the influence are likely to have reduced peripheral vision, poorer recovery from glare, poor performance in complex visual-tracking tasks, and other deficits (Hingson and Winter 2003, 66). Actual experiments both with driving simulators and on the road have found that driving skills are degraded at BACs of 0.05 percent and higher (67). Of course, in practice drinking also affects judgment; the hazards of driving fast and aggressively may be less apparent to a driver when he is drunk than sober. And despite conventional wisdom to the contrary, drinking reduces the likelihood of survival—a driver or passenger with BAC of 0.08 percent is much more likely to die from a serious crash of given intensity than a sober person (Evans 2004).

Just as we would expect, drinking drivers are more likely to be involved in serious crashes than sober drivers, even after controlling for the time and place of the trip. The likelihood of a fatal crash increases with the BAC level. These comparisons have been made possible by a series of rather remarkable field studies. The first, in 1964, was conducted in Grand Rapids, Michigan (Borkenstein et al. 1964; Hurst, Harte, and Firth 1994). Blood samples from drivers involved in fatal accidents (whether or not the drivers survived) were taken to measure BAC. To collect data on a comparison group, the police randomly stopped four vehicles at each crash location, at about the same time of day and week of these crashes (Hurst et al. 1994). In addition to asking drivers a series of questions about their drinking habits, police administered a breathalyzer to determine each driver's BAC. The resulting data were analyzed to determine the increased risk of fatal accident associated with different levels of drinking, controlling for location and time.[1]

The pioneering Grand Rapids study has been followed by several national studies. These were facilitated by the development of the Fatal Accident Reporting System (FARS) in which the National Highway Traffic Safety Administration compiles detailed information on fatal crashes nationwide. Several national surveys of drivers have been conducted to provide a comparison group for these fatalities. The most recent, the 1996 National Roadside Survey of weekend nighttime drivers, enlisted a number of police departments and civilian volunteers to collect data (Voas et al. 1997). Data collection required stopping drivers at particular times and places and administering a breathalyzer test, just for study purposes. Drivers had the right to refuse the test, and about 3 percent did.[2] Drivers who complied but were discovered to be legally intoxicated at the time of the stop were not arrested, but were required to stop driving and find another way home.[3]

The 1996 National Roadside Survey has been used together with FARS data to estimate the relative risk of a driver's involvement in a fatal accident as a function of the driver's BAC (Zador Krawchuk, and Voas 2000).[4] The results demonstrated that low BACs in the range of 0.02 to 0.05 percent were associated with an elevated risk of a fatal accident by a factor of about 3.[5] That multiple was found to increase exponentially with the BAC. Over 0.15 percent, the risk was increased by a factor of several hundred in comparison with sober drivers. The study also found that a given BAC had a much greater risk-enhancing effect on male teenage drivers than older drivers.

Estimates of the attributable portion can be generated from these data. For example, the 1996 Roadside Survey found that 17 percent of all drivers on weekend nights (between 10 p.m. and 3 a.m.) had been drinking; if drinking had no statistical association with the risk of fatal crash, then we would expect that just 17 percent of drivers in fatal crashes on weekend evenings would have been drinking. Since in fact 78 percent of fatal crashes during weekend evenings involved drinking drivers, it is clear that the drinking drivers have a greatly elevated rate of fatal-accident involvement—by coincidence, about seventeen times as high as the sober drivers.[6] If the drinking drivers had been "converted" to sober drivers (with respect to accident involvement), the fatality rate would have been just 26.5 percent of the actual rate. The portion attributable to drinking is then 73.5

percent for weekend evenings.[7] In principle we could do the same calculation for the rest of the week, although no recent national roadside survey data are available for that task.

These data demonstrate that drinking is *associated* with elevated crash risk. But a skeptic might object that this association does not prove causation, and may be—at least in part—the result of some other causal process. For example, people who drive after drinking are being somewhat reckless, a trait that may also carry over to when they are sober. That is, people who drive drunk from time to time may tend to be reckless drivers all the time, with the willingness to drive drunk as just one manifestation. That is not just a speculation: one study of FARS data found that people with bad driving records have a higher risk than drivers with a clean record of getting in a fatal crash *when sober,* and in addition are more likely to drive while drunk—at which point they are more likely than other drunks to get into a fatal accident (Levitt and Porter 2001, 1226). Personality traits that have been found to be associated with drunk driving include emotional instability, impulsiveness, hostility, and depression (Donovan, Marlett, and Salzberg 1983). Not surprisingly, those who drive after drinking from time to time are less likely to wear a seatbelt when they drive, thus increasing the chance that any serious accident in which they are involved will prove fatal (Wilson 1992).

Thus the association between drunk driving and elevated crash risk is due in part to other factors, such as the recklessness of the drivers, that influence both the likelihood that they will drive after drinking, and the likelihood that they will get into a serious crash. The apparent effect of drinking on crash risk is statistically *confounded* by the effect of recklessness, a factor that is not controlled for in the national roadside studies.

Quite a different approach to estimating the attributable portion of alcohol to crash risk is to estimate the effects of changes in law and enforcement practice. A variety of interventions designed to reduce drunk driving have been successful in reducing the number of fatal crashes. The interventions that have been studied include police crackdowns and changes in the law governing drinking and driving. A particularly vivid example is the British Road Safety Act of 1967 (Ross 1973). This Act stipulated a mandatory one-year suspension of driving privilege for those convicted of drunk driving. The intense publicity that accompanied its implementation indicated that there would be stepped-up enforcement using portable breathalyzer units. The initial effect was remarkable: Traffic fatalities dropped 25 percent overall, with the decline concentrated in the types of accidents that are most likely to involve drinking—single-vehicle crashes occurring on weekend evenings. Hence it appears that the fraction of fatal accidents that were *caused by* drinking was at least 25 percent in Britain in that era. Even then there is some ambiguity, however.

The Act created a stronger incentive to avoid driving after drinking, but it also created an incentive to avoid getting caught. One mechanism, then, may have been for those who *did* drive after drinking to drive more carefully than they would have previously.

A variety of related interventions in the United States have been evaluated and also found to have some effect on highway fatalities (Hingson and Winter 2003). Among these are raising the minimum drinking age and stepping up its enforcement, imposing "zero tolerance" for underage drivers caught drinking any amount, lowering the per se limit for driving under the influence to 0.08 percent BAC, and establishing liability for bars and restaurants when patrons become intoxicated and then cause a crash after driving away (Sloan et al. 2000; Carpenter 2004a; Hingson and Winter 2003). These evaluations all strengthen the case that a reduction in the incidence of drinking and driving reduces the highway fatality rate. But since the interventions are far from completely effective in eliminating drinking and driving, the estimated reduction in fatal crashes—typically less than 10 percent—understates the overall portion of crashes that should be attributed to alcohol.

In sum, field data demonstrate that drinking drivers are more likely to get into serious crashes than sober drivers, and that the relative risk increases with BAC. We can be confident that some portion of that enhanced risk is *caused* by the drinking. Just *what* portion remains somewhat unclear. But evaluations of interventions to reduce drinking and driving provide a direct demonstration from the field of the causal connection between drinking and driving, and also (incidentally) provide a basis for evaluating these interventions.

The remarkable reduction in drinking and driving that has occurred over the last three decades is surely responsible for part of the gains in traffic safety during this period. The National Roadside Survey in 1973 found the proportion of drivers with positive BACs was 36 percent on Friday and Saturday nights; that percentage dropped to just 17 percent in the National Roadside Survey of 1996. Alcohol-involved traffic fatalities dropped from 60 percent of the total in 1982 to 41 percent in 2002, following the same general trend as per capita alcohol consumption in the United States.

INTENTIONAL VIOLENCE

Conventional wisdom has it that drinking should get much of the blame for violence of various sorts: barroom brawls, crowd violence at sporting events. date rape, domestic battering. Scholars have documented the strong statistical association between drinking and violence, but have questioned the importance of a direct causal role (Collins 1989; Pernanen 1981); however, good evidence exists that the conventional wisdom is right (Brewer and Swahn 2005).

There are in fact several causal mechanisms by which drinking may lead to violence (Klingemann and Gmel 2001; Fagan 1990). Most obviously, alcohol has direct pharmacological effects. The initial uptake of alcohol to the brain has arousal and disinhibition effects that in some individuals are likely to lead to greater aggression. Studies confirm this possibility, and also confirm the commonplace observation that drinking is far more likely to trigger violent behavior in some people than others. Remarkably, the same sort of heterogeneity is found in animals, including rodents and rhesus macaques, where the individuals that are relatively violent when sober are more likely to become aggressive under the influence of alcohol (Giancola 2004; Exum 2002; Moeller and Dougherty 2001; Higley 2001; Miczek, Weerts, and DeBold 1993). The violence-prone trait is also associated with a taste for drinking, as is true, for example, for those with antisocial personality disorder (Moeller and Dougherty 2001).

Of course, violence does not take place in isolation, but rather is a transaction between two or more individuals. The connection between drinking and violence is conditioned by the social environment and culture, in ways that are suggested by the term *intentional* violence. Intention connotes choice, and violence under the influence is by no means purely irrational (Pernanen 1991). But intoxication may affect preferences among available alternatives in predictable ways. Enough alcohol tends to make the drinker myopic, in the sense that remote consequences of his actions become less visible or less important—immediate urges then hold greater sway in decisions (Cook and Moore 1993c; Steele and Josephs 1990). The myopia helps provide "courage in a bottle." The alcohol may also change the objective consequences, in ways that make violence more attractive. For one thing, the alcohol numbs the drinker physically, and so any injury suffered in a fight may be less painful. (Liquor was used historically as a rough-and-ready anesthetic for surgery.) For another, the interpersonal and social consequences of assault may be lessened if others judge the assailant less harshly because they attribute his behavior to the alcohol rather than his basic character. The "excuse" value of drinking shows up frequently in reports of chronic domestic violence. More broadly, some cultures tend to condone aggression and violence during drinking sessions (MacAndrew and Edgerton 1969).

Since violence is a transaction, the behavior of the victim is also relevant. (In some cases, the difference between "perpetrator" and "victim" is just who happened to win the fight!) Alcohol plays an important role in victimization. Intoxication may contribute to aggressive or provocative behavior on the part of the ultimate victim, or physically incapacitate her or him. Drunks may be easy prey to robbers and rapists.

In the most serious form of violence, homicide, there is alcohol involvement in a majority of cases (Smith et al. 1989). A 1997 national survey of state prisoners convicted of murder documented this involvement: the offender/respondent reported that he was drinking in 44 percent of the cases, his victim in 34 percent, and both in twenty-one percent (Greenfield and Henneberg 2001).

Estimating the "attributable portion" to alcohol is even more difficult here than in the case of highway fatalities, since there is no natural control group (let alone an experiment). Instead or in addition to a direct causal connection, the close association may partly reflect other causal processes, as suggested above: First, it may in part be due to reverse causation, whereby violent criminals drink in anticipation of committing violence to provide courage or an excuse. Second is the possibility that drinking and a propensity to violence may both stem from a common cause, such as a risk-seeking or antisocial personality or a social environment that encourages deviant behavior. And third, the association may simply be spurious—violent criminals who drink heavily are more likely to be caught and hence overrepresented in samples of convicts or inmates (Petersilia, Greenwood, and Lavin 1978; Collins 1986).

The best evidence in support of the importance of a direct causal role comes from aggregate interventions and policy changes—strikes that closed liquor stores, changes in the minimum age laws or excise taxes, or other policy interventions (Cook and Moore 1993c; Klingemann and Gmel 2001; Room 1983; Hingson, Merrigan, and Heeren 1985; Carpenter 2003). Much as in the case of highway fatalities, the evidence from these sources provides a clear indication that an induced reduction in aggregate drinking will result in a reduction in violence. That evidence helps cut through the Gordian knot of causal confusion.

For suicide, the evidence and issues of interpretation are quite similar. Suicide victims often have a high BAC (Hayward, Zubrick, and Silburn 1992), and being in treatment for alcoholism or alcohol abuse is a significant risk factor for suicide (Draper 1994). One review of studies on adolescent suicide concluded that between one-third and two-thirds of adolescent suicide victims suffered from substance abuse disorders (Brent 1995). One complication in sorting out causation is comorbidity—in addition to substance abuse, other forms of mental illness are very common in suicides. But one study based on a nationally representative sample of adolescents found that alcohol use is a significant predictor of suicide attempts after controlling for depression (Cutler, Glaser, and Norberg 2001). In an interesting report of a natural experiment, Wasserman and colleagues (1994) examined the relationship between male suicides and alcohol consumption in the Soviet Union during the period of Perestroika 1985–1988. The early years of this period were characterized by a very restrictive alcohol policy. Relative to the last year of the Brezhnev regime (1984), suicides and violent deaths declined sharply in 1986, falling to 65 percent of their 1984 level. By 1988, violent deaths were 72 percent of their 1984 level, and suicides, 61 percent. In 1990, the last year covered by the data, these rates of death due to violence and suicide held at 85 and 68 percent. Meanwhile, total male mortality had returned to its 1984 level by 1990. Simple regression analyses of the Soviet data indicate that the suicide rate for men falls by 1.3 per 100,000 for every 1-liter-per-year reduction in pure alcohol consumption per capita.

Changes in the Mlda as Quasi-Experiment

Some of the strongest evidence we have on the effects of alcohol-control measures arises from the "laboratory" of the states (Fosdick and Scott 1933, 150). The Twenty-first Amendment ensures that each state establishes its own alcohol-control policy. The interstate differences and changes in key policies provide the basis for assessing their effects. Many of the outcomes of interest are measured by administrative data on injuries, deaths, violent crimes, and so forth, which are compiled annually for each state.

The quasi-experimental method has been used most prominently and persuasively in the case of the minimum drinking age. As of 1970, most states had adopted twenty-one as the minimum age for legal purchase of any sort of alcoholic beverage; only two states permitted persons under the age of twenty-one to purchase liquor, and thirteen states allowed those under twenty-one to purchase beer (Males 1986). Following adoption of the Twenty-sixth Amendment (giving eighteen-year-olds the right to vote), thirty states reduced their minimum legal drinking age (MLDA).[8] That process was reversed beginning in 1976, and by 1988 every state had established twenty-one as the minimum age. The frequent changes in law generated a great deal of evidence on the consequences of the MLDA. The changes can be viewed as trials in a sort of natural or "quasi"-experiment.

The most important potential effect of these changes was with respect to traffic fatalities involving youthful drivers. A decrease in the MLDA from twenty-one to eighteen could logically increase traffic fatalities by increasing the amount of drinking by the relevant age group, and in particular the amount of drinking that was coupled with driving. But as of 1970, the public and even the alcohol experts were skeptical that the MLDA had this sort of influence, and in fact it was widely held that putting youthful drinkers on the wrong side of the law made their drinking more risky. The evidence generated by the numerous changes of the early 1970s demonstrated otherwise. States that lowered their MLDA experienced an increase in youthful highway fatalities relative to states that did not. Evidence to that effect was instrumental in reversing the trend, and eventually in establishing twenty-one as the universal MLDA. (Congress helped this process along by adopting legislation in 1984 that pressured the states with sub-21 MLDAs to get in line.)[9]

Notice that the evidence that was so persuasive came out of observations that linked changes in the MLDA directly to youthful fatalities. The logical connections via effects on drinking, and on DUI, were not necessarily documented in these analyses—but documenting these intermediate links in the logical chain is not necessary to demonstrate the result of interest. The validity of the conclusion, that the changes in MLDA were causing the observed (relative) increases in youthful highway fatalities, requires only that the states that changed their laws were not systematically different in relevant respects from states that did not—that there was no self-selection bias, and no tendency to change related laws or enforcement practices at the same time as changes in the MLDA.

A superficial inspection of the data suggests that in fact self-selection bias may be a problem. Table 6.1 provides data on the median highway fatality rates for youths age eighteen to twenty. In 1970, the eleven states with MLDA for beer of eighteen had a median fatality rate of 57.7 per 100,000, while the thirty-four states that had MLDA of twenty-one in that year had a *higher* median fatality rate of 61.2. (The remaining states had MLDA of nineteen or twenty.) As of 1975, the fatality statistics continued to favor the states with MLDA of 18. This simple difference in rates suggests that the MLDA had a perverse effect on highway safety. But on closer inspection, it is clear that this difference was not due to the MLDA itself. Rather, states which typically have lower fatality rates across all ages proved more likely to have a lower MLDA in the 1970s. In other words, there was self-selection bias with respect to the assignment of MLDA to states, when considered in terms of *levels* of the fatality rate. We get a much different impression of how MLDA affects the fatality rate if instead of comparing the rates in a single year, we analyze the state-by-state changes in fatality rates around the time of the MLDA changes.

Table 6.2 presents the medians of the *changes* in fatality rates, comparing the states that lowered their MLDA with states that did not. The sixteen states that lowered from twenty-one to eighteen during this period experienced little change in the fatality rate for those age eighteen to twenty on average. But the twenty-three states that did not change their MLDA experienced a sharp reduction. That reduction, incidentally, is in line with the national drop in the traffic fatality rate associated with the Arab oil embargo of that era. States that lowered their MLDA did not

TABLE 6.1
State Traffic Fatality Rates Per 100,000 Population, Ages 18–20

MLDA for beer	1970 Median of State Rates (# of states)	1975 Median of State Rates (# of states)
18	57.7 (11)	48.1 (30)
21	61.2 (34)	52.8 (12)

Source: Original calculations from NCHS Vital Statistics mortality data, unpublished.

share in this lifesaving trend. If they had, their average fatality rate would have been 12.9/100,000 lower (on average) by 1975. Thus, it appears that lowering MLDA caused a substantial loss of life on the highway compared with what would have happened if all states had held the MLDA constant.

This is an example of a "difference-in-difference" analysis. The before-and-after differences in the "experimental" group are compared with the comparable differences in the "control" (no change) group; the difference in differences serves as an estimate of the effect. It is a valid estimate to the extent that the states that changed their MLDA were on average similar to those that did not with respect to underlying *trends* in other factors that influence youth traffic safety. Since social, cultural, and economic trends are closely linked across the fifty states, that seems like a reasonably safe bet, but should ideally be checked to rule out self-selection bias. One type of check is to compare the difference-in-difference results for eighteen-to-twenty-year-olds with the corresponding results for the next-older age group—those in their early twenties who have much in common with the younger group when it comes to trends in drinking and driving, but are not directly affected by MLDA. The third column of Table 6.2 presents the difference-in-difference results for this group. The reassuring result is that the MLDA changes appear to have a much smaller effect on that age group. (It is reasonable that there is some effect, since the twenty-one to twenty-four-year-old age group share the road, and sometimes a ride, with those age eighteen to twenty.) Otherwise it would be reasonable to suspect that the observed patterns for the younger group were not measuring the causal effects of MLDA changes, but rather underlying changes in drinking and driving patterns that happened to be correlated in time with the MLDA changes.

This has been a rather complicated argument, but an essential one to understanding the force of the evidence on alcohol control measures. To

Table 6.2
Change in Traffic Fatality Rates Per 100,000 Population, for Two Age Groups

MLDA History, 1970–1975	Median Rate Changes, 18–20	Median Rate Changes, 21–24
Lower from 21 to 18 (16 states)	−0.8	−13.2
No change in MLDA (23 states)	−13.7	−17.6
Net "difference-in-difference" effect of lower MLDA	+12.9	+4.4

Source: Original calculations from NCHS Vital Statistics mortality data, unpublished.

recap: The fifty states have long been recognized by social scientists as a great laboratory in which policy innovations are tested. In a case like the MLDA where the state legislatures provided numerous test "trials," this laboratory can provide powerful evidence. A problem with interpreting that evidence is that the policy changes are chosen by state legislatures or regulatory agencies, rather than being imposed by random assignment. Understanding how those choices relate to the level and trend in the outcome measures—- teen traffic fatalities or the like—is key to validating any conclusions. If policy choices are systematically related to the average level of the outcome measure, then an evaluation based on a simple comparison of differences is going to confound the pattern of choice with the effect—as in the results in table 6.1. The difference-in-difference approach negates that concern by comparing changes over time rather than levels. But even with that approach, there is a possibility of self-selection bias if the policy choices made by the states are influenced by state-specific trends. That possibility can be checked in various ways. In the MLDA example, the analysis of fatality changes for the just-older group, which would logically be little affected by MLDA changes, provides one useful check.

The quasi-experimental approach to estimating the effects of alcohol-control measures on drinking-related outcomes has been used since 1981 (Cook 1981). The usual statistical method in these studies is somewhat more refined than the illustration: regression analysis applied to panel data consisting of annual observations on states. Any relevant national trend is accounted for by inclusion of yearly fixed effects. Similarly, the persistent characteristics of each state that influence the outcome variable are usually accounted for by inclusion of state fixed effects. The virtue of this approach is that it controls for myriad factors, including those that cannot easily be measured directly. For example, state highway-fatality rates differ due to weather, road quality, average miles driven, traffic rules, enforcement, and much else. Year in and year out, some states have higher fatality rates than others due to differences in such factors. Fixed-effects estimates control for all causes that don't change much over time—that account for the interstate structure of highway fatalities. The national movements in the average rate of highway fatalities resulting from the business cycle, the price of gasoline, and so forth are accounted for by the year fixed effects. And this method is flexible enough to estimate the effects of several types of policy simultaneously. It is generally valid, as explained above, as long as changes in policy are not correlated with other changes that may influence the outcome variable.[10]

Another methodological comment is in order. Previous sections of this chapter included an extended discussion of the problems of determining the causal effects of drinking on violence rates and other outcomes. The "reduced form" approach described above helps identify the causal effect of drinking even though it does not measure it directly. If changing MLDA affects some fatality rate, then as a logical matter it must be through the causal mechanism of drinking. This schematic makes the point, using the arrow ➜ to represent evidence of a causal connection:

If we observe   MLDA ➜ fatality rate
Then we can infer   MLDA ➜ drinking patterns ➜ fatality rate

This indirect inference may be more reliable than a direct demonstration of the connections, especially since the quality of the data on outcomes (such as fatality rates) is often much higher than the quality of data on drinking patterns.

This reduced-form, quasi-experimental method is relevant for any state-level policy area where there have been frequent changes in a policy that is readily characterized in one or two dimensions, such as the excise tax rate or MLDA or per se laws in drunk driving. Because of its importance in the alcohol-policy evaluation literature, it is useful to have a short-hand means of reference to this method. I propose to use "RASPP" for

Reduced-form
Analysis of
State
Panel data on
Policy Changes

The first application of the RASPP method to evaluating the effect of alcohol-control measures on drinking-related outcomes was introduced in the technical literature in 1982 (Cook and Tauchen 1982). Similar treatments by other analysts, most of them economists, have followed, providing a growing volume of evidence on the effects of alcohol policy.

RASPP Applied to Traffic Fatalities

Table 6.3 summarizes some of the RASPP studies that have analyzed the effect of various alcohol-control measures on highway fatality rates using panel data on states. Each of these studies adopts the quasi-experimental method described above, in that they exploit policy changes to estimate the effect of the policy on the outcome variable (traffic fatality rates) directly. Further, they typically do not estimate the intermediate relationships that characterize the mechanism by which the policy affects the outcome, and for that reason are appropriately labeled "reduced-form" analyses.[11] These studies have provided strong, consistent results on MLDA and alcohol taxes, and some information on the effects of other measures.

MLDA

A number of published studies have analyzed the effects of MLDA on highway fatality rates for youths (Wagenaar and Toomey 2002). The focus on fatality rates is justified by several facts. First, the data available on highway fatalities are far better than on injuries or property damage. Second, since drinking is a much larger factor in fatal crashes than others, the fatality rate is a more sensitive indicator of changes in DUI.[12] And third, fatalities are the most important of the possible consequences of DUI, accounting for the bulk of the social cost.

Different methods produce different estimates, of course. Table 6.3 summarizes some of the studies that have utilized panels of state-level data. A conservative estimate of the loss of life that occurred from lowering the MLDA (during the 1970s) from twenty-one to eighteen would be a 7 percent increase in the fatality rate for that age group and for fifteen- to seventeen-year-olds as well (Cook and Tauchen 1984; Saffer and Grossman 1987a); the younger group is affected by the MLDA both because younger teens have easier access to alcohol when the MLDA is lower, and because younger teens often ride with older-teen drivers (Cook and Tauchen 1984).

A noteworthy exception is the analysis by Michael Males (1986), who finds evidence that an increase in the MLDA does indeed reduce the highway fatality rate in the directly affected age group, only to *increase* the rate for the next older group. The driver fatality rate for the first year of

TABLE 6.3
RASPP Studies of Alcohol-Related Traffic Mortality

Authors	Years	Outcome	State & year fixed effects?	Policy Focus	Results
Cook and Tauchen (1984)	1970–1977	Fatality rates: 16–20	Yes	MLDA	—*
Males (1986)	1975–1983	Fatal crash rate: age 16–20	No	MLDA	0
DuMouchel et al. (1987)	1975–1984	Fatality rates: age 16–24	No	MLDA	—*
Saffer and Grossman (1987a, b)	1975–1981	Fatality rates: age 15–24	No	Beer tax rates MLDA	—* —*
Chaloupka, Saffer & Grossman (1993)	1982–1988	Fatality rates: total, night time, and youth	No	Beer tax rates, MLDA Dram-shop Laws, Fines	—* —* —* Mixed
Sloan, Reilly, and Schenzler (1994)	1982–1988	Fatality rate	Yes	Alcohol Price Index Dram shop Deterrent measures	—* —* —
Ruhm (1995)	1975–1988	Fatality rates	Yes	Beer tax rates MLDA	—* —*
Ruhm (1996)	1982–1988	Fatality rates: total and night time fatality rate	Yes	Beer tax rates MLDA Dram shop Deterrent measures	—* —*(18–20 only) —* Mostly insignif- icant
Eisenberg (2003)	1982–2000	Fatal crashes per cap & related measure	Yes	Beer tax rates MLDA Dram shop Other laws	Mixed —*(18–20 only) —* —*(with exceptions)

* Statistically significant effect at the p <.10 level.

legal purchase is elevated, regardless of whether that first year is eighteen, twenty-one, or some year in between. This is an intriguing finding that makes some sense if youths have to undergo a learning process about safe drinking. But Males' result has not been replicated by other analysts. In fact, the evidence suggests that the MLDA increases that began in 1976 had no discernible effect on the fatality rate of the twenty-one to twenty-four age group (Saffer and Grossman 1987a, 1987b).

Alcohol Excise Taxes

Although the MLDA has its primary effect on crashes involving youths, the price of alcohol affects all drinkers. Several authors have analyzed the effects of increasing alcohol prices by raising alcohol excise taxes. One of the most comprehensive such studies was done by economist Chistopher Ruhm (1996). He motivates his work with the mystery of why alcohol involvement in highway fatalities did not decline during the 1980s, despite diverse efforts to deter drinking and driving during that decade.

The late 1970s and early 1980s was an extraordinary time in the history of highway safety. In particular, the grassroots effort to combat drunk driving was energized with the formation of new, politically potent victims' groups, most notably Mothers Against Drunk Driving (MADD). MADD was founded by Candy Lightner in 1981 after losing her daughter to a drunk driver with a long history of DUI charges (Jacobs 1989, xv). By 1986 there were 395 chapters nationwide, providing a strong voice for taking DUI seriously in the courts and supporting new legislation (Evans, Neville, and Graham 1991). President Reagan appointed Lightner to a Presidential Commission on Drunk Driving in 1982, which supported a variety of new measures including the national MLDA of twenty-one. Numerous states adopted roadside breath testing, enacted administrative per se laws (which required license suspension or revocation by the police if a driver's BAC was found to exceed the legal limit), mandated minimum penalties for DUI conviction, and other measures (Ruhm 1996). With all of this effort, the mystery is why the percentage of crash fatalities that were alcohol related was the same in 1990 as in 1980—41 percent.

Ruhm's suggested culprit was declining alcohol prices (documented in chapter 5). They were declining partly due to the fact that excise tax rates were declining (in real terms) during this inflationary decade. The political will to raise excise taxes was lacking, and it didn't help that the DUI activists were not on board. A survey of MADD officers at the time found that they did not believe that limiting the availability of alcoholic beverages was a realistic solution or a morally appropriate strategy (Jacobs 1989; Weed 1987).

Ruhm, like others, focuses on the beer tax (as opposed to the tax on liquor or wine) because beer is the predominant source of alcohol in drunk driving. He reports robust and consistent statistical results linking variation in the state beer tax to state traffic-fatality rates. That effect remains after controlling for state and year fixed effects, unemployment rate, per capita income, and whether or not the state had adopted each of a number of other anti-DUI measures. From this analysis comes another insight into the mystery of the 1980s—the deterrence-oriented measures, with the exception of the administrative per se laws, have had little measurable effect.

The wave of anti-DUI legislation did not end with the 1980s. The following decade saw a continuing campaign that was particularly successful in getting states to adopt lower per se limits and other measures (Voas and Fisher 2001). Daniel Eisenberg (2003) conducted a comprehensive analysis covering the period 1982 to 2000. His results provide evidence in support of lowering the BAC limit above which the driver is deemed per se intoxicated and in violation to 0.08 percent. He found that it reduced fatal accidents, as have bans on open alcoholic-beverage containers and imposition of civil liability for servers. The beer tax has its expected negative effect, strongest for youthful drivers. On the other hand, mandatory jail terms for DUI conviction appears to have no deterrent value. DUI by underage youth has been targeted through "zero-tolerance" laws, which thanks to federal pressure were adopted by every state by 1998 (Carpenter 2004b). These laws have typically established a blood alcohol content of 0.02 percent (a negligible amount) as the illegal per se standard for drivers under age twenty-one, and require license suspension or revocation for those found in violation. Eisenberg finds that the zero-tolerance laws have helped reduce fatal accidents involving youthful drivers (Eisenberg 2003).

What about the possibility of self-selection bias in these results? Eisenberg employs a clever method for exploring this issue. If states adopt tougher measures at the time of growing concern about DUI, then the effect of the new laws may be confounded with the direct effect of the trend in public concern. To rule out this possibility, his statistical inquiry allows the possibility of (spurious) pre-law changes in fatalities as well as post-law effects. He also considers the possibility that the estimated effect of DUI laws is confounded by the activities of MADD, which as it grew stronger in a state could have affected legislation but also affected DUI directly by changing public attitudes. As it turns out, his estimates survive these challenges. He concludes that his estimates really are the causal effects of the new laws.

Thus, there are several policies directly aimed at drunk driving that have proven effective in improving highway safety, but so have more general measures to limit alcohol availability, including alcohol excise taxes and MLDA. A third approach, regulating on-site drinking establishments, has elements of both: these regulations are like excise taxes in restricting alcohol availability but like DUI laws in that they are more narrowly targeted and motivated primarily by a concern about drunk driving.

RASPP APPLIED TO SEX AND VIOLENCE

The link between sex and drugs, including alcohol, is pretty obvious and well documented, especially but certainly not exclusively among youths.[13] To the extent that drinking increases the likelihood of unplanned and unprotected sex, or even coerced sex, it becomes especially problematic. But just because drinking and sex often go together does not identify the causal mechanism that links the two, much less determine whether alcohol-control measures have any effect. As before, the best evidence on this matter comes from the analysis of changes in taxes and MLDA.

The first analysis of alcohol control and sex-related outcomes utilizing the RASPP method was published in 2000 by an economist at the Centers for Disease Control and two associates (Chesson, Harrison, and Kassler 2000). The authors utilized state-level surveillance data on documented syphilis and gonorrhea cases for the period 1981 to 1995. These are common sexually transmitted diseases (STDs) that can have serious consequences in themselves and, what's more, facilitate the transmission of HIV. The authors first analyzed the effects of changes in alcohol taxes on the overall rates of these diseases, finding a significant negative relationship (in a specification with fixed effects for state and year); based on their estimates, a $1 increase in the per-gallon state liquor tax (1998 prices) would result in reduction in gonorrhea rates of 2.1 percent, and a somewhat larger proportional effect on syphilis rates. They also focused specifically on adolescents, finding that both the beer tax and the MLDA had a sharply defined effect. In the latter case, an increase in the MLDA resulted in a 7 percent reduction in the gonorrhea rate during the first year, a reduction that could also be accomplished by a modest increase in the beer excise tax. The long-term effects in either case would likely be still larger, given that STDs are contagious.

The same quasi-experimental approach was used to estimate the effect of the MLDA on teen childbearing, another problematic consequence of unprotected sex (Dee 2001). The statistical results in this case are not so robust, but do point in the expected direction, especially for black adolescents. (Dee does not consider the effect of alcohol taxes or other alcohol-control measures.)

So what is the causal process that links alcohol control to STDs and teen childbearing? Finding the answer requires resorting to self-report data on sex and drinking, which inevitably are error-prone. One careful analysis of the Youth Risk Behavior Surveys found something interesting, if true: alcohol use does not increase the likelihood of having sex or of having multiple partners, but does lower the probability of using birth control and condoms among sexually active teens (Grossman and Markowitz 2001). It may be, then, that alcohol control does not lead to less teen sex, so much as less unprotected sex. But these are early days in exploring these causal connections. As of this writing, there is no direct evidence on whether alcohol controls affect the health and quality of newborn babies, or the spread of HIV.

Intentional Violence

The RASPP procedure has been applied to analyzing the effects of alcohol control on suicide rates by several authors. An early contribution analyzed the effect of an index of alcohol prices on the overall suicide rate for a panel of states 1982–1988, finding a significant negative effect (Sloan et al. 1994). A complementary result for youth suicide was estimated for a longer period (1976–1999); the authors found that the state beer tax had a sharply estimated negative effect on suicide counts for males age ten to twenty-four (considered in three 5-year age groups), but a somewhat smaller effect on female suicides (Markowitz, Chatterji, and Kaestner 2003). A similar analysis confirmed the effect of the beer tax, and found strong evidence that the zero-tolerance laws also reduced youthful male suicides. The evidence on the beneficial effect of the MLDA in this respect is fairly strong as well (Carpenter 2004b; Birckmayer and Hemenway 1999).

For interpersonal violence, the results from applying the RASPP method have been mixed. Cook and Moore (1993d), utilizing state panel data for 1979–1987 with the fixed-effects specification, find that the beer tax has no discernible effect on homicide rates, a result confirmed by a subsequent analysis (Sloan et al. 1994). But the same method indicates that increasing the beer tax does cause a reduction in robbery and rape rates (Cook and Moore 1993d).

A series of studies by Sara Markowitz and Michael Grossman has explored the effect of beer taxes and other alcohol control measures on domestic violence (Markowitz and Grossman 1998, 2000; Markowitz 2000). Since there are no good state administrative data on domestic-violence rates, these studies are based on survey data of individuals. The problem with identifying causal effects with this cross-section data on individuals is that the ability to characterize the potentially relevant characteristics of the state of residence is quite limited. That is, the analysis is more akin to the "difference" analysis discussed above in the context of the MLDA, rather than the "difference-in-difference" analysis. On the other hand, the survey data provide the ability to control for individual characteristics. In any event, the consistent finding from these studies is that increasing alcohol prices or taxes tends to reduce child abuse and other forms of domestic violence.

SOME NEW RASPP ESTIMATES

As we have seen, a number of analysts have adopted the RASPP technique, and their findings have been helpful in establishing the efficacy of some alcohol-control measures, including excise taxes, MLDA, and dram-shop liability. Of these, the policy that has the greatest promise for the future is the excise tax. Every state has long established twenty-one as the MLDA, and most states have some version of dram-shop liability in place. But excise taxes are low by historical standards and provide an open-ended opportunity for asserting greater public control over availability.

Tables 6.4 and 6.5 provides a uniform set of new estimate for five different outcome measures, in every case focusing first on ethanol consumption, and then on ethanol taxes. The outcome measures for this exercise are annual state-level fatality rates from accidents (motor vehicle and falls), violence (homicide and suicide), and liver cirrhosis. These are among the most important negative consequences of excess drinking, and have the additional virtue of being measured accurately, thanks to the Vital Statistics system.

The first set of results provides a baseline estimate of how variations in per capita drinking relate to these fatality rates. The estimates are regression coefficients on ethanol sales per capita from regressions on a twenty-year panel of the fifty states (1981–2000), controlling for average income, the condition of the labor market (through the employment-population ratio), and fixed effects for years and states. The variables were entered in log form, so the coefficients are properly interpreted as elasticities. They capture the contemporaneous effects of state-level fluctuations in drinking.

Thus, a 10 percent increase in per capita drinking is associated with a 5 percent increase in homicide and suicide, a 9 or 10 percent increase in accidents (motor vehicle or falls), and a 15 percent increase in cirrhosis deaths. Note that these estimates control for any effect that changes in economic conditions may have on both drinking and mortality. As it turns out, however, state-level fluctuations in income and employment conditions do not have much of an effect on these mortality rates: the exceptions are with motor-vehicle accidents, which increase markedly

TABLE 6.4
Short-Run Elasticity Estimates

	Elasticity with Respect to per Capita Ethanol Sales
Motor Vehicle Fatality Rate	0.92[a]
Fatality Rate from Falls	0.96[a]
Homicide Rate	0.51
Suicide Rate	0.51[b]
Cirrhosis Death Rate	1.53[a]

Source: Mortality data for cirrhosis, annual state data for 1979–2000 from Centers for Disease Control (CDC) WONDER; all other annual state data, 1981–2000, from CDC WISQARS; OLS regression results.

Note: Each regression includes fixed effects for state and year, and two covariates reflecting economic conditions—per capita real income, and the employment–population ratio.

[a]$p<.01$; [b]$p<.05$.

with employment, and cirrhosis mortality, which increases when incomes are down.

These estimates provide one basis for predicting the effects of any alcohol-control measure that was successful in reducing alcohol consumption by a certain amount. If adoption of policy X were to reduce drinking by 10 percent, the predicted result would be proportional reductions in mortality as given by these elasticities. But as we have seen, that prediction is iffy. A reduction in drinking caused by an increase in, say, the beer excise tax, may have a different effect on mortality rates than the same reduction caused by, say, the imposition of a stronger form of liability on servers. That possibility is one of the motivations for adopting the reduced-form RASPP approach.

To implement that approach for these outcome measures, I re-ran all the same regressions, but now using the excise tax rate in place of ethanol sales per capita.[14] The results are given in table 6.5, beginning with the estimated effect on per capita drinking. All the estimated coefficients are reported here as the estimated effect of an increase of 10 cents per ounce of ethanol—the equivalent of a nickel per drink. That tax increase, passed on to consumers in the form of higher prices (probably with a substantial markup), would reduce per capita consumption by about 12 percent.

Note that all these estimates are negative except for homicide (where the coefficient estimate is, statistically speaking, indistinguishable from

TABLE 6.5
Estimated RASPP Effects of Excise Taxes

	Percentage Change Associated with 10-cent Increase per Ounce*
Ethanol per Capita	−12[a]
Motor Vehicle Fatality Rate	−7[c]
Fatality Rate from Falls	−9
Homicide Rate	11
Suicide Rate	−6
Cirrhosis Death Rate	−32[a]

Source: Mortality data for cirrhosis, annual state data for 1979–2000 from CDC WONDER; all other annual state data, 1981–2000, from CDC WISQARS.

Notes: Each regression includes fixed effects for state and year, and two covariates reflecting economic conditions—per capita real income, and the employment–population ratio.

[a] $p<.01$; [b] $p<.05$; [c] $p<.10$; *2003 prices.

zero). Unfortunately, the effect sizes are not very precisely measured. Only in the case of ethanol sales, motor vehicle fatalities, and cirrhosis mortality are they significantly different from zero. The problem may be the fact that there is not much variation over time in the state alcohol excise taxes during the period under study, and the one large change in the federal excise taxes (in 1991) is absorbed by the year fixed effects. Still, the estimates are quite credible, in every case except homicide quite close to what we would expect from chaining together the elasticity estimates (table 6.4) with the proportional effect of a tax increase on ethanol per capita (first row, table 6.5). It is interesting that the effect on cirrhosis mortality is relatively large, given that cirrhosis is a proxy for the prevalence of chronic heavy drinking—a topic for the next chapter.

CONCLUDING THOUGHTS

There is no question that drinking increases injury rates from accidents and violence. Furthermore, alcohol sales and consumption fall in response to alcoholic-beverage price increases. Together these findings create a prima facie case that higher alcohol prices reduce injury rates. But a more compelling case requires direct evidence, and in particular a demonstration that price increases tend to be followed by reductions in injury rates, other things being equal. Just that sort of direct evidence has accumulated over the last twenty-five years from a series of statistical studies, many of them taking advantage of the "social science laboratory" of the states (Fosdick and Scott 1933, 150). The same is true for assessing the effects of the MLDA and other alcohol-control measures. In an era that calls for evidence-based policymaking, here is an area in which the evidence is especially compelling.

CHAPTER 7

Long-Term Effects

Hearts and Minds

> It has long been recognized that the problems with alcohol relate not to the use of a bad thing, but to the abuse of a good thing.
> —Abraham Lincoln

> One cannot judge the role of diet by starvation or excess.
> —Raymond Pearl, *Alcohol and Longevity*

THE MOST VIVID CONSEQUENCES of intoxication are immediate. The drinker gets into a wreck or a fight, or has unprotected or unwanted sex—or not. If not, then the physical harm is likely to be limited to a hangover the next morning. But that is not the whole story. A particular drinking bout may affect other people's opinions of the drinker. His behavior while drunk may affect his standing with his family, employer, and friends. Alcohol-fueled antics at fraternity parties may raise his standing among his brothers and make for a fond recollection years later. Or drinking may help an old married couple renew their relationship because they find it easier to be romantic or more inclined to get out on the dance floor when they've had some drinks. But much of what constitutes "drunken comportment" is likely to have negative social consequences, and these consequences cumulate over time. Repeated occasions when drinking leads to the neglect or abuse of important relationships, or engenders behavior that is a source of embarrassment the next day, will affect long-term relationships and reputation in the relevant communities (Klingemann and Gmel 2001).

Although this sort of "social cumulation" seems important, there has been much more systematic evidence on the cumulative physiological and medical effects of drinking. Over the course of years or decades, heavy drinking causes organ damage that may progress over time and be irreversible. Long-term heavy drinking is associated with numerous alcohol-induced disorders of the gastrointestinal tract, but it doesn't end there (Rehm et al. 2003). The liver, which does much of the work in metabolizing alcohol, is likely to be damaged by long-term heavy drinking; in the extreme, the liver may become heavily scarred (cirrhotic). About 27,000 Americans die of liver cirrhosis annually, most of them after years of heavy drinking (Yoon et al. 2003). (The fatality rate from liver cirrhosis has long been used as an indicator of the prevalence of alcoholism in a community.) Damage to the pancreas and kidneys is also common in heavy drinkers, as is impairment to the immune system with resulting susceptibility to infection. A variety of neurological abnormalities including brain damage may result from heavy drinking, either as a direct toxic effect of alcohol, or the indirect effects through liver disease or nutritional deficiencies often associated with alcoholism (Oscar-Berman and Marinkovic 2003). And of course chronic heavy drinking is the primary risk factor for the "disease of the will," alcoholism (chapter 3).

Despite this litany of problems, however, the health consequences of drinking are not all bad. That there are substantial long-term benefits of drinking, a possibility largely ignored by epidemiologists until the 1970s, is now widely accepted. The main health benefits appear to be the prevention of coronary heart disease and stroke. These and other cardiovascular diseases are the leading causes of death in the United States, accounting for nearly 40 percent of all deaths (nearly one million per year), so that even a relatively small reduction is noteworthy (Centers for Disease Control and Prevention 2004a). In fact, the best evidence suggests that the overall effect of drinking on life expectancy past age forty-five is positive. But the nature of that evidence leaves room for reasonable doubt.

Alcoholism and Liver Cirrhosis

The effects of alcohol control measures on highway safety, sex, and violence are mediated by the acute effects of drinking, although that is not the whole story. If day-to-day drinking decisions are influenced by price and availability, then over time the cumulative effect of those drinking decisions may be a habit of heavy drinking. It is only reasonable to suppose, then, that alcohol-related injury, crime, and other problems reflect not only current alcohol-control measures, but those that have been in effect for decades. These long-lagged effects are difficult to estimate using the methods discussed above,[1] but that is not to say that they are negligible. There is a real sense in which alcoholics of today are the victims of a lifetime of exposure to drinks that were too cheap and too readily available, both socially and commercially. It is worth repeating Jellinek's observation: "in societies which have an extremely high degree of acceptance of large daily alcohol consumption, the presence of any small vulnerability, whether psychological or physical, will suffice for exposure to the risk of addiction" (1960, 28–9).

Although it is difficult to trace the effects of past measures on the current prevalence of heavy drinking, it is possible to estimate the short-term causal impact of changes in alcohol control measures. The RASPP method can be readily applied because there exists a good proxy—the liver cirrhosis mortality rate.

Cirrhosis is characterized by a progressive replacement of healthy liver tissue with scarring, leading to liver failure and death. Even though it has a variety of causes, alcohol accounts for a majority of cases within population groups where drinking is widespread; indeed, the cirrhosis mortality rate has long been used as an indicator of the prevalence of alcoholism in a population (Bruun et al. 1975). The likelihood of cirrhosis is closely related to lifetime consumption. A threshold dose of alcohol for liver disease is five or six drinks per day for twenty years for men, and one-fourth to one-half of that amount for women (Maher 1997, 5).

There is considerable evidence that cirrhosis death rates are sensitive to alcohol availability, suggesting that the group at risk for alcohol-related cirrhosis, long-term heavy drinkers, is at least somewhat price sensitive. Notable cases occurred during and after the First World War. Alcohol was diverted to military purposes during the war, and several countries instituted prohibition. The results have been analyzed in Canada, Finland, and the United States, and in each case the reduction in availability was accompanied by a rapid and substantial drop in the cirrhosis death rate. In France, which ordinarily has a high cirrhosis mortality rate, sharp drops in availability occurred during both World Wars, with particularly dramatic effects on the mortality trend (Bruun et al. 1975, 43; Seeley 1960; Terris 1967).

Cirrhosis mortality is also responsive to small changes in price. My early efforts to document this effect used RASPP, as explained in the previous chapter (Cook 1981; Cook and Tauchen 1982). In a longitudinal study of state cirrhosis morality rates, we found that increases in state liquor excise taxes lead to an immediate (and statistically significant) reduction. Although this disease takes years to develop, the flow of deaths responds quickly because the progression of the disease (toward death) is slowed when drinking is curtailed. Over the long run it is logical that a reduction in heavy drinking will reduce cirrhosis mortality still further, since the rate of initiation of cirrhosis will be reduced. According to a set of assumptions that fits the epidemiological evidence, the short-term effect is about half of the eventual effect (Cook and Tauchen 1982).

Is it really necessary to demonstrate empirically that alcohol taxes affect the prevalence of heavy drinking? According to one intriguing school of thought, the answer is no. As recounted in chapter 4, the French demographer Sully Ledermann proposed the "single distribution theory" of alcohol consumption in his book, *Alcool, alcoolisme, alcoolisation* in 1956, which made several generalizations about the size distribution of alcohol consumption for any population of drinkers: first, that it is well described by a lognormal distribution (with a single peak and a long "tail" to the right); second, that any two populations with the same per capita alcohol consumption will have the same prevalence of heavy drinking; and third, that in any two populations with different consumption levels, the population with the higher per capita consumption will have a predictably greater prevalence of heavy drinking (Cook and Skog 1995). In Ledermann's theory, reducing average consumption is both necessary and sufficient to reduce the prevalence of heavy drinking. Hence, knowing (as we do) that an increase in price reduces per capita consumption implies sure knowledge that it also reduces the prevalence of heavy drinking, as proxied by the cirrhosis mortality rate.

The Single Distribution Theory achieved prominence through the efforts of Wolfgang Schmidt, Jan deLint, and colleagues at the Addiction Research Foundation in Toronto, as well as Ole-Jørgen Skog and several other Nordic researchers (de Lint and Schmidt 1968; Schmidt and Popham 1978; Mäkelä 1969; Skog 1971, 1980a; Bruun et al. 1975). The strong claims made by Ledermann have stood up quite well, and reinforce the view that heavy drinkers and alcoholics are not a distinct group, but closely tied to the environment in which they live. Nonetheless, the direct demonstration that tax increases affect heavy drinking is reassuring to those who are not sold on the infallibility of the Ledermann theory.

DRINKING AND HEART DISEASE

If smoking and eating fatty, high-cholesterol foods are bad for the heart, then why do the French, who do a good deal of both, not have a higher incidence of heart disease? This "French paradox" has long been a puzzle for epidemiologists (Criqui and Ringel 1994). An Irish physician, Dr. Samuel Black, suggested in 1819 that the low incidence of angina in France was due to "the French habits and modes of living, coinciding with the benignity of their climate and the peculiar character of their moral affections" (Klatsky 2002). More recently, the "moral affection" that has gotten particular notice is the traditional French preference for drinking red wine with meals. But the focus on wine, while welcomed and promoted by the wine industry, is perhaps misplaced. The emerging consensus, based now on decades of systematic epidemiological work, is that drinking alcohol in any form (not just wine) provides some protection against heart disease and stroke. Moderate alcohol consumption is a potent means to reduce plaque deposits in arteries by raising the "good" high-density cholesterol in the blood, while lowering the "bad" low-density cholesterol. Alcohol also "thins" the blood, reducing the tendency to produce blood clots that cause the more common form of strokes (is-chemic) (Gronbaek 2001; Rehm et al. 2003). The medical community is in agreement that moderate drinking is a healthy, life-extending practice for people in middle age and over (Dietary Guidelines Advisory Commit-tee 1995; Krauss, Deckelbaum, and Ernst 1996).

That evidence has emerged from a number of statistical studies based on systematic description but not experiment. There are no "clinical tri-als" that randomly assign one group to drink moderately for ten years while the control group is instructed to abstain. The early epidemiological reports in the medical literature go back to the beginning of the 1900s, when an inverse relationship between alcohol consumption and arterio-sclerotic disease was reported (Klatsky 2002). Physicians conducting autopsies of heavy drinkers found a pattern of a diseased liver, denoting chronic heavy drinking, associated with a particularly healthy looking heart (Cabot 1904). In recent times, over three decades of population and case-control studies have confirmed an inverse relationship between drinking and coronary heart disease (Klatsky, Friedman, and Siegelaub 1974; Klatsky 2002; Corrao et al. 2000; Mukamal et al. 2003).

To get the flavor of the evidence that has impressed the epidemiologists, consider one of the larger population studies, authored by Michael J. Thun and his associates (1997), and published in the prestigious *New England Journal of Medicine*. Their study is based on data on 490,000 men and women (average age fifty-six) from a detailed written question-naire distributed in 1982 in which subjects reported their drinking, smok-ing, and other health-related information. This sample was then tracked through national death records for nine years; by 1991, 46,000 had died, and the causes of death recorded by coroners in official records. The drinking question on the questionnaire was "How many cups, glasses, or drinks of these beverages do you usually drink a day, and for how many years?" Death rates from various causes, and overall, were analyzed as a function of this self-report on drinking, controlling for a variety of other risk factors including education, body mass index, and an index of dietary fat consumption. Without these controls, the estimated effect of drinking would have been confounded with the effect of other behaviors, particu-larly smoking: the percentage who smoked at the time of enrollment in-creased with the frequency of alcohol consumption, from 22 percent for those reporting less than one drink daily to 37 percent of those who con-sumed four or more drinks daily (Thun et al. 1997). The key result: the rates of death from all cardiovascular diseases combined were 30 to 40 percent lower among men and women reporting at least one drink daily than among nondrinkers. The largest proportional reduction was for peo-ple reporting heart disease, stroke, or some other indication of preexisting risk of cardiovascular disease at baseline.

TABLE 7.1
Estimated Probability of Death from Any Cause in the General U.S. Population,
Ages 35–69 (circa 1990)

	Males			Females		
	Abstainers %	Drinkers %	Gain from Drinking %	Abstainers %	Drinkers %	Gain from Drinking %
Not a smoker	26	22	4	17	14	3
Smoker	46	43	3	30	28	2

Source: Based on figure 2 in Thun et al. 1997.

The authors project their results to the U.S. population as a whole and derive the estimates shown in table 7.1 for death rates. What is evident from these results is that smokers, and especially male smokers, are much less likely to make it to their seventieth birthday than nonsmokers, but that drinking increases the chance of survival by 2–4 percentage points for each of the four groups defined by sex and smoking status. That increase, it should be noted, is primarily due to reductions in cardiovascular-disease deaths, and is net of estimated *increases* in mortality associated with alcohol-augmented conditions—cirrhosis and alcoholism, alcohol-related cancers, and traumatic injury.

These summary results lump all drinkers together to keep the presentation simple, but in fact death rates are influenced not only by whether someone drinks but also how much and in what pattern. Epidemiologists tend to describe the relationships they find in terms of the capital letters L, U, and J, according to the shape of the graph of mortality rate against alcohol consumption. An "L-shaped" curve is one in which abstainers have the highest death rate from some cause, while the death rate of drinkers is lower, regardless of how much they drink. For a "U-shaped" curve, mortality is lower for moderate drinkers than either abstainers or heavier drinkers, while for a "J-shaped" curve the mortality rate for the heavier drinkers exceeds the rate for abstainers.

Perhaps the first observer to describe a J-shaped alcohol-mortality curve in the medical literature was Raymond Pearl (1926), who found it in the population he was studying (tuberculosis patients) and compared his finding to a more familiar realm: "One cannot judge the role of diet by starvation or excess" (Klatsky 2002). The Thun et al. (1997) study discussed above found an L-shaped curve for cardiovascular diseases, with no indication that even the heaviest drinkers suffer. When they analyzed all-cause mortality, including death from traumatic injury, liver cirrhosis, and all else, they found the "rate of death from all causes followed a J-, U-, or L-shaped pattern in subgroups at low, intermediate, or high risk of cardiovascular disease, respectively." Those who benefit from drinking the most are those with preexisting cardiovascular problems.

Other studies have reached different conclusions concerning the shape of the risk function. One comprehensive meta-analysis of twenty-eight high-quality cohort studies that met certain criteria and were published between 1968 and 1998 concluded that the risk of coronary heart disease death followed a J-shaped curve, with lowest risk associated with one drink per day for women and two per day for men, and a "break-even" point at about six drinks per day (Corrao et al. 2000). These twenty-eight studies excluded the quitters from the "abstainer" category, so the comparison was with lifetime abstainers. Unlike the Thun et al. study (1997), these twenty-eight also excluded subjects with pre-existing disease at baseline. Another meta-analysis, this one of all-cause mortality, confirmed a J-shaped curve for middle-age cohorts (Rehm, Greenfield, and Rogers 2001), but also found that for men under age forty-five, death rates increase with alcohol consumption on a near-linear basis.

There remains a good deal of controversy about the healthiest "dose," but in a sense there cannot be any one answer, given the great heterogeneity among people. Cardiologist Arthur Klatsky (2002) cites approvingly the century-old "Anstie's Rule," which suggested an upper limit for sensible drinking of approximately three standard drinks daily for mature men, but notes that Sir Anstie, a distinguished neurologist and public health activist of his day, emphasized individual variability in the ability to handle alcohol.

One of the vital questions in this literature is whether the average daily consumption of alcohol is a sufficient statistic for describing the "dose" of alcohol, or whether it is also important to take account of day-to-day variation around the individual's average. Intuitively it seems that the physiological effects of having two glasses of wine with dinner every night would be more beneficial than the effects of drinking two bottles Saturday night after abstaining the rest of the week. The two patterns are equivalent in terms of average daily dose, but quite different in other respects (Rehm et al. 2001).

A widely cited article in the *British Medical Journal* by Patrick McElduff and Annette Dobson (1997) sought to address this issue using a case-control study of heart attack patients in New South Wales (1983–1994). The patients were interviewed while still in the hospital about their medical history and health habits; "controls" were taken from studies of medical risk factors where subjects were given self-administered questionnaires, physical measurements, and a blood sample. After controlling for smoking, age, and some medical conditions, the authors found that regular drinking is indeed protective against heart attack, and that those drinkers who did have a heart attack were less likely to die if they were regular drinkers. On the other hand, the protective effect of drinking was lost if consumption took the form of bingeing: "men who took nine or more drinks a day on one or two days a week consumed similar amounts to those who took three or four drinks a day on five or six days a week but the odds ratios [of having a heart attack] for the two groups were substantially different (2.62 (95% confidence interval 1.12 to 6.17) v 0.46 (0.27 to 0.80))" (McElduff and Dobson 1997, 6).

Although the benefits of moderate drinking of any type of alcoholic beverage seem clear, the old notion that red wine has some particular virtue continues to be debated (Gronbaek 2001; Mukamal et al. 2003). There is speculation that red wine has antioxidant and antithrombotic (anti-clotting) substances that are not much found in other forms of alcohol, and which confer health benefits. The Wine Institute has supported research to investigate this issue. One such study, of Kaiser Permanente patients in San Francisco and Oakland, California, found as usual that drinking conferred a protective effect against mortality, but also that for any level of alcohol consumption, the wine drinkers had a lower mortality rate than those who drank beer or liquor (Klatsky et al. 2003). Whether the wine itself should get the credit, or whether it's the lifestyle associated with wine drinking, remains an open question. The authors note some of the possible confounders in this study: "Persons in Northern California who drink preponderantly wine are more often women, college graduates, nonsmokers, and temperate drinkers, characteristics even more pronounced in persons drinking wine exclusively" (2003, 590).

SECOND THOUGHTS ABOUT THE BENEFICIAL EFFECTS

Scanning the epidemiological literature on the health effects of chronic consumption, one cannot help but be impressed by the scope of the studies and the consistency of the finding that drinking can be good for you; that taking one or two drinks per day is the equivalent of a powerful anti-cholesterol drug and confers other benefits as well for those of us who are no longer young. Completely lacking is the kind of experimental or quasi-experimental evidence relating drinking to highway-crash risk.

This is not just an academic point. Ready at hand is a vivid example, from the pharmaceutical field, of how such chains of logic can lead to widely accepted conclusions that prove devastatingly false when subjected to direct test. The example is Hormone Replacement Therapy (HRT) for women past menopause. The remarkable history of this therapy is recounted by Harvard physician Jerry Avorn (Avorn 2004). Hormone replacement in the form of estrogen supplements has been prescribed for decades, not just to relieve hot flashes and other acute symptoms of meno-pause, but in a belief that it protects against disease. Brief experiments have demonstrated that women who are given Premarin or a similar form of estrogen thereby lower their "bad" cholesterol (LDL) and increase "good" cholesterol (HDL) in the blood, changes known from other re-search to be associated with reduced risk of cardiovascular disease. Nu-merous epidemiological studies (based on observation, rather than experi-mental intervention) have reported that post-menopausal women who were taking estrogen had lower rates of heart disease than women of the same age group who were not taking this hormone. But for decades what was lacking in this chain of evidence was direct experimental evidence connecting estrogen replacement to a reduction in heart disease. Dr. Avorn reports that the first large, well-conducted, controlled clinical trial of HRT was not published until 1998; it found that estrogen replacement actually *increased* the rate of heart attacks in the patients studied (2004, 23). Another trial in 2002 found an increase in the risk of heart disease, stroke, and cancer.

The HRT story, in sum, is of fatally misleading conclusions derived from the combination of suggestive evidence from observational studies, and some plausible inferences from short-term experimental evidence. That can only be called bad luck—in many other cases evidence of this sort has pointed in the right direction. But a *confident* conclusion should have awaited a large controlled clinical trial sustained over a long enough period to provide direct evidence on the incidence of disease. The funda-mental problem with the nonexperimental, observational studies on HRT was that they were comparing two groups that emerged from the volun-tary choices made by individuals, rather than dictated by the experimenter using a random assignment process. The women who chose to take estro-gen replacement were in important medical respects systematically differ-ent from those who didn't. Even after the statisticians adjusted for age and other observable characteristics, it appears that healthier women were more likely to choose HRT—perhaps because they tended to be more health-conscious. There was, in short, a large element of *self-selec-tion bias*. On the other hand, in the clinical trials the hormone "takers" and "nontakers" were guaranteed to be comparable with respect to preex-isting medical conditions, attitudes toward their health, and everything else through the power of random assignment.[2] Subsequent differences in disease incidence could then be confidently attributed to whether the sub-ject was receiving estrogen or the placebo. Self-selection bias was ruled out by the experimental procedure.

In the case of drinking and heart disease, unlike, say, alcohol-involved crashes, the causal mechanisms are still somewhat speculative, lacking the direct evidence that comes from experiments—such as those conducted with driving simulators. For another, where the Roadside Surveys can collect objective data from breathalyzers, the epidemiologists in chronic-drinking studies are forced to rely on highly unreliable data on drinking—typically self-report data from a single survey that is used to characterize a lifetime of drinking. As pointed out in the previous chapter, self-reports on drinking are unreliable in the extreme; average self-reported consumption averages half of the true total. The epidemiological studies typically include no audit or check on self-report, and there is every reason to believe that some substantial fraction of the self-reported abstainers, aren't, and some fraction of the self-reported "one drink a day with dinner" respondents are failing to report the heavy drinking they do on weekend evenings. Errors in self-report are bound to distort estimates of those L-, U-, and J-shaped curves.

Of even greater concern is that we don't really know why some people drink and others abstain. Whether and how much and in what pattern and what type of beverage one drinks are all choices. Those choices may be influenced by a variety of factors, and some of those factors may well be related to the likelihood of early death. Some of these potential confounders have been mentioned already. Among the most important is the association between drinking and two very important risk factors—being male, and being a smoker. More subtly, the epidemiologists have been concerned about the possibility that some of the abstainers are former drinkers who choose to give it up after becoming sick—indeed, the data indicate abstainers who are former drinkers do have a higher mortality risk than lifetime abstainers and the best epidemiological studies exclude former drinkers from the comparison group (Gmel, Gutjahr, and Rehm 2003).

But the question remains as to whether the self-reported lifetime abstainers are really comparable to drinkers of the same sex, age, race, education, and smoking status. The basic presumption of the epidemiological studies is that after controlling for readily observable characteristics and self-reported behavior, the only important remaining difference is the amount of alcohol consumption. It doesn't take much creativity to imagine confounding possibilities. Perhaps the abstainers have an allergy to alcohol that is also associated with circulatory problems. Or perhaps they tend to include a disproportionate number of social misfits, a condition that is likely to be bad for their health—people who are socially isolated tend to die young—but will not be controlled for in these studies. Indeed, a comprehensive analysis of risk factors for cardiovascular (CVD) disease found that "After adjusting for age and gender, nondrinkers were more likely to have characteristics associated with increased CVD mortality in terms of demographic factors, social factors, behavioral factors, access to health care, and health-related conditions. Of the 30 CVD-associated factors or groups of factors that we assessed, 27 (90%) were significantly more prevalent among nondrinkers" (Naimi et al. 2005, 369). The authors of this study conclude that "These findings suggest that some or all of the apparent protective effect of moderate alcohol consumption on CVD may be due to residual or unmeasured confounding."

In addition to the possibility that these studies fail to control for important confounding variables is the possibility that in some sense they control for more of the observed variables than is really appropriate. The result could be to underestimate the beneficial effects of drinking (Corrao et al. 2000) or overestimate them. Take the case of smoking. The data on death rates in table 7.1 suggest that smoking has a powerful negative influence on the chance of surviving middle age. It is only after controlling for smoking status that the life-enhancing effects of drinking are revealed. In practice, however, smoking and drinking are not so easily separated. Smoking and drinking tend to go together. Imagine a forty-year-old smoker who is trying to quit, and to make it easier, gives up drinking as well. But then her doctor (or a public service ad) touts the heart healthy advantages of drinking. If she takes that information seriously, she may decide to continue her drinking after all, but then fail in her effort to give up smoking. Most likely the benefit of continuing drinking would be less than the harm from continuing smoking.

Better evidence on the physiological mechanisms by which alcohol affects the cardiovascular system and various organs will continue to emerge from the laboratory, with short-term observations on people and longer-term observations on animals. But organizing relevant long-term human experiments in the field seems out of the question. What's left is to seek out natural experiments, but that too is problematic. Consider some possibilities. Groups who are enjoined to abstain from alcohol by their church (Mormons, for example) can be studied to see if they have a higher-than-expected incidence of cardiovascular disease—but such comparisons are of little use, given all the other health-related behaviors that may also be affected by such religious affiliation. Another possibility is to look at the consequence of sharp disruptions in alcohol availability that are sustained for an extended period. Again, most of those that come to mind, such as wars, are embedded in circumstances that are bound to affect other health-related factors as well.

Epidemiologists have taken a particular interest in President Gorbachev's program to reduce drinking in the former Soviet Union during the mid-1980s. Of course, the Gorbachev reforms, and their rescission, were far from a controlled experiment, coming as they did during a tumultuous period leading up to the dissolution of the USSR. Still, the evidence from that period has been seen by some observers as casting doubt on the beneficial effects of drinking:

Numerous measures were implemented to limit access to alcohol, including banning alcohol at the workplace, limiting alcohol sales hours, restricting the number of alcohol outlets, reducing alcohol production, and increasing prices by 25 percent in 1985 alone. . . . During the period from 1984 to 1987, when estimated total alcohol consumption fell by about 25 percent, age-adjusted male deaths from circulatory disease fell by 9 percent. . . . After the end of the campaign, alcohol consumption increased by about 36 percent (from 1987 to 1993) and the circulatory disease death rate rose by 29 percent. (Rehm et al. 2003a, 43)

It seems fair to say that the evidence on the long-term effects of drinking on health and longevity is less complete than one would like as a basis for formulating alcohol-related policy. And new findings are to be expected as research in this area continues. For example, there is evidence that moderate drinking protects against dementia, including both vascular dementia and Alzheimer's disease. In one epidemiological study, moderate drinking reduced the risk of dementia past age sixty-five by over half (Mukamal et al. 2003).

The Overall Burden of Mortality and Morbidity

In the United States and other wealthy industrialized countries, drinking increases the incidence of serious injury and traumatic death, while possibly offering some protective effect against cardiovascular disease. Standard estimates of deaths due to drinking indicate that most of the "problem" is the result of acute intoxication rather than chronic heavy drinking. For example, the Centers for Disease Control estimates that in 2001, 63 percent of all potential live years lost due to drinking were due to the acute effects of drinking, namely injuries resulting from assault, suicide, traffic accidents, poisoning, and so forth. The remainder were due to chronic excess consumption.[3] Some estimates of the number of lives saved because of long-term moderate drinking are in the same ballpark as the number lost, but with an important difference—the victims tend to be quite young, whereas it is older people whose lives are extended by drinking. (The age pattern of deaths from injury and heart disease is depicted in figure 7.1.) If the calculation of gains and losses is based on life-years gained and lost, or life-years adjusted for disability, then the losses greatly exceed the gains (Murray and Lopez 1997).

Eric Single and colleagues (1999) confirm these generalizations for Canada, offering specific estimates of the relevant numbers for 1992. For that year, they estimate that 6,701 Canadians lost their lives owing to alcohol consumption, from impaired driving (1,477), cirrhosis (960), alcohol-related suicides (918), and other causes. That amounts to 3 percent of total

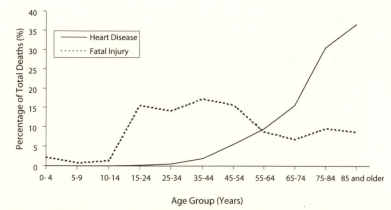

Figure 7.1. Distribution across Age Groups of Total Deaths by Fatal Injury and Heart Disease (2003).
Sources: CDC WONDER and WISQARS databases.

mortality in that year, but 6 percent of total years of potential life before age sixty-five lost. They found that alcohol prevented an estimated 7,401 deaths, including 4,205 due to ischemic heart disease and 2,965 due to stroke. Thus, the deaths prevented slightly exceeded the deaths engendered. But the number of potential years of life lost due to alcohol was over twice the potential years of life saved by alcohol use, 186,000 vs. 89,000. Thus, by these estimates drinking shortens life expectancy in Canada. Such estimates are interesting, but based on the discussion above, should be viewed as point estimates from a very wide distribution of plausible possibilities.

Concluding Thoughts

Despite the difficulties of extracting reliable conclusions about causation with respect to long-term effects, it is still possible to be quite confident of certain conclusions. First, drinking is heavily implicated in injury deaths and in a variety of chronic diseases. Second, there is no known health benefit to youths from drinking, and notable harms; before middle age, the acute risks of injury associated with intoxication are pretty much the whole story.[4] Third, in the middle and older years when arteriosclerosis and stroke become major risks, alcohol is a potentially beneficial drug that when used properly (regular, moderate "doses") quite possibly extends life—but on that score the evidence is far from definitive.

The bottom line is that if alcohol were just medicine, then the appropriate minimum age for a prescription would be something like forty years old.

CHAPTER 8

The Drinker's Bonus

> Even though a number of people have tried, no one has yet
> found a way to drink for a living.
> —Jean Kerr

DOES DRINKING AFFECT THE productivity of the labor force? Common sense, backed by a good deal of evidence, says yes. In fact, estimates of alcohol-related social costs are typically dominated by the value of lost productivity (Harwood Fountain, and Livermore 1998). Historically the concern with the quality and quantity of work provided by the labor force was a major factor in nineteenth-century temperance movements in the United States and Europe (Roberts 1984; Rumbarger 1989). Clark War-urton (1932) stated the argument concisely:

> Prohibition, if it actually resulted in the cessation of use of alcoholic beverages, might be expected to affect the efficiency of industry in several ways. The principal effect of alcohol is on the central nervous system, and experiments show that a decrease in the consumption of alcohol during, or immediately preceding, working hours is accompanied by greater skill at work. The finer co-ordination made possible by the absence of alcohol tends to reduce the accident rate. The elimination of drinking bouts should tend to eliminate absenteeism, especially on Monday, and irregularity in reporting at work. The impossibility of drinking to excess should result in less sickness and absence on account thereof, and in a longer average working life. (195–6)

In recent times, a majority of large corporations in the United States have established occupational alcoholism programs or employee-assistance programs to improve productivity (Walsh 1982).

Curiously, however, the link between drinking—even heavy drinking—and reduced productivity does not receive unambiguous support from the econometric work on this subject. In fact, drinkers tend to earn *more* than those who abstain, and that "drinker's bonus" is not necessarily limited to moderate drinkers. The striking parallel with the epidemiological findings on drinking and heart disease bears close scrutiny.[1]

DIRECT EVIDENCE ON THE ACUTE EFFECTS OF DRINKING

Yale economist Irving Fisher undertook early efforts to estimate the productivity costs of drinking (Fisher, 1926). His view was that drinking slowed down the "human machine" (118), and he noted, "All of us know that industrial efficiency was one of the chief reasons for Prohibition" (158). He supported his claim of impaired productivity by citing experiments which showed that drinking reduces proficiency or speed at some task. In particular, he noted an experiment in which four typesetters were studied over a four-day period; two of them were given drinks, and the other two were used as a control group. The conclusion was that drinking three glasses of beer in a day reduced typesetting output by about 10 percent. Fisher made a heroic extrapolation from this result, projecting a 5 percent increase in national productivity as a result of reduced drinking caused by Prohibition.

There have been surprisingly few modern-day experiments to study how drinking affects work, perhaps because it seems obvious. Several laboratory studies have been conducted on the effects of hangovers on job performance in industrial settings (Howland et al. 2000). Subjects drank till intoxicated, slept it off, and then the next morning performed tasks in simulated work situations (Wolkenberg, Gold, and Tichauer 1975). Even as much as eighteen hours after the drinking bout, experimenters observed detrimental effects of the residual effects of the drinking bout on reaction time, motor skills, perception, and other performance attributes.

But outside of the factory setting, circumstances arise where drinking—even drinking on the job—may actually enhance productivity, especially when the "job" requires socializing. For example, in sales and contract negotiations, a few martinis at lunch may help close the deal (and hence, incidentally, be a justifiable charge to the corporate expense account). After-hours drinking sessions with work mates may be the best opportunity to air out grievances and make new connections, as is reputedly the tradition for office workers in Japan.

Such mechanisms do not lend themselves to experimentation, but there is some relevant nonexperimental evidence. One of the largest observational studies, the Worksite Alcohol Project, found that *problematic* drinking (but not drinking per se) was associated with work-related problems (Mangione et al. 1999). Sixteen work sites belonging to seven different corporations, spanning the gamut from professional office to factory, were included, with over nine thousand individual survey respondents interviewed in the early 1990s. The respondents were asked about job-related problems during the previous year, including having missed work; done poor quality work; arrived late or left early; done less work than expected; had an argument with a coworker; or been hurt on the job. The combined frequency of these work performance problems was regressed on self-reported measures of drinking and alcohol-related problems, controlling for demographic characteristics, life circumstances, and job characteristics. Three drinking measures had a significantly positive effect: drinking on the job, at times drinking to get drunk, and dependence on alcohol (as indicated by the CAGE instrument). Interestingly, given these other measures, the weekly quantity of alcohol consumed had no discernible effect on problem frequency.[2]

Finally, several surveys have asked respondents whether their drinking has caused them any problems. For example, in a national survey conducted in the United States in 1984, 2.9 percent of men stated that their drinking had harmed their employment opportunities, and 0.8 percent reported they had lost or nearly lost a job as a result of their drinking (Hilton and Clark 1987). The corresponding percentages for women were about half those of the men. These percentages seem remarkably small relative to the prevalence of alcohol abuse.

Drinking and Earnings

The possibility that drinking is actually rewarded in the labor market was first documented by economists Mark Berger and Paul Leigh (Berger and Leigh 1988). They compared the hourly wages of drinkers and nondrinkers,[3] finding that for males the drinkers earned 10 percent more, while for females the drinkers earned 35 percent more. After controlling for experience, education, occupation, race, and marital status, the differences shrank somewhat but remained large.

This finding that abstainers earn less than drinkers, or at least moderate drinkers, has been replicated in a variety of other studies (van Ours 2004; Zarkin et al. 1998; French and Zarkin 1995; Hamilton and Hamilton 1997; Kenkel and Ribar 1994). As further illustration, figure 8.1 displays the drinker's bonus using data on annual earnings and drinking in 1992 for full time workers ages twenty-seven to thirty-four. The data are from the National Longitudinal Survey of Youth. The median earnings for both males and females who reported at least one drink in the month before the survey were greater than for those who abstained. Figures 8.1 and 8.2 also indicate that the likelihood of being a full-time worker is higher for drinkers than abstainers.

How should these results be interpreted? Economists are inclined to equate earnings (hourly or annual) with productivity, albeit with a number of qualifications (Bowles, Gintis, and Osborne 2001; Kenkel and Wang

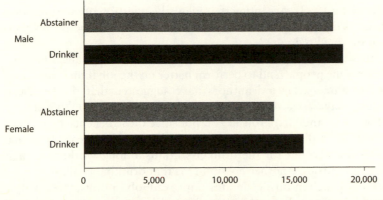

Figure 8.1. Median Earnings for Full-Time Workers by Gender and Drinking Status for Population, Ages 27–34.
Source: National Longitudinal Survey of Youth 1979.
Note: Drinking status and earnings from 1992 wave of survey. Sample: Respondents who worked at least 1,500 hours and earned at least $1,000; "drinkers" had at least one drink in the previous 30 days; dollars are adjusted to the 1982–1984 level.

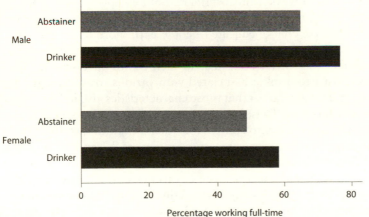

Figure 8.2 Full-Time Status by Gender and Drinking Status for Population, Ages 27–34.
Source: National Longitudinal Survey of Youth 1979.
Note: Drinking ststus and hours of work from 1992 wave of survey. Full-time status is defined as worked at least 1,500 hours and earned at least $1,000; "drinker" had at least one drink in the previous 30 days.

1999; Mullahy 1993). Accepting that view, the question of interpretation becomes, "Why should workers who drink be more productive on average than those who don't?"

One answer, of course, is that drinking itself actually enhances productivity; that some people tend to perform better on the job if they are drinkers than abstainers. Several authors have suggested that the beneficial mechanism may be via the health benefits of moderate drinking (Heien 1996; Hamilton and Hamilton 1997). But since those benefits are primarily through heart-disease prevention in middle age, the "health" mechanism does not account for the drinker's bonus among workers in their twenties and thirties. Another possibility is that drinking facilitates social networking, which in turn generates improved job options; most people find their jobs through word-of-mouth, and having a wide network of friends and acquaintances is an important aspect of one's "social capital."[4] In an environment where drinking is a routine aspect of socializing, drinkers may be more productive because they find better jobs on average.

Influence of Other Variables

Another interpretation of the "drinker's bonus" is that the observed association is a coincidence, the result of some "third cause" that influences both drinking and productivity. Drinkers are a self-selected group who differ in all kinds of ways from abstainers. For example, people with college degrees are more likely to drink than those who are high school dropouts, and of course college-educated people earn more on average than dropouts. So one reason that drinkers earn more than nondrinkers may be that drinkers are better educated. In fact, as we have seen (chapter 4), the propensity to drink is associated with various socio-demographic characteristics; it's a good bet that those characteristics also influence productivity and earnings. To isolate the direct causal influence of drinking on earnings, it is necessary to control for other variables that affect both. Hence, I refine the comparisons presented in figures 8.1 and 8.2 by use of a multivariate regression analysis, a method for controlling for a number of characteristics simultaneously. The covariates in this analysis include demographic characteristics (age, race/ethnicity, metro/nonmetro residence), ability (as measured by the Air Force Qualification Test), education, family circumstances, one aspect of the respondent's personality (outgoing or shy), work experience, and several descriptors of the economic condition of the local labor market.[5] Also, instead of simply distinguishing between "drinker" and "not drinker," this specification includes indicators for the number of times the respondent reports bingeing in the previous month (having six or more drinks on one occasion). The estimates are based on all the relevant NLSY data going back to the survey wave in which drinking items were first included (1982).

TABLE 8.1
The Drinker's Bonus Refined: Earnings by Full-Time Workers, Ages 21–34

	Percentage Increase in Annual Earnings in Comparison with Abstainers			
	Drink in Last 30 Days, No Binges	1–3 Binges Last Month	4–5 Binges Last Month	6+ Binges Last Month
Males	5.4	2.2	0.3	−8.4
Females	6.9	7.2	1.1	−2.8

Source: Computed from Cook and Peters (2005), table 4, short form 2.
Note: Numbers calculated by use of multivariate regression on 7 waves of NLSY79 data, 1979–1993. "Binge" means 6 or more drinks on a single occasion.

TABLE 8.2
Odds of Being a Full-Time Worker, Ages 21–34

	Percentage Increase in Odds of Full-Time Work in Comparison with Abstainers			
	Drink in Last 30 Days, No Binges	1–3 Binges Last Month	4–5 Binges Last Month	6+ Binges Last Month
Males	41.3	40.2	49.4	31.6
Females	54.8	81.0	77.8	50.4

Source: Computed from Cook and Peters (2005), table 5, short form 2.
Note: Numbers calculated by use of multivariate logit regression on 7 waves of NLSY79 data, 1979–1993. "Binge" means 6 or more drinks on a single occasion. "Full-time workers" are those who report working at least 1,500 hours in the previous calendar year, and earning at least $1,000 in 1983 dollars.

The estimated effects of being a drinker (having at least one drink in the previous thirty days) and of binge drinking during that period, are summarized in table 8.1. Thus, the drinker's bonus is not simply the result of confounding by demographic variables, ability, and other readily measured characteristics. Other things equal, drinkers who do not binge have an advantage in annual earnings of about 5 percent, over their nondrinking counterparts (with little difference between the sexes). In both cases the effect is estimated quite precisely. As shown in table 8.1, occasional bingeing does not eliminate the bonus, although frequent bingeing does. Furthermore, the likelihood of working full time is much higher for drinkers than abstainers, especially for women, and that difference persists even for those who are frequent binge drinkers (see table 8.2).

Of course in a nonexperimental analysis of this sort, we can never be sure that the regression specification controls for the variables that would otherwise confound the relationship between drinking and earnings.[6] Drinkers and abstainers may differ in hard-to-measure ways, such as the ability to get along well with other people, or their personal priorities between home life and career. The literature includes heroic efforts to deal with this "omitted variables" problem (Kenkel and Ribar 1994), but the possibility of bias remains.

To further complicate the situation, in addition to genuine confounders are problems that may arise as artifacts of the measurement process. For example, self-reported drinking may be affected by how trusting the respondent is of the survey interview process. A spurious correlation between drinking and earnings will arise if more trusting respondents are more likely to admit their drinking in the NLSY interviews and also tend to earn more (or be willing to report a higher percentage of their income).

It must be pointed out that the sort of multivariate analysis reported here, for all the statistical problems and reasonable doubts, is similar to the analysis of epidemiological data that supports the claim of health benefits from drinking (chapter 7). Why are medical experts now (mostly) convinced of these health benefits, but almost no one is convinced that drinking enhances productivity? The answer is *not* a difference in the quality of the empirical evidence. Rather, the difference is that medical researchers believe that there is a plausible mechanism by which drinking could protect against heart disease; on the other hand, the most plausible mechanism linking drinking to earnings predicts a *negative* relationship (since for some people, drinking obviously impairs productivity). The difference, then, is not in the strength of the statistical associations, but in the prior beliefs of the relevant scientific community concerning what's plausible and what isn't.

Reverse Causation

Although it is logically possible that being a drinker improves productivity and earnings, the most likely explanation for the drinker's bonus is just the reverse—increased earnings result in more drinking. When their earnings increase, some drinkers increase their alcohol consumption, and some people who usually abstain become regular drinkers.[7] Of course, it's not an either-or proposition—the drinking–earnings link may result from several causal mechanisms.

At this point, it may be helpful to have a scorecard to keep track of all the various relationships under consideration (Cook and Moore 2000). In the schematic diagram (figure 8.3), current drinking (both on and off the job) may affect productivity, which in turn determines individual earn-

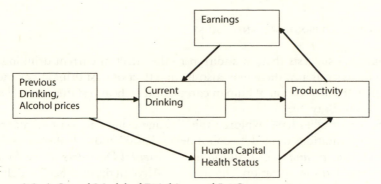

Figure 8.3. A Causal Model of Drinking and Its Consequences.
Source: Cook and Moore 2000.

ings. The diagram also depicts an indirect effect via the influence of drinking history on the accumulation of human and health capital (Grossman 1972; Grossman 2000)—more on this topic below. The final link represents "reverse causation," in which current consumption is affected by earnings.

The diagram identifies several mechanisms by which current drinking and earnings could be correlated. To distinguish between them using nonexperimental data is, as we have seen, a challenge. One statistical method that promises to solve some of the problems is instrumental-variables estimation. This approach is intended to eliminate the influence of reverse causation, and in particular to isolate the variation in observed drinking that is not influenced by earnings. If that variation, so identified, is still positively associated with earnings, then it is reasonable to conclude that drinking really does have a causal effect.[8]

When the regressions on earnings and work are re-run, now replacing the individual-drinking variables with a price-index variable (namely the index of state excise taxes introduced in chapter 5), the drinker's bonus disappears. Instead, higher prices (which reduce drinking) have the effect of *increasing* full-time work and perhaps earnings as well (Cook and Peters 2005).

From this evidence, we may reasonably conclude that the drinker's bonus is due to reverse causation—it is not the effect of drinking on earnings that we are observing, but rather the effect of earnings (or occupation) on drinking. Or perhaps the positive association is the result of unobserved characteristics of the workers' personality that result in an alignment between drinking and earnings. In any case, common sense suggests that drinking is unlikely to enhance productivity, and the best evidence does not contradict that view.

ALCOHOL DEPENDENCE AND ABUSE

Figure 8.3 suggests that, in addition to the effect of current drinking on productivity, if any, there may also be an effect of past drinking as mediated by the acquisition of human capital and by health status (mental and physical) (Bray 2005).

Several studies have explored this linkage using data on two alcohol-related conditions termed "alcohol dependence" and "alcohol abuse" in the *Diagnostic and Statistical Manual of Mental Disorders* of the American Psychiatric Association (chapter 3). "Alcohol dependence" is defined by symptoms indicating psychological and physical dependence on alcohol and neglect of responsibilities at work or home. "Alcohol abuse" is defined by continued drinking despite alcohol-related problems and risky behavior associated with bouts of heavy drinking.

John Mullahy and Jody Sindelar (1993) utilize data from the Epidemiological Catchment Area survey of the New Haven area, which includes diagnostic questions on mental illness. Twenty percent of their primary sample (males age thirty to fifty-nine) had at some point in their lives experienced the symptoms defining alcohol dependence or abuse. This group of problem drinkers had a substantially lower employment rate and lower earnings—results that held up after controlling for other characteristics. (Strangely, alcoholic males in their twenties and sixties actually had higher earnings than nonalcoholics.) In another analysis, Mullahy and Sindelar used Epidemiological Catchment Area survey data for four cities, finding that for both genders, nonalcoholics had higher educational attainment, and were more likely to be working, more likely to have white-collar jobs, and had higher incomes (Mullahy and Sindelar 1991).

Of course these statistical associations do not tell us much about causation. The problems of inference are the same as with determining the influence of drinking on productivity. Whereas problematic drinking probably affects labor force participation, productivity, and earnings—in fact, the mechanisms by which this could happen are blindingly obvious—isolating this effect is not easy from nonexperimental data. Mullahy and Sindelar note that "Other factors may cause both employment and alcohol problems; such factors could include psychiatric problems, congenital or chronic health problems, injuries, physical pain, lack of ability to cope, problems with friends or family, frustration of various forms, or an unstable upbringing" (Mullahy and Sindelar 1996, 413). Further elaboration on this theme comes from another pair of economists, Don Kenkel and David Ribar:

> Studies have consistently found that alcoholics are more likely than nonalcoholics to have been raised in a home with heightened marital conflict, inadequate

parenting, and lack of child–parent contact. The parents of future alcoholics are also more likely to have been alcoholic, antisocial, or sexually deviant. In addition, depression and antisocial personality are so strongly associated with alcoholism that alcoholism has been considered a manifestation of these disorders rather than as a separate disorder. It seems reasonable that people with deficient family backgrounds or personality disorders may suffer socioeconomic disadvantage independent of whether they develop alcohol problems. (1994, 125)

Depending on the data source, it may be possible to use multivariate methods to control for aspects of nature and nurture that may lead to drinking problems and have an influence on schooling, acquisition of other forms of human capital, and work. But usually the available measures in population surveys are inadequate or unreliable.

The statistical challenge is further compounded by the fact that alcohol problems develop over a number of years, influencing the life course in a variety of ways. There is some evidence that problem drinking in youth affects school completion (Mullahy and Sindelar 1989; Mullahy and Sindelar 1991) and family formation (Kenkel and Ribar 1994). Hence the contemporaneous effect of alcoholism on work—controlling for education and family circumstances—may miss much of the long-term effects. Kenkel and Ribar report a series of multivariate-regression results that help make the point: they find that alcohol-dependent women (age twenty-four to thirty-four) earned 11 percent more than those who were not dependent, while alcohol-dependent men earned 10 percent less. But when they add controls for marital status and children, earnings for both males and females are unaffected by alcohol dependence. The apparent reason: alcohol dependence reduces the likelihood of getting married, and marriage has opposite effects on work outcomes for men and women—men work and earn more, women less.

Michael Moore and I followed up on the Mullahy-Sindelar findings on the education deficit among people who had been alcohol-dependent as adolescents (1993b). We suggested two possible mechanisms by which drinking and schooling may interact for adolescents:

1. Drinking problems may interfere with learning and classroom performance, thereby reducing the contribution to human capital of an additional year of schooling and hence the incentive to continue.
2. To the extent that higher education is rationed according to past scholastic performance and reputation, heavy drinking may have consequences that increase the cost of continuation. (414)

Thus, a forward-looking student would make drinking and schooling decisions together; a myopic student would make them sequentially; but in either case alcoholic-beverage prices and other determinants of high school drinking are thereby also a determinant of school persistence. We utilized NLSY data for high school seniors in 1982, which allow inclusion of an extensive list of covariates. We found that the beer tax and minimum legal purchase age in the respondent's state had a direct effect on school persistence, as measured either by the number of years of college or the likelihood that the respondent will eventually graduate from college.[9]

These results suggest that much of the effect of drinking on productivity may be indirect, mediated by the accumulation of human capital. If so, controls on youthful drinking become particularly important in influencing the course of the economy.

Concluding Thoughts

The long debate among economists over the effects of drinking on productivity serves as a cautionary tale concerning the pitfalls of working with nonexperimental data. We know that drinkers are more likely to work than abstainers, and if they do work they earn more. These findings hold up even after controlling for demographic characteristics, education, and other observable characteristics. But that doesn't mean that you should encourage your underachieving friends and relatives to start drinking. It probably won't help, and it may well hurt their performance.

In fact, it has proven exceptionally difficult to estimate the impact of drinking on workforce productivity. Without a doubt hangovers and on-the-job drinking detract from productivity, and some heavy drinkers become too ill to work at all. But any attempt to use econometric estimates to project the overall burden of drinking on the economy—and there have been more than a few—should not be taken too seriously at this point. The causal mechanisms embedded in the data are simply too difficult to unravel. What the analysts need in order to make progress on this problem is an abrupt, Gorbachev-like change in alcohol-control policy. If alcoholic-beverage prices doubled, what would be the effect on workforce productivity?

PART III

Assessing Policy Options

CHAPTER 9

Evaluating Interventions

> That among these [inalienable rights] are Life, Liberty and
> the pursuit of Happiness.—That to secure these rights,
> Governments are instituted . . .
> —Declaration of Independence

> Why should the Devil get all the good tunes,
> The booze and the neon and Saturday night
> —A. E. Stallings

IN MY STATE, NORTH CAROLINA, it is commonplace for convenience stores
to sell single beers on ice, positioning them in a big barrel located near
the cash register. This presentation encourages customers to buy a ready-
to-drink beer on impulse. Someday the state legislature may get around
to debating a ban on this practice. Predictably, advocacy groups such as
Mothers Against Drunk Driving would argue for a ban to make the highways safer by reducing drinking-while-driving. On the other side, representatives of the convenience store owners might make the case that they
are simply providing a service to anyone who relishes the idea of a cold
beer when they arrive home—and besides, the proposed ban would reduce revenues and force some convenience stores to lay off workers. Op-
eds would appear in the local newspapers by libertarians, arguing that a
ban would just be another example of government nannying at the cost
of individual freedom, and by public health experts arguing that if the
ban saved lives, it would be worth it.

There is assuredly no consensus about how to evaluate such measures.
The use of government authority to restrict commerce and choice in the
name of enhancing safety is inevitably contentious, because it taps into
profound disagreements about the public interest, and about the proper
role of government in promoting that interest. Are (adult) individuals the
best judge of their own interests? Is the collective interest just the sum of
individual interests, or something more? In assessing costs and benefits,
how are these interests to be translated into dollar terms? And is government the right place to turn when the collective interest requires changes
in individual behavior? Many a tome has been written on such questions.

But the greatest influence on public rhetoric derives from the classical liberal tradition that has been incorporated into mainstream economics, and the more communitarian perspective of public health.

THE HARM PRINCIPLE AND PUBLIC HEALTH

When it comes to regulations that restrict freedom of choice, the great distinction in classical liberal thought is based on what type of harm the regulation is intended to remedy. If the choice carries risks to the person making the choice, that is of much less public concern than if bystanders are also put at risk.

This principle was given powerful voice by John Stuart Mill, a British philosopher and political economist of the nineteenth century. In his essay *On Liberty* (1859), he asserts, "the only purpose for which power can be rightfully exercised over any member of a civilized community, against his will, is to prevent harm to others. He cannot rightfully be compelled to do or forbear because it will be better for him to do so, because it will make him happier, because, in the opinion of others, to do so would be wise, or even right." Mill was a utilitarian, and as such he derived this conclusion from the claim that each of us is the leading expert on our own interests: "With respect to his own feelings and circumstances, the most ordinary man or woman has means of knowledge immeasurably surpassing those that can be possessed by any one else." In this view he echoed Adam Smith's observation ninety years earlier in *The Theory of Moral Sentiments* (1759) that "every man is certainly, in every respect, fitter and abler to take care of himself than of any other person." If true, then any paternalistic restriction on adult choices, no matter how well meaning, is likely to make some people worse off and reduce the sum total of happiness.

Of course, most of us have family who would experience an emotional loss (and perhaps a financial one) if we made choices that were harmful to our health, productivity, or reputation—for example, the choice to drink too much. Such interconnections seem at first glance to open the door to a variety of regulations that are otherwise ruled out by the "harm" principle. In response, utilitarians assert that mutual concern and the opportunity for direct negotiation among family members will assure some balancing of interests in the individual's decisions. Adam Smith again:

> "After himself, the members of his own family, those who usually live in the same house with him, his parents, his children, his brothers and sisters, are naturally the objects of his warmest affections. . . . He knows better how every thing is likely to affect them, and his sympathy with them is more precise and determinate, than it can be with the greater part of other people. It approaches nearer, in short, to what he feels for himself."

The situation with friends is similar, although generally more muted. In any event, empathy and mutual concern for those who are closely connected, together with a presumed ability to make their views known, suggest that their sentiments will not be ignored. If nonetheless the individual makes a choice that may result in disability or early death, it is because the utility that choice brings her is greater than her concern about their possible bereavement. Hence, a choice-restricting regulation would be ill-advised if based on family welfare considerations.

It is easy to think of instances where this conclusion falls flat. Few of us would credit the alcoholic father who fails to provide financially or emotionally for his children with making the "right" decision, utility-enhancing though his dereliction may be from his perspective. Even more compelling is the urge to intervene in the case of a pregnant woman who is drinking heavily, thus placing her baby at risk of being born with severe defects (Armstrong 2003). But government agencies are reluctant to intervene in such cases. The classical liberal concern for preserving the autonomy of the family continues to hold sway, and not just for utilitarian reasons. Even Mill suggested that preserving individual autonomy was an important guide to policy, *not only* because it allowed individuals to further their own ends most effectively, but also because autonomy is valuable in itself. The modern-day philosopher Gerald Dworkin says it well: "To be able to choose is a good that is independent of the wisdom of what is chosen" (Dworkin 1971, 117).

That an individual's choice has the potential of harming others then becomes a necessary but not sufficient condition for intervention in this philosophical tradition (Dworkin 1971, 107). Preserving freedom is desirable and may be warranted even at some net cost (of harm to others). Further, the quality of the intervention, and who is doing the intervening, are both relevant. The threshold for intervention by a government agency should rightly be higher than the threshold for intervention by employers and friends, let alone by pastors, physicians, and others whose job description includes an obligation to speak up when they believe that people under their care are acting unwisely. Government interventions that seek to compel a change in behavior are to be used more sparingly than interventions designed to inform, persuade, or influence without the use of compulsion.

This perspective does not always carry the day in our public decision making—for example, state laws mandating use of seatbelts and motorcycle helmets seem justified only out of a paternalistic belief that anyone who doesn't buckle up or wear a helmet is making a mistake. But from another quite different philosophical perspective, closely associated with the public health profession, such regulations further a *collective* interest in preserving life. As Dan Beauchamp (1980, 158) notes in his monograph on alcohol control policy, "The question for public health here is not the distribution of specific benefits to identifiable individuals, but rather the improvements of levels or rates of health among the entire population or among specific groups . . . public health stands closer to a communitarian ethic than does the stark individualistic perspective of most treatments of social justice." In this view, the community interest is not just the sum of self-regarding individual interests; the untimely death of a community member harms all its members, including those who did not know the victim.

More generally, the appeal of the communitarian perspective is suggested by President Kennedy's stirring words in his inaugural address in 1961: "Ask not what your country can do for you—ask what you can do for your country." The most influential modern economist writing in the classical liberal tradition, Milton Friedman, notes in his book *Capitalism and Freedom* that the second half of this invocation "implies that government is the master or deity, the citizen, the servant or the votary. To the free man, the country is the collection of individuals who compose it, not something over and above them" (Friedman 1962, 1–2). Both the Kennedy assertion of a transcendent community interest, and Friedman's utilitarianism, have resonance in public discourse, even though they are often contradictory.

Still, there is something like consensus on some matters. Few would argue against the view that individual preferences deserve respectful consideration in making policy, and that government interference in private decisions requires compelling justification. In evaluating government actions intended to limit risky behavior, the voluntary risks (to the person making the choice) are of less salience than involuntary risks (for those unwittingly exposed).

How would John Stuart Mill view a proposed ban on selling those cold singles at the convenience store checkout? In any discussion of highway safety, he would insist on distinguishing between the safety of the people who actually buy the beer and consume it while driving, and the safety of everyone else who might be on the road with them. The public interest in protecting those innocent bystanders must be weighed against the utility provided to beer drinkers of having easy access. The presumption is against government regulation unless clearly demonstrated to be in the collective interest.

In modern terminology, the effects on bystanders are called "externalities." An "externality" of a transaction occurs when people who are not party to the transaction are affected; a "*negative* externality" occurs when those effects are harmful. The sale of cold beers to drivers generates a negative externality to the extent that it increases the chance that people who share the road with those who buy the beer (and drink it while driving) will collide with the beer buyer. Over the course of a year, with thousands of convenience stores selling those cold beers, the total increment in the negative externality associated with drinking while driving may add up to something substantial.

The Behavioral Science Challenge to the Harm Principle

The utilitarian tradition implies an accounting framework for evaluating government restrictions on alcohol that focuses on externalities of drinking, including the direct threat of injury to others, and the socialized financial consequences of disability and early death. The "internalities" of drinking, both good and bad, are ignored in this accounting on the grounds that the drinker himself reckons on them when deciding whether and how much to drink. If someone of "mature years" believes that the pleasures of a heavy bout are worth the likely hangover and possible injuries, then who are we to second guess (assuming that we're not married to this person) (Mishan 1971)?

In sum, this perspective is grounded in three assumptions, each subject to challenge:

1. The proper role of government is to enhance the sum of individual utilities of its citizens;
2. Utility flows from the individual's activities according to his own subjective preferences;
3. Individuals choose their activities from available options in accord with their true preferences.

Of course, these assumptions don't make sense in the case of children. Parents and other adults have authority over children because their preferences have not matured, and their choices are likely to be impulsive and poorly informed. Take the case of smoking. Most adults who smoke started during adolescence, a time when choices tend to be shortsighted and heavily influenced by peers. Even though adolescents typically know that smoking may be harmful to their health over the long run, they fail to foresee the difficulty of quitting later in life (Gruber 2002–2003). If an effective device were developed for preventing smoking initiation before age twenty, parents would line up to buy it. And some day their children would thank them for doing so. As the psychologist William James said a century ago, "Could the young but realize how soon they will become mere walking bundles of habits, they would give more heed to their conduct while in the plastic state" (James 1900).

Although adults tend to be more mature, the fact is that there's not a complete discontinuity between childhood and adulthood—adults aren't necessarily wise or consistent in their decisions (as many a teenage child has pointed out), and the same concerns that lead us to endorse restrictions on children may also support restrictions on adult behavior. Under some circumstances, it is simply human to act in a shortsighted fashion that is likely to be regretted later. The behavioral scientists have learned a lot about these tendencies in recent decades.[1]

For activities like drinking and smoking, the consequences are spread out over time, with the pleasure first and the pain later. The drinks that made a Friday-night party more enjoyable may be followed by a deadly lottery (where the "prize" is crashing while driving home) and if that risk is avoided, a headachy, unproductive Saturday. Although in the utilitarian view the pleasures of getting drunk must have exceeded the subsequent risks and discomfort—or why would he have chosen to get drunk?—it would not be surprising to learn that he cursed his stupidity the next morning and vowed to drink less at the next party.

The importance of the timing with which consequences occur has been documented in a wide array of experiments that in some respects contradict the presumption of rational choice. There appears to be a hard-wired tendency toward inconsistency in decisions involving delayed consequences. That decision to drink heavily on Friday night might have turned out quite differently if the individual had been able to make the decision of how much to drink the day before. From Thursday's vantage point, the pleasures of getting drunk on Friday night are unlikely to be worth the risks and the pain on Saturday. Yet when Friday night comes, that prudent judgment is overwhelmed by the immediate payoff of elevated mood, reduced social anxiety, and camaraderie that comes from drinking. Thursday's decision to abstain or drink lightly is difficult to enforce on Friday.

Part of the maturation process is to recognize this power of immediate rewards in distorting decisions and thus violating one's true interests. Self-control is not just a matter of willpower, but also experience and technique. Thomas Schelling (1980) coined the term "egonomics" (self-management) to capture the array of methods that we are taught while growing up or learn by experience. These include *precommitment* devices that provide some mechanism for sustaining the prudent decision made earlier. A number of scholars who have written on this subject allude to Homer's tale of Ulysses' encounter with the Sirens (Elster 1984). Ulysses wanted to experience the extraordinary song of the Sirens but did not want to be seduced by that song to steer his boat onto the rocks, as had many sailors before him. Ulysses' solution was to have his men lash him to the mast and fill their ears with wax, with the direction that they sail on no matter what.

Someone who knows himself well enough to know that he'll drink too much if he goes to that party Friday night may decide to go to a movie instead—even if he knows that he would enjoy the party sober. Or he may go to the party after vowing to his wife that he will abstain (thus attaching negative consequences to the first drink he takes), or seek out other people once at the party who are not drinking. When the drinks must be purchased, there is another practical alternative: Several of my students have told me that when they go out drinking they leave their credit cards at home and take a limited amount of cash, imposing an artificial budget constraint on their evening's consumption.

Self-management, like management of others, is a costly and imperfect craft, and some people are better at it than others (Thaler and Shefrin 1981). For those who have slipped into alcoholism, the problem is especially daunting. Alcoholics Anonymous provides an array of egonomic devices—a bright line (abstention) to guide behavior that cannot be fuzzed, a daily social occasion that does not include drinking cues, guidance about how to get through the rough times ("one day at a time"). Alternatively, modern medications help by reducing craving for a drink. Inpatient programs are a temporary escape from day-to-day temptations. Self-management help in these and other forms is often sought by alcoholics, but the impulse to drink is still likely to overwhelm the genuine desire to stay on the wagon.

The challenge to John Stuart Mill's harm principle here is not so much that people tend to make mistakes occasionally, but that the nature of the mistakes and the circumstances in which they occur are predictable. The well-established bias toward pursuing present payoffs, only imperfectly controlled by self-management devices, suggests that society should not be neutral on these matters, but rather take a parental perspective. Institutional arrangements that facilitate self-management can be helpful to all concerned.

Richard Thaler and Cass Sunstein (2003) have coined the term "libertarian paternalism" to capture some of the less intrusive possibilities. The notion is that bad choices can sometimes be curtailed by subtle arrangements that are not coercive but do weigh in on the side of impulse control. The hostess for a large party may place the drinks table in a room separate from the main social mix and hire a bartender to introduce a social barrier to repeated trips. Although in Japan it is possible to buy beer from outdoor vending machines, in the United States we are spared that temptation—but those cold beers at the cash registers may have the same effect. Removing cues to alcohol abuse and posing small barriers to purchase and consumption will facilitate self-management.

This line of reasoning leads us again to the question of the proper accounting framework for evaluating interventions. If we cannot fall back on the presumption that individual choice is a faithful representation of true preferences, then interventions may have social value in reducing mistakes people make when unregulated. In that case, restrictions on availability may make them better off *by their own preferences*.[2] What's more, some people with drinking problems may welcome restrictions and seek out restricted environments as a way of shoring up their own will-power. In this view, some portion of the foreseeable death and disability suffered by the abusive drinkers themselves should be taken into account when evaluating a restrictive policy. In short, "internalities" should count. Smoking is an especially compelling case in point, since most smokers regret their habit and express an interest in quitting (Gruber and Köszegi 2004). But the same logic can also be applied to drinking.

The liberal tradition, embodied in the harm principle, claims to promote the greatest good by leaving the (adult) individual free to make his own choices as long as others are not harmed. As we have seen, the case that those choices cannot be improved upon by government regulation rests on unfounded claims about the quality of individual decision making. In a sense, the stronger basis for the liberal doctrine is the intrinsic value of freedom—especially freedom from *government* coercion. Family and friends will continue to meddle in each other's affairs, especially when it comes to drinking, and that is as it should be.

NONCOERCIVE REGULATIONS

The discussion so far has focused on evaluating government regulations that restrict the choices available to consumers with the goal of improving health and safety. But it should be noted that there are policy options for improving health and safety that do not restrict individual choice, and hence do not pose the stark trade-off between life and liberty (Vaupel and Cook 1978). Many of the possibilities here can be categorized as either "harm reduction" or "information provision."

Just as the name suggests, harm-reduction measures are aimed at reducing the harmful consequences of some unhealthy or unsafe activity, such as drinking too much (MacCoun and Reuter 2001). To put it baldly, the goal is to make the world safer for drunks. Note that harm reduction for drinking is often a by-product of generic safety measures. Requirements that vehicles come equipped with air bags, padded dashboards, safety glass, collapsible steering columns, and so forth protect all motorists, but especially the drunk drivers since they are vastly more likely than others to get into a serious crash. A wide array of other safety measures have similar effect: to name just a few, breakaway light poles along highways, smoke alarms and fire-retardant materials in homes, the

911 emergency-response system. The consequences of long-term heavy drinking can also be ameliorated. Harm reduction for alcoholics entails such efforts as providing homeless shelters and requiring a vitamin additive to liquor to prevent Korsakoff's psychosis, as well as research into developing effective medications for treating addiction, easing withdrawal symptoms, and so forth.

Harm-reduction measures benefit the drinkers themselves. The value of these measures would presumably be reflected in the consumer demand for alcoholic beverages, an effect known as "moral hazard" because it is an unintended and unwanted consequence of harm reduction. For example, an easy "cure" for alcoholism would provide assurance for youths who currently limit their drinking for fear of becoming addicted, with the result that they may be inclined to drink more. The outward shift in their demand curve is an accurate representation of the value of that cure to drinkers who are not (yet) alcoholic.

Information provision is another noncoercive approach, in some ways the least controversial. Included here are warning labels on alcoholic-beverage bottles, public service ads on television and radio, restrictions on advertising, and alcohol curriculums in school health classes. These measures seek to improve the decisions made by consumers without actually limiting their choices. It is an open question whether at-risk drinkers themselves place value on such measures, but it is a safe bet that parents support them.

QUANTIFYING COSTS AND BENEFITS

In evaluating proposed regulations, it may be enough for some purposes to quantify the risks by simply tabulating the reduction in the number of additional instances of injury (of various degrees of seriousness) and deaths, as well as the property damage and medical costs. But often it is important to be able to combine these dimensions of harm into a single number. In the example of regulating sales of individual cold beers, we would like to be able to compare the value of improved highway safety with the cost of imposing and enforcing the possible ban—including the subjective cost to the beer lovers.

Two accounting frameworks are in general use for translating injury and death into dollars, the "cost-of-illness" (COI) method and the "willingness-to-pay" (WTP) method. The COI method is the norm in government reports. It distinguishes between "direct" costs (primarily medical treatment) and "indirect" costs resulting from the loss of productivity by the victims (measured by how much they would have earned in the labor market).[3] The COI method is not grounded in an explicit theory of the public interest, but it can be interpreted as "implicitly based upon the maximization of society's present and future production" (Landefeld and Seskin 1982, 556). An Institute of Medicine (1981) committee referred to this basic approach as "output accounting," noting the similarity to national product accounting methods. It is also closely related to the problem facing juries in wrongful death cases; the goal is to make the victim's estate "whole" based on an assessment of his future earnings and other contributions (Cohen 1988).

The WTP method is generally preferred to COI by economists because economic theory assumes that utility flows from consumption rather than production. In this view, the value of a person's life and health is not measured by her present and future earnings, but rather by the value she places on enjoying a safe environment. That enjoyment is subjective and somewhat difficult to measure because "safety" is not a commodity that is bought and sold in the marketplace by itself. However, safety is one aspect of myriad economic decisions involving both big decisions—where to live, what car to buy—and small ones, such as whether to spend extra for the smoke detector that includes a carbon monoxide detector.

To be precise, such decisions entail a judgment, not about the value of life, but rather the value of a small increase or reduction in the probability of death. Thomas Schelling begins his famous essay on this subject with the following distinctions: "It is not the worth of human life that I shall discuss, but of life-saving—of preventing death. And it is not a particular death, but a statistical death" (1968, 127). If a million people are each willing to spend $5 on a device that will reduce the probability of death for each of them by one millionth (a "microrisk"), then the total of $5 million expended saves one life on the average; we conclude that a "statistical life" is worth that amount for this group of people. Five million dollars may be more than any one of them would or could pay to avoid certain death. But this "ransom" value of an *identified* life is not our concern: The public's willingness to pay for small increments of safety is what's relevant for valuing safety-enhancement programs. After all, when such programs are undertaken, no one knows which lives will be saved. Instead, the service provided by the safety program *ex ante* is that a large number of people enjoy a small reduction in risk.

A variety of techniques have been used to estimate how much people would be willing to pay for reducing a risk to their lives. One approach is simply to ask them, and there have been a number of "contingent valuation" studies that have done just that, posing hypothetical questions to a random sample of the public (Ludwig and Cook 2001). A parallel approach involves analyzing legislative decisions involving the public value of safety, such as each state's choice of how high to set the speed limit on interstate highways (Ashenfelter and Greenstone 2004). But a more common method is to value lives by using an estimate derived from the analysis of relevant prices in the marketplace. For example, a widely used approach is to examine the extra wage compensation that workers require in order to take risky jobs (Thaler and Rosen 1975; Moore and Viscusi 1990; Viscusi 2004). Other areas of study include prices of real estate (Portney 1981; Gayer, Hamilton, and Viscusi 2000) or consumer goods (Viscusi 1993) as related to health risks. Estimates range widely for both substantive and statistical reasons, but typical estimates place the average value at several million dollars. Based on such studies, the U.S. Environmental Protection Agency was using a value of $6.1 million per life in its evaluations of environmental regulations (http://ostpxweb.dot.gov/policy/EconStrat/treatment of life.htm).

These market-based studies can provide useful information about how people value safety if they have accurate information regarding the risks associated with different jobs, residential locations, and consumer products. Economists assume that the market will provide an accurate indication of the public's trade-off between safety and money; if the risk premium for a job were not sufficient given the preferences of the relevant group of workers, then the employer will have trouble recruiting an adequate supply of labor, and if too generous, there would be more applicants than needed. Of course if workers are generally misinformed about the risks of a particular job, then the risk premium will misrepresent those preferences.[4]

Financial Externalities

Willingness to pay for enhanced safety for oneself and loved ones is not the whole story. Each of us has some financial stake in the health and safety of strangers, and hence may be concerned about the choices they make for that reason, if no other (Arthur 1981; Cook and Ludwig 2000). A variety of government programs, including taxation and public support for health care and income maintenance, ensure that decisions that affect earnings and longevity create financial externalities, both positive and negative. For this reason other people's productivity matters (as in the COI studies), but only after deducting personal consumption. In the aggregate, production and consumption are close to equal (since in the United States the savings rate is close to zero), so the financial externalities tend to be of less importance than the direct valuation of safety (Manning et al. 1989).

For a life saved or disability averted, the community may be viewed as gaining whatever the individual produces over her remaining lifetime plus the medical costs associated with the averted injury, net of that individual's consumption expenditures over her remaining lifetime. In this calculation, an individual's contributions are equivalent to wage and salary earnings gross of income and payroll taxes. Her "consumption" includes personal expenditures, the cost of her medical care (however financed), and the value of public services for which she does not pay directly (public schooling). She might run a deficit by this standard because she is receiving non-wage income (pensions, income from investments) or spending down her net worth, or using subsidized medical care.[5]

To this calculation of net contribution to the community's assets we would want to add an accounting of contributions she would make outside of the marketplace. That would logically include both positive and negative contributions: performing volunteer work (on the positive side) as well as criminal predation (on the negative side). The monetary equivalents of such nonmarket services should be combined with the net financial consequence to get the bottom line.

Individual production and consumption both tend to vary over the life course. Children and elderly people are likely to consume more than they produce, while in the years between school completion and retirement the reverse is true. When someone is killed in an alcohol-related accident at age sixty-five, society saves the cost of providing Social Security pension payments, private pension payments, Medicare, and that person's use of his personal savings; when someone is killed at age twenty-five, those savings are far in the future (and hence heavily discounted) while society loses forty years of tax payments and possible personal savings. Ignoring the subjective value of safety for a moment, interventions that save younger lives tend to have a positive effect on the collective standard of living, while interventions that primarily extend life expectancy after retirement pose a financial drain on society (Manning et al. 1989, 1991).

Among the causes of death and disability associated with drinking, traffic accidents, important by any metric, become all the more so because they disproportionately affect young adults (see chapter 6). For example one-quarter of traffic fatalities in 2003 were in the fifteen to twenty-four age group. On the other hand, the long-term health effects of drinking—reduced heart disease associated with moderate drinking, or liver cirrhosis and other organ damage associated with chronic heavy drinking—are going to have their greatest consequences much later in the life cycle.

Impact on Employment

Often the most prominent argument against government regulation and taxation is the impact on business. Although a ban on selling cold beers at the cash register is unlikely to cause many stores to go out of business, broader regulations and higher taxes on alcohol sales could cut into alcohol beverage sales and related employment.

A quick check of the Web sites of relevant trade associations confirms the importance of the "economic impact" argument. For example, the beer industry supports a site called "beerservesamerica.com," where we learn under "Economic Impact" that:

> The U.S. brewing industry is a dynamic part of our national economy, contributing billions of dollars in wages and taxes. . . .

> The industry today includes more than 2,400 brewers and beer importers, 1,908 beer wholesalers, and 551,000 retail establishments. The industry's *economic ripple effect* benefits packaging manufacturers, shipping companies, agriculture, and other businesses whose livelihood depends on the beer industry.

> Directly and indirectly, the beer industry employs approximately 1.78 million Americans, paying them $54 billion in wages and benefits.

It goes on to point out that "The brewing industry has a presence in every state of the union and every congressional district." And finally: "The brewing industry is actively supporting a *rollback of the 1990 excise tax increase*. This would provide relief for the lower and middle classes, allow brewers and wholesalers to expand and hire more workers, and ultimately boost the American economy."

The problem with this argument is not in the statistics, but in the claim that an expansion of the beer industry would "boost the American economy" as a whole. In fact it is more accurate to see this as a zero-sum situation, at least in the aggregate. Whereas taxes and regulations may influence the industrial composition of the labor force, it is macroeconomic conditions that determine the growth in overall employment. Lower beer prices would cause a series of adjustments across the economy, with higher employment in complementary activities—medical trauma care, for example—and lower employment in connection with substitutes, such as the production of other beverages.

Without a doubt regulatory changes that affect the growth and prosperity of the alcoholic beverage industry will create winners and losers—in employment, and perhaps also in the stock market and the value of dedicated assets. An assessment of the public interest requires a summing up, recognizing that while the flow of economic activity is directed to some extent by regulations, the overall volume of that flow is not. That lesson should have been learned when the repeal of Prohibition in 1933 had no noticeable effect in bringing the nation out of the Great Depression.

The National Cost of Alcohol Abuse

For some purposes it is useful to estimate the total costs of alcohol abuse, rather than to assess just those costs affected by a specified intervention.

In fact, total cost estimates are routine in the descriptions of public health and safety problems. Thus, we are told that drug abuse cost the nation $143.3 billion in 1998 (Office of National Drug Control Policy 2001); that highway crashes cost $346 billion in 1993 (Miller, Lestina, and Spicer 1998); that indirect and direct costs of diabetes in 2002 were $132 billion (National Institute of Diabetes and Digestive and Kidney Diseases 2004); and that medical costs due to being overweight or obese cost $78.5 billion in 1998 (Finkelstein, Fiebelkorn, and Wang 2003). Numbers of this sort may serve policymakers as a rough guide to the relative magnitudes of different problems, and whether a particular problem is worth worrying about. In that respect it serves as an alternative to public health measures such as the number of lives or life-years lost.

Detailed estimates of the national costs of alcohol abuse have been commissioned by federal agencies for the years 1977, 1980, 1985, and 1992 (Harwood et al. 1998). The last estimate was extended to 1998, and came in at $148 billion (Harwood 2000). All of these estimates have used the cost-of-illness accounting framework described earlier. The most recent estimate offers the following breakdown of the total:

4 percent	Specialty alcohol services
11 percent	Medical care
13 percent	Crashes, fires, criminal justice expenses, etc.
5 percent	Lost earnings due to alcohol-related crime (incarceration)
20 percent	Lost earnings due to premature death
47 percent	Lost earnings due to alcohol-related illness

These estimates can be challenged on several grounds. First is the COI framework itself, which (as already discussed) equates the value of health and life to earnings. Second, the estimates of lost earnings due to "alcohol-related illness," almost half the total, are based on regression estimates of the effect of drinking on earnings—estimates that, as explained in the previous chapter, are highly suspect. Third, there is no distinction in these numbers between the costs borne by the drinker himself and consequences to others.

There is another problem with this and other such total cost estimates: it is unclear just what question they are intended to answer. A first thought is that we are being told the value of eliminating all excess consumption of alcohol that could result in injury or disease or crime. But there is an implicit proviso that this change occurs without curtailing moderate drinking of the sort that may prevent cardiovascular disease and increase longevity in middle age. A second thought is that it might be important to specify what everyone is doing instead of drinking to excess. What do we assume about their diets, exercise, use of other intoxicants, and other activities that might affect productivity, health, and longevity? Of course, the same problems arise with estimating the total number of lives lost or other measures of the magnitude of the problem.

A number of economists (Myrdal 1930; Österberg 1983; Cook 1991) have suggested that it would make more sense to estimate the costs and benefits of specific real-world interventions than attempt to come up with a sensible total cost. In any event, by any measure the alcohol problem is big enough to be worthy of our attention and concern.

Concluding Thoughts

The Declaration of Independence invokes the "inalienable rights" of life, liberty, and the pursuit of happiness, but does not discuss the trade-offs that sometimes arise in attaining them. The liberty to drink as much as we want facilitates the pursuit of happiness for some but can also lead people in quite a different direction—and sometimes comes at the cost of lives cut short. If liberty is the paramount concern, as preached by John Stuart Mill, then government's proper role is to step aside and let individuals and private institutions rule when it comes to self-hazardous behavior. (Government restrictions are only justified for drinking that poses an immediate threat to bystanders.) But when it comes to the pursuit of happiness, the answer is not so clear—many of us might welcome some restrictions on availability and price for alcohol, as an aid to whatever willpower we can muster to resist the allure of too many drinks. The public health communitarians would broaden the argument, pointing out that we have a stake in the well-being of family, friends, and neighbors.

The controversies here are ancient and will not be resolved any time soon. Fortunately, however, it is not necessary to agree on principles regarding the proper scope of government in order to set a direction for alcohol policy. Even within the freedom-loving principles of John Stuart Mill, alcohol is currently undertaxed and in some respects under-regulated.

CHAPTER 10

Regulating Supply

> The Supreme Court has identified several "core interests" reserved to the states under the Twenty-first Amendment. These interests include promoting temperance, ensuring orderly market conditions, and raising revenue.
> —Judge Marsha J. Pechman, U.S. District Court, Seattle, in *Costco v. Hoen* finding, April 2006

THE STATES HAVE BEEN IN the business of taxing and regulating alcoholic beverages since Repeal. As we have seen (in chapter 3), the systems put in place during the 1930s were guided by the goals of promoting temperance, collecting revenue, and preventing the crime and corruption associated with Prohibition and the infamous pre-Prohibition saloons. In practice the temperance goal never had much sway, and in the post-War period state officials came to view alcohol control as irrelevant to alcohol-abuse prevention (Medicine in the Public Interest 1979; Room 1984). But evidence to the contrary has been accumulating in recent years. As documented in chapters 5 and 6, the terms on which alcoholic beverages are supplied to the public affect consumption, abuse, and consequences.

Alcoholic-beverage prices and availability are the result of the choices made by producers, distributors, and retailers of alcoholic beverages. With some exceptions, these suppliers are private for-profit firms that are responding to market forces in the context of government regulation and taxation. Assessing the likely effects of alcohol-control measures requires some understanding of how the relevant markets are structured.

If we are to assess alcohol-control measures from the perspective of promoting temperance—or, in more modern terms, of reducing social costs—it is useful to first address a common objection to this approach: that it burdens the entire drinking public rather than focusing on the people and occasions for which drinking is likely to engender negative consequences.

ALCOHOL CONTROL VERSUS TARGETED POLICIES

The Gospels observe that the sun rises alike on the evil and on the good, and the rain falls on the just and on the unjust (Matthew 5:45). Likewise, taxes and other restrictions on alcohol supply impose on both the moderate and immoderate drinker. Such measures, in short, are indiscriminate. If the goal is to reduce abuse and its consequences, the same tax rate that is appropriate when applied to a bottle of wine destined to be shared at dinner by four adults, is far too low if applied to a bottle that is to be consumed by two teenagers while they are driving around town (Kleiman 1992, 249). Similarly, when stadiums stop serving beer in the middle of baseball games so that fans are less likely to be tipsy when it is time to drive home, the fan who plans to go home by bus and wants a beer with her seventh-inning hot dog is deprived for no reason. Generally speaking, the risks of drinking are heterogeneous, influenced by the individual's drinking proclivities and the circumstances in which the alcohol is consumed. Supply controls do not make such distinctions. The partial exceptions help prove the rule.

Consider the traditional "tot of grog" that was doled out daily to British sailors at sea and consumed on the spot. This uniform ration did something to ease the harsh conditions of life on a cramped sailing ship without creating a risk of intoxication. The rationing scheme suited the rather homogeneous population and circumstances. It was only possible due to the regimentation of navy life.

A much more elaborate rationing system was instituted throughout Sweden in 1919, thanks to the efforts of Ivan Bratt, a physician and politician. (He probably gets the credit for the defeat of national prohibition in a 1922 plebiscite, although it was a close call—49 percent voted in favor!) The "Bratt system" limited liquor purchases to adults who held a *motbok* in which all purchases were recorded. Under this system individuals filled out an elaborate application for the chance to purchase alcohol, and if successful were awarded a ration that depended on their sex, marital status, social responsibilities, and community of residence (Thomasson 1998). The maximum purchase for upper-class married males was four liters per month, with single people and those with fewer social responsibilities getting less, and married women simply ineligible. *Motbok*-holders who abused the drinking privilege were further restricted or cut off entirely. The system was feasible in part because all package sales were through the government monopoly stores. Although it was possible to buy alcohol by the drink in some restaurants, such sales were strictly limited and prices were much higher there (Nycander 1998). The effectiveness of the Bratt system was revealed after it was terminated in 1955. Abuse rates surged despite a considerable increase in tax rates (Nycander 1998; Thomasson 1998). The 50 percent increase in cirrhosis mortality rates was greater than would be expected from the increase in per capita consumption, suggesting that consumption became more concentrated among heavy drinkers when rationing ended (Norström 1987).

Can we imagine a scheme that could work in twenty-first century America for rationing consumption of alcohol on an individual basis? Mark Kleiman has suggested a system of personal licensure for drinking (1992). Adults could apply for the license with a requirement that they pass a test of some kind (presumably not a road test!), or the license could be awarded to all who qualify by some set of minimum conditions. In either case the license would be subject to revocation due to abuse of the privilege, such as providing alcohol to an unlicensed individual. Although this approach seems well suited to the problem, the notion of drinking as a privilege rather than a right would be a hard sell to the voters.

The indiscriminate nature of real-world alcohol-control measures practically ensures over-regulation, in the sense that some—perhaps most—of the drinkers or drinking occasions that are affected pose little or no cost to others. If these measures are effective, then the safer, healthier environment that results may make them worthwhile, even to people whose drinking behavior poses no risk. But other things equal, a more precisely targeted system would be preferable.

Much of the external costs of drinking stem from bad or foolish behavior while intoxicated, including those costs stemming from transportation-related crashes, brawling, criminal predation, domestic violence, and so forth. If these consequences of drinking could somehow be curtailed through other means, the case for supply controls would be much weaker. That observation has led some observers to suggest that what's needed is not higher taxes and the like, but rather a greater public effort directed at reducing the consequences of alcohol abuse (Whitman 2003). For example, the array of DUI interventions championed by MADD and other such advocacy groups have reduced the incidence of DUI and fatality rates, and more could be done in this regard: stiffer penalties for DUI violators, more anti-DUI patrols and special roadblocks, a requirement that vehicles belonging to any DUI violator be equipped with an ignition interlock activated by an alcohol-breath analyzer, and so forth. Similarly, for alcohol-related crime and violence a greater investment in criminal law enforcement would help deter criminals (or incapacitate them), including those whose crimes are linked to their alcohol abuse.

Although targeting the harmful behavior associated with alcohol abuse has obvious appeal, it falls short of an adequate response to the array of alcohol-related problems. First, enforcing DUI and criminal laws is a costly enterprise. At some point the costs to the public of additional enforcement become greater than the gain in terms of reduced crime, violence, and reckless driving. The burgeoning prison population makes this point all too clearly. What economist Gary Becker defined as the "optimal" crime rate is not zero crime, but rather the rate associated with a balancing of marginal costs and benefits of law enforcement (1968). At the point where additional enforcement effort costs as much or more than the value of the resulting reduction in crime, a further expansion in the crime-fighting budget would be wasteful. But at that point there remains more crime prevention that could profitably be done using other policy approaches—such as instituting some degree of regulation of the availability of alcohol (Cook and Leitzel 1996).

An example may help illustrate: consider a violence-prone alcohol abuser who tends to act impulsively. The threat of punishment may be simply irrelevant to him when drunk. But he may drink less and hence cause less harm in the face of higher alcohol prices or restricted availability. Acting on this theory, the mayor of the Dutch city of Eindhoven ordered that only half-strength beer be served during the Euro 2000 soccer championships. The British soccer "hooligans" were there in force but remained peaceful for the most part. In contrast, they rioted the next week in Belgium, where the beer was full strength and readily available (Babor et al. 2003, 119). It seems likely that the citizens of Eindhoven, even those who were frustrated by the ban on their usual brew, benefited from the mayor's action on balance.

Second, some of the harmful consequences of alcohol abuse are largely beyond the reach of a targeted consequence-oriented approach. For example, while domestic violence is subject to criminal penalties, parental neglect and mistreatment are only actionable by public officials in extreme cases. Likewise, there is little that law enforcement can do to prevent risky sex and the associated spread of STDs. The organ damage from chronic excess drinking is entirely beyond reach. Limiting availability and raising the price of alcoholic beverages, crude as this approach may be, is an effective means for government to reduce the harmful consequences of drinking that are not cost-effectively reached through targeted efforts.

Of course there are other options than law enforcement and supply controls for combating heavy drinking and harmful behavior associated with abuse. Prevention and treatment play some role in the overall mix. But even with a considerable increase in public expenditures in subsidizing treatment and sponsoring public service ads and the like, much of the "problem" would remain. Thus, alcohol-control policy should not be viewed as an alternative to other approaches to reducing the social costs of alcohol abuse, but as one important element of the portfolio of policies, all of which have some role.

INDUSTRY STRUCTURE AND PRICING

Alcohol-control measures interact with market conditions to influence prices and availability to consumers. The markets and market regulations for beer, wine, and liquor differ in important ways, but have some things in common. All three beverage categories are regulated by the federal government and each of the state governments. The federal government licenses and collects excise taxes from importers and manufacturers through the Treasury Department's Alcohol and Tobacco Tax and Trade Bureau. This agency also investigates allegations of illegal trade practices in the marketing of alcoholic beverages (together with the Federal Trade Commission), and enforces the federal requirement of a specific alcohol warning label on all bottles. Illegal production and trafficking is policed by another federal agency, the Justice Department's Bureau of Alcohol, Tobacco, Firearms, and Explosives—the direct descendent of Elliott Ness's "Untouchables." The Food and Drug Administration monitors the purity of the products.

For the most part, however, the Twenty-first Amendment assures that the state governments take the lead in regulating the alcohol industry. This amendment, in addition to repealing national Prohibition, states: "The transportation or importation into any State, Territory, or possession of the United States for delivery or use therein of intoxicating liquors, in violation of the laws thereof, is hereby prohibited." Thus, each state can elect its own taxes and regulations, no matter how stringent, without being (legally) undercut by laxer alcohol regulations in other states.

The states have generally adopted a three-tier regulatory system that distinguishes between producers, distributors, and retailers. Eighteen states maintain public monopolies over the second "distribution" tier, and in most of these monopoly states the retail sale of package liquor is restricted to government ABC stores. There is a licensing system for on-premise sale of drinks and for retailing of package goods in all fifty states.

Although the alcohol industry is regulated more than most, the private profit motive remains important. Market conditions have considerable influence on pricing, product, and availability. These conditions differ among the three beverage types.

Beer

America is predominantly a beer-drinking country. Beer provides well over half of the ethanol consumed by the public (55 percent in 2003). Pricing in the beer industry is influenced by the fact that production is highly concentrated. Anheuser Busch is the industry leader, supplying over half of domestic production with Budweiser, Michelob, and several other brands. Miller is the next largest brewer, and then Coors. Between them this big three accounted for 89 percent of domestic beer production in 2000 (Tremblay and Tremblay 2005).

This remarkable concentration is relatively new. According to one account, the thirteen most influential American brewers all were founded in the mid-1800s, somehow survived Prohibition, succeeded as large national or regional producers through 1971—and thereafter failed (Tremblay and Tremblay 2005, 100). Anheuser Busch is the lone exception in this group. It became the world's largest brewer, the "King of beers," in 1957, and continued to grow in both absolute and relative terms since then. It was challenged for preeminence in the 1970s when Phillip Morris bought Miller and started the "beer wars" of that period. Miller advertised intensively and brought out new brands, including Miller Light—the first successful brand in a product category that now outsells all others.[1] But Anheuser Busch met the challenge and has continued to thrive. Meanwhile, Coors transformed itself from a regional to national brewer and was successful in capturing third place in the national market while other brewers went bankrupt or were taken over.

Just why the beer market has become so concentrated is not entirely clear. Technological change in production and shipping have had the effect of expanding minimum efficient scale over time, but according to one estimate, Anheuser Busch is five times as large as required to achieve full-scale economies, and Miller is twice as large (Tremblay and Tremblay 2005, 47). Marketing has played an important role: Anheuser Busch was an innovator in doing market research (beginning in 1961), and the Budweiser name has been developed into a huge asset. Of course Anheuser Busch is now in a position to protect its market position by matching its rivals' price cuts, new-product introductions, or other strategic moves.

This increasingly static structure has been coupled with the emergence of an active fringe of over one thousand specialty brewers (Tremblay and Tremblay 2005, 104). The rapid growth in the number of microbreweries was facilitated by a change in the federal tax law, which reduced the beer excise on small producers starting in 1977 and greatly expanded this tax break in 1991.[2] What's more, all states have legalized brew pubs, which in effect merge the three tiers into a single entity.

But the industry that provides beer *ordinaire* to the masses is a highly concentrated oligopoly, with Anheuser Busch as the price leader. That is not the same thing as having a monopoly, and while beer prices are higher than if the industry were more competitive, they are less than what a profit-maximizing monopoly would choose. The evidence for this conclusion is that at current prices, overall beer demand is highly inelastic, implying that if all producers raised their prices together, then combined industry revenues (and hence profits) would increase. The fact that the brewers have not been able to fully exploit this possibility is evidence that their rivalry remains strong. If Anheuser Busch announced a large price increase, Miller or Coors might decide not to go along, since by holding the line they could obtain a larger market share. The threat that the large producers in Mexico, Canada, and Europe could enlarge their share of the U.S. market (12 percent by volume in 2003)[3] may also be relevant in pricing decisions by the big three domestic producers.

In this context, theory does not provide a sure guide to the effect of a tax increase on prices. Producers could choose to swallow the increase, or pass all or part along in the form of higher prices. It all depends on how the tax increase plays out in the context of the pricing game among the rivals—the decisions by each of whether to cooperate, given the common interest in higher prices, or defect, given the individual interest in expanding market share. In practice, as suggested by evidence over the course of several decades, beer excise taxes are not only passed along to consumers, but actually engender price increases *larger* than the tax increase (Young and Bielinska-Kwapisz 2002). Apparently the rivals find it relatively easy to cooperate in raising prices around the common stimulus of a tax increase.

A full account of pricing in the beer industry must include the other two tiers. Producers and importers contract with distributors, who warehouse the product, deliver to retailers, engage in local advertising and point-of-sale promotions, and monitor the freshness of beer on store shelves (Sass 2005). All the large brewers assign exclusive territories to their distributors so that retailers have only one source for each brand. To ensure their distributors' interests are closely aligned with theirs, in 1997 Anheuser Busch began requiring that its distributors devote their primary effort to its brands (Sass 2005). In some cases distributors carry only one brewer's product line, or are actually owned by the brewer. The quest for vertical integration sometimes crosses over the legal line to include retailers; for a while in the 1970s it was common for brewers to give bars and restaurants kickbacks in exchange for exclusive sale of its products (Tremblay and Tremblay 2005, 203). That sort of "tied house" arrangement is illegal and is just what the reformers of the 1930s were trying to prevent.

The continuing quest for greater market power is one motivation for advertising by producers. Beer ads on television are more about image than factual information, creating subjective differentiation among products that are objectively very similar. The introduction of premium brands helps further differentiate the market. It is plausible that a ban on image advertising would result in lower prices as customers' brand loyalties eroded and they became more sensitive to price. Of course, some advertising provides factual information about product and price, and that may strengthen competition. A study by economists Tim Sass and David Saurman found that state laws restricting price advertising in local beer ads during the 1980s had the effect of strengthening the hand of the larger producers, with a resulting increase in market concentration at the state level (1995).

Thus, beer production and distribution is far from the competitive-market ideal celebrated in economics texts. It seems reasonable to suppose that there are several areas of government policy that could influence prices: antitrust, advertising restrictions, and the regulation of relationships between the three tiers. And the empirical evidence demonstrates that both state and federal governments have direct influence on beer prices through the choice of excise tax rates.

Wine

A look at the wine market demonstrates the importance of the distribution network in influencing alcohol prices. Whereas beer production has become more concentrated, wine producers have proliferated, with the leading winery, E.& J. Gallo, playing a much less dominant role in the wine industry than Anheuser Busch does in beer.[4] By 2002, there were 2,700 bonded wineries in the United States, a 500 percent increase from thirty years earlier (Wiseman and Ellig 2004). And imports play a larger role (nearly one-quarter of domestic consumption volume in 2003) than for beer (Adams Beverage Group 2004, 28). But wine *distribution* has gone through an extraordinary consolidation, from nearly 5,000 distributors in the 1950s to approximately 400 in 2002 (Wiseman and Ellig 2004). The top five distributors account for a third of the market (Freedman and Emshwiller 1999). These divergent trends have placed the distributors at odds with the producers over at least one prominent issue—direct shipment of wine to customers. As of 2003, half the states banned direct shipment from out of state. The result was to protect the market position of licensed distributors, often to the chagrin of small wineries that have trouble getting on the distributors' lists, and of connoisseurs who can't buy the vintage that they want. The noted wine writer Robert Parker observed, "I can buy an assault weapon at a gun show more easily than I can order a coveted bottle of Chardonnay" (Freedman and Emshwiller 1999).

The constitutional issue here comes down to the conflict between the Commerce Clause, which limits the power of the states to erect barriers against interstate trade, and the Twenty-first Amendment, which appears to make alcohol the one exception to this rule (Douglass 2000). In May 2005, the Supreme Court ruled in a 5–4 decision (*Granholm v. Heald*) that the states could ban direct shipment, but only if they did so for in-state producers as well as out-of-state. The laws of Michigan, New York, and by extension twenty-two other states were thereby ruled unconstitutional (Stout 2005).

Although much of the publicity in connection with this case had to do with small wineries being able to access a national market, the consequence may be downward pressure on wine prices generally. The whole-salers' cut typically amounts to about 18–25 percent of the price to the retailer for wine, and a similar percentage for liquor. A *Wall Street Journal* article reported that wine and spirits have the most expensive distribution system of any packaged-goods industry by far, with margins more than twice those in the food business (Freedman and Emshwiller 1999). For temperance advocates, lower prices are not necessarily welcome, but when the Court announced its decision, a lawyer for the winning side observed that "This is the best day for wine lovers since the invention of the corkscrew."

Competition from direct shipment of wine and liquor may end up squeezing the distributors' margins and driving down prices. And this is just one aspect of a broader legal attack on the three-tier system. For example, in April 2006, a U.S. District Court judge in Seattle ruled on behalf of the plaintiff (Costco) that Washington State's restrictions on pricing discretion by beer and wine distributors were in conflict with the federal antitrust law, and in particular that volume discounts and pricing flexibility should be allowed. In this case the judge asserted that the state had a legitimate interest, protected by the Twenty-first Amendment, in promoting temperance, but that the regulations on distributors did not serve that interest to any great extent, and hence must give way to other interests.[5] In any event, the result of this and other cases may be reduced prices engendering an increase in consumption and abuse. That problem could be readily resolved by raising taxes.

Distilled Spirits

Spirits have always been viewed as the most problematic of the beverage types due to the high concentration of ethanol, and remain more closely regulated than beer or wine. Perhaps the most surprising feature of government involvement in the liquor trade is that eighteen states continue to control wholesale distribution as a public monopoly. Five of these states also monopolize the retail sale of package spirits; most of the other "control" states, while licensing some private outlets, run ABC stores as well.[6] In some cases the monopoly has extended beyond spirits to include wine, but the trend since the 1960s has been to privatize wine sales (Holder and Wagenaar 1995).

The other thirty-two states and District of Columbia license wholesale distributors and retail outlets to sell packaged liquor. In those states, retail price is influenced by the state excise tax and, presumably, the conditions under which retail licenses are issued. In the absence of a comprehensive study of how such regulations affect pricing, all that can be offered here is a simple comparison of license and control states. Price data for a popular brand of scotch are available for samples of retail outlets in most states.[7] In 2000, the median price in control states was 10 percent higher than in license states; the mean difference was also 10 percent. It is interesting to note that this gap had widened since the early 1980s, during which time the real price in license states declined by more than in the control states.[8]

On the supply side, the liquor business is quite competitive. The leading supplier, Diageo, has only 20 percent of the market by volume; the top four suppliers account for less than half the total.[9]

AVAILABILITY

A large percentage of drinking occasions that lead to DUI occur at bars and restaurants. These establishments have a duty to manage their alcohol service responsibly, and in particular to refuse service to minors and cut off service to adults who are becoming intoxicated. The goal is preventing damage by drunken patrons, either while they are on premise or after they drive away.

Of course, the history of public regulation of drinking establishments goes back well before the advent of automobiles. As we have seen, the temperance movement was mobilized against saloons as a source of personal and public corruption and various sorts of vice. Following repeal of Prohibition, there was a determination to constitute a new order that would prevent the excesses of the saloon. Every state eventually instituted a system for organizing and regulating both off-site package sales and on-site sales by the drink (Medicine in the Public Interest 1979, 23; Sloan et al. 2000). These systems specify the rules governing issuance, renewal, and possible revocation of licenses, as well as the rules governing the operations of licensees. From the public's perspective, the result is to influence the availability of alcoholic beverages—not just prices, but also what sorts of retail outlets will sell what sorts of alcoholic beverages at what hours of the day and week. The resulting environments range over the spectrum defined by "dry" and "wet." At the dry end are the (generally rural) counties, Indian reservations, and public parks that maintain a prohibition on sale and in some cases even the possession of alcohol. At the wet end are states where grocery stores have off-premise liquor licenses, and on-premise licenses are readily procured.

The key question is whether availability really matters as a causal factor in alcohol abuse and its consequences. Certainly it does in extreme cases— American troops involved in the Gulf War in 1991 were cut off from alcohol, to generally good effect; troops stationed in Saudi Arabia had a very low rate of discipline problems due to the stringent prohibition in that country (Shenon 1991). But that doesn't imply that a modest reduction in the density of liquor outlets in a typical American city would make much difference. Several reviews of the literature have been skeptical or have concluded that the evidence is just not strong enough (Saffer, Grossman, and Chaloupka, 1998, 47; Sloan et al. 2000).

Of course, estimating the effects of availability on alcohol-related outcomes is made difficult by the lack of experimental evidence. The statistical association between the density of outlet licenses and drinking is hard to interpret, since a variety of causal processes could account for it (Watts and Rabow 1983; Scribner, MacKinnon, and Dwyer 1994; Giacopassi and Winn 1995; Gruenewald and Ponicki 1995). But sometimes a dramatic policy change has the effect of producing a natural experiment with clear evidence.

Local Option

When the states were sorting out their ABC laws in the 1930s, thirty-four of them legislated local option for counties and sometimes municipalities to ban the sale of alcoholic beverages. The counties that chose to remain dry in the 1930s were, with only a few exceptions, also dry in 1915, prior to national Prohibition (Strumpf and Oberholzer-Gee 2000). That fact serves as a reminder that a simple comparison of alcohol-related problems in dry jurisdictions with others would confound the effects of the local prohibition with the effects of historical local sentiment about drinking. But in most jurisdictions, that sentiment was contested and subject to drift over time. In fact, there were over five thousand elections between 1934 and 1939 in which voters were asked to choose whether to ban or permit alcohol sales, and thereafter hundreds of elections annually until 1970 or so—by which time the "dry" county population had dwindled from 38 percent to about 6 percent (Strumpf and Oberholzer-Gee 2002). The effects of numerous abrupt changes from wet to dry and back again may someday provide grist for an analyst's statistical mill.

Some states have also instituted local option about whether restaurants and bars should be licensed to serve liquor by the drink.[10] James Blose and Harold Holder have analyzed the consequences in North Carolina (Blose and Holder 1987; Holder and Blose 1985), and their positive findings, based on the natural experiment of county adoption, seem both reliable and surprising. In a sense the switch to liquor by the drink was not that great. Even before local option was adopted in 1978, people could drink when dining out. Restaurants in counties that permitted alcohol sales could obtain licenses to serve beer, wine, and "set ups"—ice and mixers to go with the spirits that patrons brought with them. There was even speculation that this "brown bagging" tradition caused more trouble

than would serving liquor by the drink, since some patrons were inclined
to finish the bottle they brought with them before driving home (Holder
and Blose 1985). Blose and Holder analyzed patterns in alcohol-related
traffic crashes before and after adoption, comparing the early adopters
with jurisdictions that were similar in some respects but did not elect the
liquor-by-the-drink option. This evidence suggests an increase of about
20 percent in alcohol-related crashes involving male drivers age twenty-
one and over. (The minimum drinking age for liquor was twenty-one
throughout this period.) Apparently the increased availability of liquor at
restaurants, and the change in drinking environments—some establishments opened bar or lounge areas for the first time—led to a sharp increase in DUI.

Privatizing Package Sales

As we have seen, the eighteen control states have maintained a public
monopoly on wholesale distribution, but have taken different paths when
it comes to retail sales. Several states that monopolized both wine and
liquor sales elected at some point to privatize the off-premise retail sale
of wine (Holder and Wagenaar 1995). Iowa has been unique in privatizing
both wine (in 1985) and spirits (1987). The result of switching to a retail
licensing system was to greatly increase the number of outlets and hence
the convenience to the public of buying wine and spirits, with attendant
differences in marketing practices (Mulford, Ledolter, and Fitzgerald
1993).

A number of evaluations of the effects on alcohol sales have been published, with conflicting conclusions (Mulford and Fitzgerald 1999). A
careful look at the data provides a strong indication of a large and lasting
impact on the wine market, and little effect on spirits sales. It is illuminat-
ing to compare per capita sales in 1990 (after the new regime was fully
established for both wine and spirits) with the baseline year of 1984. Wine
sales in Iowa increased 50 percent during this time, while in the Midwest
region as a whole wine sales were actually declining. (The six states that
border Iowa experienced modest changes, plus or minus, with nothing
comparable to the surge of sales in Iowa.) On the other hand, spirits sales
during the same period *declined* by 11.5 percent in Iowa, very much in
line with the 11.9 percent decline across the Midwest, and well within
the range of changes experienced by the border states. It should be noted
that wine is a small part of the mix in Iowa, even after that large proportional increase, and it is not clear that the overall sales and consumption
of ethanol changed as a result of privatization.

Licensing Retail Sales

The broader question of whether states are well advised to restrict the number of licensees remains open to debate. Certainly the states differ in this respect. Several dimensions of licensing stringency are noteworthy, including fees, nature of the licensing authority, and regulatory enforcement. License fees for the principal licenses range widely. Among the ten largest states, the annual fee for a retail off-premise license to sell beer ranged from less than $100 in New Jersey to $252 in Ohio and $500 in Illinois. The annual fee for a mixed-drink license in a restaurant ranged as high as $6,000 (in California); New Jersey let municipalities set the fee within a legislated range ($250–$2,500), while several of the states adjusted the fee to size of the local population.

The ABC authorities responsible for licensing differ in a number of respects. The typical authority is a commission, board, or agency headed by a political appointee, with the power to investigate applicants (Sloan et al. 2000, 36). Local jurisdictions can limit new establishments through zoning ordinances. In several states it is local governments that take the lead in licensing: in Illinois, all state licensees must first be licensed by their local jurisdictions; in New Jersey, municipalities set fees and issue licenses subject to limits specified in the state law; in Wisconsin there is no state licensing authority, and localities handle licensing subject to broad state-level guidelines.

State licensing procedures are not especially stringent. One survey with responses from twenty-seven states found that the application-rejection rate averaged just 4 percent (Sloan et al. 2000, 39). Furthermore, while every state has some procedure for enforcing state regulations, it is rare in practice to impose severe penalties: the same survey found that only 1.5 percent of on-site licenses had been suspended or revoked over the course of a year.

Several states, including Florida, New Jersey, and Pennsylvania, have actually capped the number of some types of licenses. The result has been the creation of a private market in which licenses are bought and sold (subject to state approval), much like the taxi medallions in New York City. For example, New Jersey and Pennsylvania both limit the number of licenses for retail sale of beer and liquor to one license for every three thousand inhabitants in the county. In counties that have hit this cap, a new entrant must buy a license from an existing license holder. One interesting consequence in Philadelphia has been the phenomenon of upscale restaurants opening without a license. Patrons must "brown bag" their own wine and liquor until the restaurant is well enough established to afford a license from the open market.

There are several different enforcement systems for ABC regulations. A majority of states have a dedicated enforcement staff organized as an independent state agency, or, more commonly, part of the ABC agency (Sloan et al. 2000, 37). A survey of commercial servers found that the perceived likelihood of being cited for serving underage or drunken patrons was somewhat higher for states with this sort of dedicated enforcement, as opposed to states that assigned this task to the state or local police.

Licensing systems support zoning requirements designed to prevent taverns from operating near schools or churches or in residential areas. Operating hours, credit provision, serving food as well as alcohol, happy hours and price promotions, advertising, and much else are closely regulated (Moore and Gerstein 1981, 75), and violations may result in administrative penalties including fines and license suspension or revocation. Some violations are actually crimes that can, at least in theory, result in jail terms for the server and her manager. In particular, serving a minor or an intoxicated person is a criminal offense in all but four states (Sloan et al. 2000, 78).[11] In any event, the objective probability of an arrest or fine is low, since enforcement resources are stretched thin everywhere. One survey found that fewer than 10 percent of bars reported that a liquor authority had taken disciplinary action against them or their employees during the previous year (Sloan et al. 2000, 62). (The most common violations were serving minors, gambling, and indecent exposure or lewd conduct.) When there is an action against a licensee, penalties are usually mild—inadequate to create a strong deterrent.

It seems likely that it is the *unlicensed* establishments that are the worst offenders when it comes to alcohol regulations, not to mention providing a venue for other vices such as drugs and prostitution. Such "shot houses" are likely to flourish in direct relation to the stringency of licensing rules and regulations on service. But there has been little research about this feature of the underground economy.

Dram-Shop Liability

One important solution to the problem of enforcement has been, in effect, to privatize it through imposition of civil liability. In states that have adopted "dram-shop" liability, establishments can be sued if a patron is served alcohol illegally—because he is underage or intoxicated—and then because of his intoxicated state causes injury or property damage after departing the premises. As of 1998, forty-three states had dram-shop liability in place, most by statute, a handful by judge-made case law alone, and eighteen with both (Sloan et al. 2000, 120). The rationale for imposing liability is twofold: first, to provide compensation for the victims, and second, to create a stronger incentive for establishments to refuse service to drunks and minors (Mosher 1988). That incentive must be strong enough to overcome the normal propensity of an establishment to accommodate patrons' wishes and sell as much alcohol as possible.

Dram-shop liability has long been controversial. In traditional common law, dispensers of alcoholic beverages were not liable for injuries caused by their drunken customers, since the drinkers themselves were deemed the proximate, and hence legally culpable, cause (Jacobs 1989, 139). Under pressure from the temperance movement, eleven states adopted dram-shop liability by the mid-1870s, at a time when the concern (and the potential plaintiffs) was primarily the families of habitual drunkards who were squandering their livelihood at the local saloon. Liability fell out of favor following Repeal. In 1978, California became the first state to enact a dram-shop liability statute in the post-war period, and that statute was later repealed. Opposition has come not only from the "hospitality" industry, but also from those who are concerned that making the server liable will somehow undermine the principle that the drinker should be responsible for his own actions. But the pendulum has now swung so far that in many states, the drinker himself can under some circumstances sue the bar that served him if he has an accident (Holder et al. 1993).

Dram-shop lawsuits are not limited to drunk driving accidents, but those constitute the bulk of such cases (Mosher 1988). Several of the RASPP studies summarized earlier (table 6.3) have found direct evidence that the imposition of dram-shop liability reduces traffic fatalities in a state.

Economist Frank Sloan and his associates conducted a survey of drinking establishments to provide a basis for looking inside the "black box" of how liability might affect serving practices. They found that managers and owners were aware of the possibility of a lawsuit and perceived it as a greater threat in states that had dram-shop liability. More than the threat of regulatory enforcement actions, the threat of a lawsuit appears to influence management policies. "Bar owners who perceived a higher risk of tort suit tended to monitor their employees more closely. They were significantly less likely to allow employees to drink on the job and were more likely to provide services for intoxicated customers, check the references of job applicants, cover more subjects in server training programs, and provide employees with procedures for serving alcohol" (2000, 251).

Of course, the service staff are on the front lines in this effort. They are the ones expected to recognize when patrons have drunk enough and find some way to cut them off—a difficult job, especially in a crowded establishment, and one that works against the interests of anyone whose earnings are primarily in the form of tips (Liang, Sloan, and Stout 2004). To some extent, techniques for identifying and dealing with inebriated patrons can be learned. Server-intervention training programs became popular during the 1980s with the growth of liability and accompanying pressure from insurance companies (Jacobs 1989, 141). Several states, beginning with Oregon, mandated server training as part of licensing. Whether such programs are effective is not entirely clear (Holder and Wagenaar 1994; Grube 1997).

The ongoing effort to regulate or persuade bars and restaurants to take greater account of public safety is multifaceted, and often spearheaded by local activists. Some guidance for this effort comes from a five-year demonstration project in the early 1990s, evaluated by Harold Holder and his associates. Theirs was a comprehensive, community-based environmental intervention to reduce rates of alcohol-related injuries resulting from motor-vehicle crashes and assaults. Working in three communities with populations around 100,000, it sought to mobilize community support for preventive interventions, convince licensees to adopt responsible beverage service, engender increased enforcement by local police against sales to minors, set up roadside police checkpoints for DUI, and assist communities in developing local restrictions on access to alcohol through local zoning powers (Holder et al. 2000). The apparent result of this comprehensive effort was to reduce alcohol-related crashes by around 6 percent, and perhaps cause a small reduction in serious injuries from assault.

Federal Role

Finally, it should be noted that whereas the main regulatory action is with the states, the federal government has some role in influencing alcohol availability (Mosher and Mottl 1981). The National Park Service and National Forest Service impose and attempt to enforce rules governing sale and possession of alcohol for federal parks and other lands. The Bureau of Indian Affairs traditionally had a role in setting policy for tribal lands, although now it is up to the individual tribes to decide alcohol policies. Probably most important in practice is the role of the Department of Defense (DoD). All three services operate package stores in connection with Post-Exchange Stores, and on-premise sales through service clubs on bases. Cheap, readily available alcohol used to be one of the perks of military service, but the DoD has tightened up its policies in this regard— a subject for the chapter on youths.

CONCLUDING THOUGHTS

Even if public officials responsible for ABC regulation accepted as part of their task to reduce alcohol abuse and its attendant costs, research would not provide them with enough guidance. We can't be sure whether the social costs of alcohol abuse are reduced by mandated closing hours, requirements that food be served with the alcohol, or limits on outlet density (Babor et al. 2003, chap. 7).[12] Regulations against serving underage or drunken patrons and maintaining order are on firmer ground. But even there, the systematic evidence is not adequate to determine whether increasing the enforcement efforts would pass a cost-benefit test. Still, it is only common sense that good regulations should be backed up with a credible enforcement system, one with sufficient teeth to elicit compliance from licensees and shut down unlicensed vendors.

CHAPTER 11

Taxing the Alcohol Industry

> Taxes should be levied not with the idea of filling the public
> treasury at whatever cost to public morality and efficiency,
> but as a method of reducing the consumption of alcohol.
> —Raymond B. Fosdick and Albert L. Scott,
> *Toward Liquor Control*

OF ALL THE ALCOHOL-CONTROL measures, taxes have unique advantages. They help curtail alcohol abuse and its consequences without a direct restriction on freedom of choice. They can be set high or low or anywhere in between, providing the possibility of a calibrated response to the costs of alcohol-related problems. And rather than competing for resources with other government priorities, alcohol taxes enhance public revenues. As we have seen (chapter 2), it was this last advantage that was the immediate motivation when the first Congress imposed a whiskey excise tax in 1791, and the revenue motive has remained paramount in federal and state tax policy ever since. (Federal alcohol tax collections currently amount to over $8 billion, and state collections over $4 billion, per year.) But one important justification for special tax treatment of alcohol has always been the unique, problematic qualities of alcohol. As it was over 200 years ago, the question now is not *whether* alcoholic beverages should be subject to higher taxes than other commodities, but just *how high* these taxes should be. The U.S. Congress's answer to this question in recent years has been "far lower than they used to be." For example, looking back fifty years from 2005, the federal excise tax on liquor (adjusted for inflation) was 5.7 times as high, and the excise tax on beer 3.6 times as high. The states also tax alcohol, and they too have allowed rates to decline in real value. The reasons for this dramatic decline are something of a mystery, but surely are not due to a corresponding decline in alcohol-related problems. By a number of standards, beginning with this historical standard, alcohol taxes are now too low (Cook 1988).

THE HISTORICAL STANDARD

Alcoholic beverages are subject to a variety of specific federal, state, and local taxes. The most important of these are the federal and state excise taxes. (Most states also include alcoholic beverages in the list of items subject to state sales tax.) The excises differ from the standard sales tax in that excises are usually unit taxes, defined in terms of volume rather than value of the product, and are paid by the manufacturer or distributor rather than the retailer. As of 2006, the federal excise on liquor stands at $13.50 per proof gallon (the volume of liquid containing 64 ounces of ethanol), while beer is taxed at $18 per 31-gallon barrel and table wine at $1.07 per gallon.[1] To facilitate comparison, it is useful to calculate the average tax per ounce of ethanol from each beverage type: 7 cents for wine, 10 cents for beer, and 21 cents for liquor.[2] States also impose alcohol excise taxes. With a handful of exceptions, the state excise rates are lower than the federal rates; for example, the median of the state beer excise rates is about one-quarter the federal rate (Factbook on $State Beer Taxe$ 2004).

Because excise taxes are typically assessed on volume rather than value, the rates have no automatic inflation protection. Maintaining the real value of the excise tax rates would require that Congress and the state legislatures act to increase the nominal value with inflation. However, between 1951 and 2005, Congress legislated increases in the beer and wine excises only once, in the budget bill of 1990; there were just two increases in the liquor excise tax during that period, both small. As a result, inflation has greatly eroded the real value of the federal excises on beer and liquor. By 1990, the rates were only about 20 percent of their value four decades earlier; the legislated increase beginning in January 1991 regained part of this ground, but it has been lost since then. Figure 11.1 depicts this history since 1970.

The real value of state excise tax rates has also declined during this period. One tabulation found that only eleven states legislated a beer tax increase in the decade before 2003, and thirteen states had not raised their tax rates since 1975 (Factbook on $State Beer Taxe$ 2004). The slide in real tax rates accounts for a good deal of the decline in alcohol prices (relative to other consumer prices) during the 1970s and 1980s (see chapter 5).

The historical standard for evaluating current excise tax rates can be expressed something like this: If in 1951, Congress saw fit to establish a tax rate equivalent in 2005 dollars to $12.60 per fifth of (80 proof) liquor, then why have subsequent Congresses allowed the tax to drop to the 2006 level of just $2.16 per fifth? Similar calculations for the federal beer tax, and for the state excises, lead to the same puzzle. It is too easy to answer that we live in a time when politicians have become allergic to tax increases. Although that may indeed be part of the answer, it must be noted that the "allergy" has not extended to *tobacco* excises, which numerous state legislatures—and Congress—have raised in recent years, often by substantial amounts. The political case for higher tobacco taxes

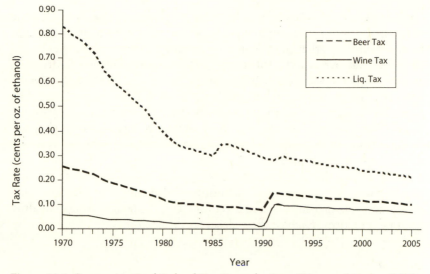

Figure 11.1. Comparing Real Federal Tax Rates for Beer, Wine, and Liquor (1970–2005).

Note: Nominal tax rates converted to cents per ounce of included ethanol and converted to 2005 dollar values using the CPI.

has been abetted by the growing consensus that tobacco taxes promote the public health. The argument, and the evidence, seem just as strong or stronger in the case of alcohol.

PUBLIC HEALTH AND SAFETY

The evidence that alcohol prices and hence taxes matter in influencing alcohol consumption, abuse, and short-term negative consequences was developed in chapters 5 and 6. (The "laboratory of the states" has provided much of this evidence as a sort of quasi-experiment.) Our experience with Prohibition, carefully considered, in no way contradicts that conclusion (chapter 2). Quite simply, alcohol taxation and other measures that increase the price of ethanol are effective in promoting the public health and safety. Higher prices are conducive to lower rates of underage drinking, traffic fatalities, and sexually transmitted disease. There is less direct evidence on the effects of higher prices on the prevalence of chronic excess drinking and related medical conditions, but the indirect evidence is compelling on that score as well.

Note that these conclusions are based on empirical evidence rather than intuition, anecdote, and speculation. It is easy to imagine plausible scenarios under which an increase in alcohol prices would have little effect on abuse, or even a perverse effect. In the face of higher prices for alcoholic beverages, consumers could make a variety of substitutions in an attempt to maintain their ethanol consumption without paying more; they could switch to cheaper brands, substitute at-home consumption for drinking at bars, or make their own. Furthermore, it seems plausible that heavy drinkers, especially those who have become alcohol dependent, would be especially determined to maintain their drinking in the face of higher prices. Some of these speculations may well be correct as far as they go. But according to the empirical evidence, the net effect of higher prices is salutary for public health.

What about the unintended consequences of increased taxes and prices? Three come to mind: substitution from alcohol to other drugs, the creation of a dangerous black market for alcohol, and a decline in healthy drinking practices. Each of these deserves discussion.

Substitution?

The intuition that alcohol may be a substitute for illicit drugs rests on the belief that the fundamental goal of the drinker is intoxication, without much regard as to the type of "high." Deprived of alcohol, the would-be drinker will then seek an alternative such as marijuana or other intoxicating drug. That view is probably most plausible for youths, and that group has been the focus of research in this area. But a number of empirical studies have found that contrary to expectation, marijuana and alcohol are complements, not substitutes (Pacula 1998; Williams et al. 2001; Farrelly et al. 1999). Youths who smoke marijuana (and cigarettes—see chapter 5) are likely to drink as well—it is not an "either- or" situation, but more akin to "both" or "neither." One account of complementarity focuses on the "gateway" phenomenon, whereby use of one illegal substance (alcohol) results in greater interest in and opportunity to try others (marijuana). In any event, some direct evidence based on econometric research of survey data indicates that when it becomes more difficult or costly to acquire either marijuana or alcohol, the youthful consumption of both tends to decline.[3]

Of course there is no reason to suppose that consumers are uniform in this regard. Some may be inclined to shift among intoxicants depending on relative prices and availability, while others exhibit more of an all-or-nothing approach. Further, the initial response may be qualitatively different than the long-run effect on behavior (as suggested by the gateway story). In any event, it is important to note that regardless of how the various intoxicants relate in consumer choice, the relevant consequences for injury rates are already incorporated in the RASPP studies (chapter 6). For example, the demonstration that an increase in alcohol taxes or MLDA reduces the youthful highway fatality rate implies that even if there is some substitution from alcohol to other sources of inebriation, the net effect is reduced incidence of dangerous driving by youths.

Creation of a Black Market?

A large increase in alcohol taxes could be a boon to the few moonshiners who are still in business. Illicit production of distilled spirits was a non-trivial problem in the 1950s (when federal liquor taxes were far higher than today) and has virtually disappeared in more recent times with the decline in price of "government whisky." When the moonshine business was thriving, there were health risks caused by the lead and other poisons introduced by backwoods distillers. But at no time—even during Prohibition, when illegal production was rampant—did the health problems associated with the impurities of moonshine compare with the injuries and deaths caused by consuming ethanol itself.

Decline in Healthy Drinking Practices?

As discussed in chapter 7, there is a growing body of epidemiological evidence suggesting that moderate drinking in middle age offers some protection against coronary heart disease and several other conditions. One meta-analysis of the evidence on the relationship between alcohol consumption and all-cause mortality, based on dozens of studies of various population groups (average age, forty-five), found that a J-shaped curve fit the results best (Gmel et al. 2003). For women, average consumption of somewhat less than one standard drink per day was ideal, while for men the mortality rate was minimized at about two drinks per day. A reasonable concern is that raising alcohol taxes would have the effect of causing some middle-aged drinkers to abstain or drink too little, raising their overall mortality risk.

I and two colleagues explored this possibility by combining survey data on drinking among middle-aged Americans with the J-curve of mortality (Cook, Ostermann, and Sloan 2005). We estimated the mortality effect of a 1 percent reduction in per capita consumption by people in the middle-age range, under three different assumptions about how that reduction occurs: at the extensive margin (a one percentage point increase in the number of abstainers), the intensive margin (an across-the-board reduction of 1 percent in consumption by drinkers), or a mixture of the two. The result was pretty much the same regardless—a negligible net effect on mortality. Our conclusion was that small reductions in per capita drinking by people age thirty-five to seventy, of the sort engendered by moderate increases in tax rates, are unlikely to make much difference on balance from a public health perspective. The good effects of reduced drinking (reduced injury deaths and cirrhosis mortality) are balanced by the alleged harmful effects (increased heart attacks). Since the epidemiologists are quite sure that there are no health benefits from drinking by people younger than thirty-five, for that group the acute injury–reducing effects dominate. Hence, the overall all-age effect of a tax increase is to reduce mortality rates.

Note that the simulation results presume that the J-curve from the meta-analysis of epidemiological studies is valid as a description of the *causal* effect of drinking. The discussion of the evidence in chapter 7 was intended to raise questions about that presumption. In brief, the problem is that the epidemiological evidence presumes that lifetime abstainers are equivalent in all other medically relevant respects to moderate drinkers (after accounting for demographic characteristics, smoking, and known preexisting conditions). If that is not the case, then the fact that moderate drinkers have lower mortality in middle age than abstainers may say nothing at all about the medical benefits of drinking *per se*. It is quite possible that alcohol is of no greater life-saving value for middle-age people than, say, hormone replacement therapy.

In the face of this uncertainty concerning the long-term effects of drinking, it is difficult to calibrate the overall mortality effects of a tax increase. The short-term effects are easier to estimate. My preferred estimate of the short-term effects of the alcohol tax on overall mortality rates is based on a RASPP estimate utilizing a thirty-year panel of state data (Cook et al. 2005). We found that an increase of 10 cents per ounce of ethanol would result in a short-term reduction in all-cause, all-age mortality rates of about 3.4 percent (plus or minus 2.0 percent).[4] (Note that about 2.5 million people die each year, so that each 1 percent reduction comprises 25,000 lives.) That estimate captures only the short-term effects of a change in drinking stemming from injuries and acute effects for people who have organ damage. Over the long run, the higher tax could have a variety of effects on drinking careers both for better (with reduced prevalence of dependence and long-term organ damage) and possibly worse (with reduced protection against heart disease). If the RASPP estimate is in the right ballpark, the implication is clear: if Congress doubled the beer tax and raised the taxes on wine and liquor by a similar amount, one result would be tens of thousands of lives saved every year.

FAIRNESS

A conclusion that higher alcohol taxes would improve the public health and safety does not settle the issue of whether they should be raised, and if so, by how much. These taxes should be evaluated on the same basis as others, with careful attention to fairness and economic efficiency. "Fairness" is a particularly slippery term, and certainly means different things to different people. An appealing case for the inherent fairness of taxing alcohol differently than most other commodities is captured by the notion of a "user fee"—a term that also provides some guidance as to the appropriate magnitudes.

People who abuse alcohol benefit from certain government programs more than nonabusers. For example, heavy drinkers have elevated morbidity, disability, and criminal victimization, and hence claim a disproportionate share of government expenditures on medical care, long-term care, and criminal justice services (Rice et al. 1990). Revenues from alcohol taxes help defray these and other alcohol-related public expenses. It may seem only fair that the drinker should pay for the costly consequences of his or her drinking, and the alcohol excise tax is a mechanism for accomplishing that result.

Given that much of the alcohol-related costs are associated with rare events such as traffic accidents, this "user fee" is akin to an insurance premium. Insurance premiums are set according to a schedule that reflects individual characteristics correlated with the likelihood and magnitude of a claim. Alcohol taxes differ among individuals in direct proportion to how much they drink, which is a strong predictor of the likelihood of drinking-related problems. However, they do not discriminate with respect to any of a number of other correlates of alcohol-related problems, such as age, sex, prior history of problems, or drinking pattern. A twenty-one-year-old man who drinks seven beers a week in a single session and then attempts to drive home pays the same tax as a forty-year-old woman who drinks one beer with dinner every night. Thus, this tax is not perfectly calibrated to risk (which can also be said about insurance rate schedules). But broadly speaking, the incidence of this tax makes sense. The majority of the population who abstain or drink very little will pay little or no tax; in any given day or year, most of the tax will be incurred by the relatively small group who drink heavily.

The "drinker should pay" standard can be extended beyond drinkers' disproportionate draw on government programs to include privately borne external costs of drinking. A comprehensive study of this matter conducted in the 1980s by Willard Manning and his associates (1989, 1991) found that most of these costs are not financed by government programs, but rather by private insurance companies or by innocent victims. The study concluded that the present value (using a 5 percent discount rate) of external costs per ounce of ethanol consumed was about 48 cents, double the average state and federal tax per ounce—suggesting that the "user fee" of that time was not nearly high enough. A subsequent study amplified this conclusion by noting that Manning and colleagues had failed to account for nonfatal highway injuries (Miller and Blincoe 1994). Including injuries increased the estimate of external costs to 63 cents per ounce.

The analysis by Manning and colleagues attempts to sort out alcohol-related costs between those that are borne by the drinker or his household (internal) and those that are borne by those outside his household (external). The normative importance of this distinction stems from John Stuart Mill's "harm principle," discussed in chapter 9. By this reckoning, earnings lost as a result of heavy drinking are internal costs, whereas payroll taxes not paid as a result of early death or retirement are external costs. Medical and disability costs that are reimbursed by insurance are internal if the insurance premium is paid by the drinker and reflects his true risk status, and external otherwise. Traffic fatalities and injuries are also divided between internal (where the injury is to the drunk driver himself) and external (where someone else is injured in an accident involving a drunk driver). The question of where the line should be drawn between internal and external is especially difficult with respect to intra-family effects. Family members have individual interests that are sometimes in conflict, though these differences remain "internal" to the extent that they can be negotiated within the family (Heien and Pittman 1993; Heien 1995). Nonetheless, there is a clear public stake in preventing alcohol-induced family violence, child abuse and neglect, and fetal damage. The "fairness" problem with including these costs in the justification for higher excise taxes is that the other family members may end up paying twice if the drinker does not change his or her behavior—the higher tax reduces money left over for other members of the household.

Another gray area between internal and external costs is with respect to injuries to passengers of vehicles driven by drunk drivers. If the passengers are consenting adults, then their choice reveals their judgment that accepting the ride is preferable to the next-best alternative. This argument appears to generalize to all users of the road, who presumably know there is some chance of encountering a drunk driver when they choose to drive on it, and choose to accept that risk. But voluntary acceptance in this case does not imply that there is no externality. If other users of the road were able to negotiate directly with the drunk, they would likely find room for a bargain that kept the drunk from driving. That is less clear for the case of vehicle passengers, who presumably do have the opportunity to negotiate with the drunk (Cook and Moore 2000, 1661).

Finally, there is some ambiguity concerning the "drinker should pay" criterion. Suppose the alcohol excise tax was increased so that total collections were equal to the external costs associated with drinking. The increase in these tax rates would cause a reduction in tax collections from other sources (Sammartino 1990). Boyd and Seldon (1991), using a computable general equilibrium model, estimate that an increase in alcohol and tobacco taxes will increase net government revenue by only 60 percent of the increase in collections on those taxes. The "loss" of 40 percent is the result of the tax consequences of the reallocation of economic activity induced by the tax increases.

The appeal of the "user fee" argument is stronger if the excise tax revenues (net or gross) are dedicated to financing relevant activities, such as supporting emergency medical response, trauma care, and alcoholism prevention and treatment. An analogy is the federal excise tax on gasoline, much of which is dedicated to the Highway Trust Fund. Former Surgeon General C. Everett Koop advocated for an alcohol-tax increase as a source of funding for programs to redress drinking problems: "I strongly recommend that states consider 5 cents a drink to be the minimum tax increase. After all, who could quarrel with a 'nickel a drink' user fee that will generate billions of dollars to help save lives?" (Center for Science in the Public Interest 1990). But even if the revenues go into the general fund, as they do in most states, it is still true that these taxes provide compensation by either reducing other taxes or increasing government services.

Incidence and Vertical Equity

A common objection to alcohol excise taxes is that they are "regressive." In a literal sense this is just a technical term meaning that on average, a larger percentage of the income of poorer households goes to pay this tax than is true for richer households. That's true, without a doubt. But the *connotation* of the term "regressive," that the alcohol tax is therefore unfair, seems misplaced. Reframing the alcohol tax as a user fee clarifies the situation. Without these taxes, or with the tax rates too low, drinkers pay less than the true cost of their drinks. The public is in a sense subsidizing the heavy drinkers and alcohol abusers. The user fee then serves as a correction. If we deem it fair and equitable that each consumer pay the full costs of her choices—especially those choices involving purely recreational activities such as drinking—then the regressivity of the alcohol tax is of much less concern than the regressivity of the sales tax on, say, food. A lower-income household can escape the burden of this tax by adopting the drinking habits of the large majority in every income category who abstain or drink so little as to ensure that alcohol tax payments are a negligible part of the household budget.

Still, since the concern about regressivity is part of the debate about alcohol taxes, it is useful to review the evidence on the subject. As a first approximation, it is enough to know how quantity of drinks consumed maps onto household income. In chapter 4 we saw that the prevalence of drinking increases with income, from around 50 percent for the lowest income category (less than $20,000 per year in 2001) up to near 80 percent in the top category (greater than $80,000 per year). Thus, the likelihood of paying *any* alcohol taxes increases with income. Average quantity of drinks per year also tends to increase somewhat with income. But the increase is less than proportional, ensuring that excise (unit) taxes are regressive by the standard technical definition—alcohol excise taxes constitute a declining percentage of household budgets as income increases. In contrast, several studies have documented the fact that an *ad valorem* tax (such as a sales tax) on alcohol would be far less regressive, and in fact near proportional over the broad middle range of household incomes (Sammartino 1990; Poterba 1989; Lyon and Schwab 1995). Expenditures increase more strongly with income than does consumption, because of increases in "quality" of alcohol purchased. But the excise tax rates are not affected by quality.

A deeper inquiry into the distributional effects of an increase in alcohol excise taxes would be interesting but very challenging. Since the taxes are passed along to consumers in the form of higher prices, and with a substantial markup, it is doubtful that higher taxes have much effect on the profitability of the industry (chapter 10). But the higher prices will engender a reduction in drinking and its consequences, which will have manifold benefits including such possibilities as a general reduction in auto insurance rates. It is also true that higher taxes would reduce alcoholic-beverage production, importation, and sales, with the result that some jobs may be lost. Although this effect is front and center when the alcohol industry lobbies for lower taxes, it is mostly irrelevant to the public interest. Higher alcohol taxes will not shrink *overall* employment. Jobs lost in the alcohol industry will open up elsewhere. So even though there may be transition costs for some workers, the overall scope and health of the U.S. economy does not depend on preserving employment in the alcohol industry.

EFFICIENCY

In the normative framework of public health, a high priority is placed on reducing morbidity and mortality; if an increase in alcohol taxes helps achieve that purpose, then that is sufficient justification (Beauchamp 1980). In contrast, the normative framework traditionally favored by economists defines the public interest in terms of individual preferences, as revealed by choices in the marketplace and elsewhere. If people choose to place their own health and safety at risk by drinking too much, that choice is to be respected and is not in itself an argument for raising alcohol taxes. But the external costs of drinking do provide a justification, not only because it is "fair" for the drinker to pay (as discussed in the previous section), but also because it is "efficient." If alcohol prices are too low (less than the full cost of production and consumption), then people will tend to drink too much—not necessarily in the medical sense, but in the sense that the personal utility provided by some of those drinks (those at the margin) will be less than the full costs of production plus consumption externalities associated with those drinks.

Taxes imposed as a correction for free-market prices that do not reflect full social costs are called "Pigovian" in honor of Arthur C. Pigou, who developed the theoretical justification for such taxes (1962). In practice, the Pigovian tax would likely be somewhat larger than the "user fee" tax. Rather than cover the average external costs of per capita alcohol consumption, the ideal for the sake of efficiency is to set the tax rate high enough to cover the marginal social costs. Since for both individuals and communities the social cost per drink tends to increase with total consumption, the marginal cost exceeds the average cost.

The application of the corrective tax principle to drinking has the same difficulty as in setting the user fee: unlike the tax rate, the external cost of a drink differs depending on various characteristics of the drinker, the time and place of consumption, and how many drinks have been consumed already. It is possible to institute some crude differentiation in tax rates, such as on-premise versus off-premise, but not enough. Peter Diamond (1974) demonstrated that when social costs differ with circumstances, the value of that uniform tax which maximizes social welfare (under certain assumptions) is equal to a weighted average of the marginal external costs. Pogue and Sgontz (1989) applied this theory to the case of alcoholic beverages, with a model that assumes all drinkers can be classified as either "abusers" or "nonabusers." In that model, the correct tax depends on the proportion of the drinking population who are abusers, and their price elasticity of demand relative to nonabusers. An alternative approach that does not require this artificial dichotomy and takes better advantage of the empirical literature utilizes direct estimates of the effects of a change in tax on alcohol consumption, and on highway fatalities and other damages. The former is the basis for estimating incremental loss of consumers' surplus, while the latter can be used to estimate the reduction in social cost. Taxes should be increased as long as the latter exceeds the former.

A number of authors have suggested that the principle of corrective taxation be extended to account for the tendency of consumers to underestimate the internal costs of their drinking (as discussed in chapter 9). If consumers tend to disregard certain costly consequences of their drinking out of ignorance or myopia, then a higher tax may bring their drinking closer into line with their "true" preferences (Atkinson and Meade 1974;

Phelps 1988; Godfrey and Harrison 1990; Kenkel and Manning 1996; Gruber and Köszegi 2004).

This analysis of efficiency presumes that the price system functions well in other respects. In fact, numerous distortions are introduced by taxes, monopoly power, and externalities. For one example, taxes on income have the effect of reducing the incentives to work. Taxes reduce take-home pay and may distort such choices as how much to work, how much effort to expend while working, and how much to invest in education and training (Rosen 1980). One approach to correcting for the disincentive effects of income taxation is to impose special taxes on commodities that are complements to leisure and substitutes for investment in human capital (Kay and Keen 1986, 88; Slemrod 1990, 159; Corlett and Hague 1953). Alcohol is believed to be one such commodity, a conclusion supported by the results reported in chapter 8. The taxes on labor income then support an efficiency argument for higher taxes on alcohol. On the other hand, it can be argued that alcohol beverage prices are inflated above marginal costs by the market power of producers and the artificially costly requirements of the three-tier distribution system. The analyst faces a daunting task in attempting to identify and quantify all relevant inefficiencies in the economy that could influence the calculation of an "optimal" set of alcohol taxes. But current taxes are so low relative to external costs that we can be confident in the "right" direction to take them—upward.

Since the bulk of the external cost results from drunk driving, alcohol-induced violence, and other behavior that is subject to sanctions, then it might be more efficient to increase the price imposed on violators than to increase the alcohol tax (Kenkel 1996). For the case of drunk driving, that "price" includes legal and private penalties if apprehended and convicted, as well as the expected cost of causing an accident, which in the United States may include an increase in insurance-premium rates and civil liability (Sloan and Githens 1994; Sloan, Reilly, and Schenzler 1995). Still, imposing stiffer sanctions is socially costly in itself, and constrained by various practical and ethical considerations.[5] And no matter how stiff the sanctions, there will be some who will ignore them and drive drunk or fight anyway. Given these concerns, there would remain an important role for taxes to preempt problematic drinking even if the authorities were doing everything appropriate to sanction bad behavior. (See chapter 9 for additional discussion of this point.)

The Case for Uniform Taxes

A can of beer, a glass of wine, and a shot of liquor all contain approximately the same amount of ethanol, but are taxed at different rates; the federal excise tax on a shot of liquor exceeds the tax on a can of beer by a factor of two and on a glass of wine by a factor of three. Why these large differences? The case for taxing ethanol at a uniform rate regardless of the type of beverage is quite compelling (Center for Science in the Public Interest 1990). A strong move in that direction occurred in 1990 during the first Bush administration, when Congress doubled the federal tax on beer while the tax rate on spirits was pushed up by just 8 percent. (The wine tax was increased from 7 cents per gallon to $1.07 per gallon.) But there's still a long way to go.

The tax principles discussed above help organize the discussion. The one clear source of support for the current large differences is historical convention. The practice of taxing spirits higher than other beverages has been a feature of U.S. tax practice since the beginning. But the principles of fairness and efficiency offer more support for uniformity.

The historical myth is that beer should be taxed more lightly than spirits because it is the "drink of moderation," and what's more, the drink of the "working man"—of "Joe Six-Pack." Be that as it may have been, these notions don't get much support in modern times. Expenditures on beer and spirits both tend to be proportional to income over the broad middle range of incomes (Sammartino 1990). And the notion that spirits are in some sense more intoxicating than beer, and hence more subject to abuse, receives little support from the evidence. In fact, one summary of the literature concludes: "The consistent observation is that most drinkers prefer beer, and that drinkers who prefer beer are more likely to drive while intoxicated (DWI) than those who prefer wine or distilled spirits" (Berger and Snortum 1985, 232). This same study concludes that beer is disproportionately preferred by higher risk groups: men far more than women, youths far more than older people, those who drink a lot during a typical session far more than those who drink moderately. Although these results do not imply that tax uniformity is the best policy, they do challenge the current structure, where beer is taxed much lower than spirits.

Application of the efficiency principle leads to a similar conclusion. If the structure of taxes across the three types of alcoholic beverage does not reflect differences in external costs, then consumers will be induced to purchase an inefficient mix of beverages. There is no reason to believe that the marginal social cost of beer consumption is less than the marginal social cost of spirits consumption, and the reverse may well be true. One analysis that took careful account of external costs and the possibility of substitution among beverage types concluded as a "best guess" that efficient beer taxes would be 1.25 times spirits taxes and wine taxes would be about 1.08 times spirits taxes (Saffer and Chaloupka 1994, 39). Unless historical precedent is given a great deal of weight, then, there is a strong case for raising beer and wine taxes relative to spirits taxes.

Concluding Thoughts

Alcoholic beverages are too cheap for our own good. The obvious solution is to raise excise taxes. That conclusion is supported by historical precedent—federal tax rates on spirits and beer are lower as of 2006 than at any time since the Korean War. And it is supported by principles of fairness and efficiency. If tax rates are so low that drinkers do not pay for the damage they do, then those costs are distributed unfairly among everyone, without regard to their contribution to the problem. What's more, if alcoholic beverages are in effect subsidized by the public, then too much of our resources are devoted to producing and consuming alcohol. The result is a lower standard of living across the board.

For some, the arguments about fairness and efficiency enhancement are of less interest than improving the public health. Often the argument is that alcohol taxes should be raised and dedicated to financing programs to prevent alcohol abuse and underage drinking, finance stepped-up effort against DUI, and so forth—and ten states do earmark these taxes. But whether or not it makes sense to dedicate alcohol tax revenues in this fashion, raising tax rates would help accomplish these purposes *even without the stepped up expenditures on prevention and enforcement*. Alcohol taxes promote the public health and safety.

The empirical evidence in support of this conclusion is quite clear, even if it does contradict much intuition (Grossman et al. 1993; Chaloupka, Grossman, and Saffer 2002; Cook and Moore 2000). It is a great challenge to coach that prevalent intuition so that it conforms with what the data tell us. Somehow that battle has been won in the case of tobacco, but has scarcely been engaged when it comes to alcohol. Maybe it helps to think of it this way: There are all kinds of institutions seeking to combat alcohol abuse, including families, churches, schools, health departments, workplaces, and law enforcement agencies. Is their job harder or easier if alcohol is cheap?

CHAPTER 12

Youth as a Special Case

> Those who are still in a state to require being taken care of
> by others, must be protected against their own actions as well
> as external injury.
> —John Stuart Mill, *On Liberty*

> We gamble when we extend choices to the not-yet-adult. If
> we win, the experience gained in decision-making becomes an
> integral part of a process of achieving adulthood. If we lose,
> harm can come to the adolescent and the community.
> —Zimring, *The Changing Legal World of Adolescence*

MY STUDENTS AGREE ON TWO things—the transcendent importance of
Duke basketball, and the absurdity of campus drinking regulations. On
the latter issue they sound much like critics of social policy through the
ages, whose arguments, as Albert Hirschman has documented, can be
summarized as "futility," "perversity," or "jeopardy" (1991). They assert
that the effort to ban drinking by underage students is futile, and even
perverse in that it pushes the party scene off campus where it is more
dangerous and strains town-gown relationships. A deeper criticism is that
these control measures jeopardize the effort to create a sense of community on campus. More than a few faculty members are sympathetic to
these arguments, perhaps in some cases due to fond memories of their
own college years when the de facto (or even de jure) policy was more
tolerant.

But for better or worse, youths live under a more stringent regime these
days, and not just on campus. The national minimum legal drinking age
has been twenty-one since the 1980s. States have adopted zero-tolerance
polices for drivers under that age, and alcohol law enforcement agencies
give top priority to combating sales to underage customers. Liability concerns have emerged as a powerful influence for colleges and even parents
who may otherwise be inclined to allow drinking at, say, a high school
graduation party. In short, alcohol control has been embraced by legislators and advocates as an important part of the answer for combating
youthful drinking. The main argument in its favor is simple—regardless
of the problems it may cause at residential colleges, this approach has had

some success in reducing drinking and abuse nationwide. Still, there are limits to what can be accomplished by a youth-only focus. Regardless of the regulations, underage drinking is closely linked to adult drinking.

THE PROBLEMS OF YOUTH

Adolescents are dangerous to themselves and others. The physical attributes of their emerging adulthood—size, strength, sexual maturity—typically develop prior to the cognitive attributes—perspective, judgment, sense of responsibility, impulse control, ability to resist peer suggestion. Parental authority tends to give out long before youths make the transition to adult roles, leaving an awkward hiatus (Room 2004, 656). Crime- and violence-commission rates, unwanted pregnancy rates, and risk of causing a fatal traffic accident all peak during this stage of life; in fact, "adolescents are overrepresented statistically in virtually every category of reckless behavior" (Arnett 1992, 339). That would probably be true even if youths didn't drink—but the fact that they do drink, and drink heavily, multiplies the risk.

The primary source of data on youthful drinking and drug abuse is Monitoring the Future, a survey conducted annually since 1975. In this survey, about one-half of high school seniors admit to drinking in the past thirty days, and almost one-third indicate that they got drunk—troubling statistics that have remained steady since the early 1990s.[1] For both college students and college-aged youths generally, the thirty-day prevalence of drinking has been about two-thirds during that period, without any noticeable trend. (Drinking and bingeing were still more common among youths during the 1970s and 1980s.) The thirty-day prevalence of binge drinking (five or more drinks in a row) was 41 percent for full-time college students, and 36 percent for others of college age, in 2002 (Windle 2003, 82). Approximately one in six drinks sold nationwide is consumed by someone under twenty-one years old.[2]

An analysis by Ted Miller and his associates provides a summary of the social costs of underage drinking (2005). Based on results from the epidemiological literature, they estimate a total of 3,170 deaths attributable to underage drinking in 2001, of which 55 percent were due to traffic crashes and 35 percent to interpersonal violence (homicide). Once account is taken of nonfatal injuries and the age of the victims, the relative importance of interpersonal violence increases, accounting for 67 percent of lost quality-adjusted life-years (QALYs). By this measure, then, the social costs of underage drinking reside predominantly with criminal violence—injuries from assault, robbery, and rape that would not have occurred in the absence of alcohol abuse by those under twenty-one. Traffic crashes contribute 19 percent. One conclusion is that most of the immediate damage done by underage drinking is not to the drinker himself, but to those who are victimized by the drinker, although self-inflicted injury deaths—suicide, poisoning by overdose, and drowning—make notable contributions to the overall toll.[3]

The longer-term developmental effects of youthful drinking are also noteworthy, albeit difficult to quantify. Ongoing research offers evidence that alcohol can do permanent damage to the development of the adolescent brain. Some background is helpful to understand what's at stake here. Although the brain achieves its full size well before adolescence, it continues to mature through age twenty or later (Zeigler et al. 2005). The prefrontal area of the brain becomes more efficient as it matures, and better able "to execute such tasks as planning, integrating information, abstract thinking, problem solving, judgment, and reasoning" (Zeigler et al. 2005, 26).[4] The hippocampus and other limbic-system structures also develop during this period. From experiments on animals, and from brain scans and cognitive tests of human adolescents, it appears that drinking may interfere with the brain's development and cause impairment that continues into adulthood. The evidence of damage is particularly strong with respect to learning and memory (Brown and Tapert 2004; Zeigler et al. 2005). But it is not clear at this time what the "dose response" curve looks like, and in particular whether moderate drinking has any deleterious effect.

The possibility of permanent alcohol-induced brain damage adds to a well-established list of concerns associated with youthful alcohol abuse. In addition to the heightened risk of injury and criminal involvement, youths who drink heavily are more likely to engage in risky sex with resulting exposure to STDs and unwanted pregnancy, and according to some studies they are more likely to drop out of school (but see below). Of particular concern are individuals who begin drinking regularly before age fifteen—in addition to various other risks, they have an elevated chance of becoming alcohol dependent as adults (Grant and Dawson 1997). None of these statistical associations is necessarily the result of a direct causal process. If this were the only evidence, one possible interpretation would be that alcohol abuse results from a general taste for risk taking that is also conducive to engaging in risky sex, or that an innately strong taste for alcohol engenders both early drinking and later dependence.

The 1997 National Longitudinal Survey of Youth is one of the best sources of data with which to further describe the extent to which youthful drinking is predictive of subsequent problems. This federal survey has a representative sample of individuals age thirteen to seventeen at the time of the first interview in 1997. Subsequent interviews have been conducted with the participants on an annual basis, and cover demographic characteristics, family, school, work, criminal activities, and substance abuse. Tracking respondents from junior year in high school, we find that most graduated the following year (71 percent of males and 77 percent of females), and over a quarter matriculated in a four-year college or university in that year (26 percent of males, 33 percent of females).[5] From an analysis of the individual characteristics predictive of school continuation, it appears that drinking in junior year is largely irrelevant, with the exception (for females only) of those who are frequent binge drinkers (Cook and Hutchinson 2005). To be precise, in a logit regression that controls for family characteristics,[6] cognitive ability, and smoking, those juniors who reported drinking in the previous month were just as likely to complete high school and go on to college as those who reported that they did not drink. The small group of females (7 percent) who report having five or more drinks at least once a week were at heightened risk of not graduating or going on to college. For male respondents, this sort of frequent bingeing (11 percent of respondents) had little or no effect on the likelihood of graduation or the likelihood of college matriculation. That null result does not rule out the possibility that drinking impairs cognitive ability, since the regressions control for ability.[7]

In the same analysis, smoking, unlike drinking, proves to be a strong predictor of ending school early, either by dropping out of high school or not going on to college. Since it is hard to imagine that smoking has much direct effect on school performance, that result reminds us once again that choices like drinking and smoking are at least in part *signals* rather than *causes*. A sixteen-year-old who smokes is sending a signal (perhaps unwittingly) of being off track in school, whereas drinking does not convey any additional information unless the drinking is heavy and frequent—and then only for females. Whether drinking has a direct *causal* effect on the likelihood of school continuation is a different question, one that is better answered by a quasi-experimental approach. An analysis by economists Thomas Dee and William Evans of the effect of changes in the MLDA on high school graduation rates is just such a study (2003). They report that increases in the MLDA during the 1970s and 1980s had no measurable effect on high school graduation or college matriculation rates.

Finally, there is some quasi-experimental evidence on the question of habit formation. My research with Michael Moore (2001) demonstrated that youths who at age fourteen were living in a state with a minimum drinking age of eighteen were more likely to engage in weekly binge drinking years later than those who were living in states with a higher minimum age. This result holds even after controlling for individual characteristics and circumstances. Experiments on animals also point to habituation from youthful drinking (Yoshimoto et al. 2002).

In sum, adolescence is a risk-filled time of life, made more so by drinking. Drinkers who survive adolescence may suffer lingering cognitive deficits, although drinking per se is not predictive of completing high school or going on to college. Early drinking is habit forming, so that those who start early have a stronger taste for alcohol than they otherwise would later in life. The greatest immediate cost of youthful drinking is increased involvement in violent crime.

DILEMMAS OF REGULATING YOUTHFUL BEHAVIOR

For governments, schools, and parents alike, regulating youthful behavior poses a variety of dilemmas. The first dilemma results from the conflict between two important goals: keeping adolescents from harming themselves and others, and providing them with the opportunity to gain experience. Franklin E. Zimring notes, "a few of the things we cannot learn to do well without practice: making decisions, making love, driving, flying, practicing law, parenting, taking risks, saying no, and—most important— choosing the path of our lives in a free society" 1982, 89). He continues: "We gamble when we extend choices to the not-yet-adult. If we win, the experience gained in decision-making becomes an integral part of a process of achieving adulthood. If we lose, harm can come to the adolescent and the community." The chances of losing this gamble can be limited by finding ways to provide opportunity to gain experience in circumstances that offer special limits and protections. He suggests the image of the learner's permit for new drivers as a model (1982, chapter 7).

Of course, the learner's permit notion applies to activities that are a legitimate, normal part of adult life, such as driving, having sex, and managing money. Drinking is such an activity for most American families, while smoking and drug use are not. Following this line of reasoning, parents might be well advised to teach their teenagers about drinking, for example by giving them a chance to experience wine or beer with dinner at home. That could help demystify alcohol and model safe drinking practices (assuming that the parents themselves drink moderately). But as sociologist Robin Room points out, alcohol has a variety of "use values," and teaching the use of wine or beer as a complement to a good meal does not necessarily provide the youth with the experience to make good decisions about whether and how much to drink while out with friends on a Saturday night, where intoxication is the principal use value (2004).

A second dilemma arises from the obvious fact that kids don't follow the rules, and their stratagems for evading the rules may make things worse. Just because parents, schools, or state authorities decree that youths shall abstain (from alcohol, sex, tobacco, violent videos, gambling) until a certain age does not make it so. Prohibition may create an allure, as in the old English proverb "forbidden fruit is sweet." The reference, of course, is to the apple from the tree of knowledge that proved to be Eve and Adam's downfall. Morris Chafetz, the first director of the National Institute of Alcoholism and Alcohol Abuse, stressed the dangers of the "forbidden fruit" effect. "One thing is clear: admonitions never to drink, particularly in the complex societies of today, frequently bring about the opposite results" (Chafetz and Demone 1962, 185). He goes on to say that "Alcohol should not be set up in the family as the motivation for rebellion. If the adolescent wishes to revolt (and most American youngsters do) he will most often turn to whatever is forbidden—in this case, alcohol" (1962, 233).

Contrary to Chafetz's prediction, prohibition of drinking by youths through state minimum-age laws has had the effect of reducing the likelihood that they will drink or abuse alcohol. And, contrary to the conventional wisdom, American teens tend to be less likely to drink frequently or get drunk than European teens, where laws and public attitudes concerning youthful drinking are far more permissive and tolerant (Currie et al. 2000; Cook and Moore 2001). The allure of a forbidden activity is apparently trumped (on balance) by the reduction in availability.

Of course that does not settle the matter of whether the minimum age reduces alcohol abuse. When youths are barred from drinking legally, many drink anyway; since they are forced to drink on the sly, they may choose a place and manner more dangerous than if they could drink at clubs or chaperoned parties—exactly the point my students insist on. So even if we accept abstinence as the ideal for youths up to age twenty-one, the effort to achieve that ideal through prohibition may have unintended, damaging consequences. A plausible argument—but once again, the evidence points the other way. In particular, although there may be exceptions for some groups of youths (possibly including students at residential colleges), the overall net effect of the minimum age laws is to reduce DUI and other risk taking associated with drinking.

A third dilemma is whether to support institutions that have responsibility for youths, or to preempt their authority with direct government regulation. Instead of a blanket minimum-age law, exceptions could be made for military bases, college campuses, and, most compellingly, families. These institutions are in a position to provide a relatively safe environment with rules that are suited to the youths in question. In fact, nineteenth-century minimum age laws allowed parents to provide their children with drinks (Mosher 1980), and in modern times some states have continued this tradition by carving out parental exceptions to the minimum age laws. But most states impose a blanket prohibition.

Finally is the familiar dilemma that arises whenever freedom conflicts with safety. As we saw in chapter 9, John Stuart Mill's harm principle provided one answer to this dilemma—that protection of the individual was never justification to use the coercive power of government to restrict his choices. But Mill did not apply this stricture to youths, who he thought must be protected against their own actions (Zimring 1982, 16). The question, then, is at what age (or other indicator of adulthood) should government policy become more concerned with freedom than safety when it comes to self-hazardous behavior?

The spectrum of age-based rights and responsibilities grants or imposes adult status by age eighteen for all but a few activities. At that age individuals can vote, serve on juries, and hold most public offices, enlist in the military or work at any job without parental consent, undertake contractual obligations including marriage, and buy lottery tickets, cigarettes, and shotguns. By age eighteen or before (depending on the state) they have adult status in the criminal justice system, are entitled to obtain an unrestricted driver's license, and are no longer subject to protection from the statutory rape laws. But in every state, the legal purchase of alcohol is restricted to those who have had their twenty-first birthday. This law appears out of line with the other markers of adulthood, and is definitely out of line with European countries, almost all of which have adopted a minimum age for alcohol purchase of eighteen or younger (Room 2004, 662). (Canada's provinces have set theirs at eighteen or nineteen, and Mexico at eighteen.) In America, a 20-year-old soldier can be arrested for celebrating his safe return from war by drinking with friends; a 20-year-old bride cannot legally toast her new husband with anything stronger than grape juice. It is not surprising that the minimum drinking age and its enforcement have been contentious. The events that led to a national political consensus in support of twenty-one as the minimum age suggest a narrowing of the debate to just one of the various concerns—highway safety—to the exclusion of other issues. The arguments for a lower minimum age still have some appeal, and not just to the college students (Scrivo 1998).

The Ascendance of Twenty-one as the Minimum Age

Following Repeal, most states set the minimum age for legal purchase of alcohol at twenty-one. New York and Louisiana were outliers, with a MLDA of eighteen, while a dozen other states had a split age, lower for beer than liquor. These age limits remained quite static through the 1960s, albeit with some changes in the scope and penalties associated with the prohibition (Mosher 1980). But that was not to last. The coming of age of the Baby Boomers and the political pressures engendered by the Vietnam War led to adoption of the Twenty-sixth Amendment in 1970, giving eighteen-year-olds the right to vote. In the five years following, a number of states lowered the age of adult legal status for contracting a financial obligation to eighteen. And twenty-nine states lowered their minimum age for drinking. By 1975, most states had established eighteen or nineteen as the minimum age for all beverages.

At the time, lawmakers' concerns about the consequences of a possible increase in youthful drinking gave way to wartime rhetoric. As Michigan state Senator Daniel Cooper observed, "If he is responsible enough to serve as a platoon leader with eight or 10 men under him in a life or death combat situation, you can't tell him he's not responsible enough to drink."[8] Besides, there was little systematic evidence on the effects of minimum age laws on public safety. Obviously they were routinely violated by millions of youths. Arrests and punishments were few. The laws appeared a primarily symbolic expression of official views regarding appropriate behavior (Bonnie 1978).

But evidence started accumulating that these laws had more effect than previously understood. States that lowered their minimum age limits experienced an increase in traffic fatalities resulting from drinking by young drivers. The evidence was sufficiently persuasive to reverse the political tide, helped by the end of the Vietnam War. No states lowered their minimum age after 1976, and a number reversed previous reductions. In 1983, President Reagan's Commission on Drunk Driving recommended that Congress establish a national minimum age of twenty-one, citing the evidence on the beneficial effects of raising the MLDA and the particular problems stemming from neighboring states with different MLDAs. For example, Illinois college-aged youths often drove north to drink legally in Wisconsin bars and then returned home drunk; the result became known as the "Blood Border." Subsequent congressional hearings made much of a study by the Insurance Institute for Highway Safety which estimated that a national minimum of twenty-one would save 730 lives per year (Williams et al. 1983; Males 1986; Wagenaar 1993). Congress did not legislate the minimum directly, but rather enacted a provision that pressured each state to adopt twenty-one as the minimum age by threatening to withhold federal highway funds. The Supreme Court eventually ruled this law constitutional, despite the Twenty-first Amendment's stricture that the authority to regulate alcohol was a state prerogative.[9] By 1988, the last state (Wyoming) had complied, and twenty-one was the minimum age of purchase and public possession everywhere in the United States.

It should be noted that the state MLDAs are not entirely uniform.[10] State laws generally outlaw selling or furnishing to a minor; purchase, possession, and consumption by a minor; and use of false identification by a minor to obtain alcohol. But a handful of states create exceptions to the prohibition on possession and consumption. The exceptions specify circumstances in which a parent is present or gives consent, or the drinking occurs in a private residence. (In a few states a legal-age spouse can authorize drinking.) More common are exceptions for religious, medicinal, or educational purposes (think culinary school!). A number of states allow eighteen-year-olds to sell and even serve alcoholic beverages. Despite these differences, relatively minor in practice, it is reasonable to say that there is a national minimum drinking age.

As discussed in chapter 6, the churning of state minimum age laws during the 1970s and 1980s created a natural experiment that provided considerable information on the effects of such laws. The "experimental" feature is important because a valid "control group" was needed. There were strong trends in national drinking practices during that period which could and did get confounded with the effect of the MLDA changes. Nationwide per capita consumption peaked around 1980 and dropped steeply during the 1980s. Drinking by youths followed this same pattern. The predominant reason was not changes in state MLDA laws, but rather the close link between youthful and adult alcohol consumption (Cook and Moore 2001). Increasing the MLDA did make some difference, but not as much as might be guessed from a simple "before and after" comparison.

One review article summarized dozens of peer-reviewed studies (Wagenaar and Toomey 2002). Most of the seventy-nine high-quality studies of MLDA on traffic crashes found the expected result that a higher age was associated with a lower rate; none of these studies found the opposite. Several reputable studies found evidence that MLDA reduced other problems, such as suicide and drinking problems. Various speculations about possible harmful effects of a high MLDA—that it might aggravate drinking problems later in life, or increase marijuana use—appear unfounded (Wagenaar and Toomey 2002; Males 1986; Pacula 1998). A variety of statistical methods have been used in these evaluation studies. In cases where state-level data are available on outcome measures, the RASPP method discussed in chapter 7 has provided particularly strong evidence.

The qualitative conclusion is clear: If a state decided to reduce its MLDA this year, additional lives would be lost in traffic crashes. Just how many lives are at stake is not known or even knowable, since the estimates are out of date. But it appears that the stakes are lower now than they were in the 1980s, in part because the campaign against drunk driving has been so successful. Back when states were changing their MLDAs (and thus generating statistical evidence), there was higher per capita consumption and a considerably higher alcohol involvement in fatal crashes.

In the national roadside surveys (discussed in chapter 3), the percentage of drivers under age twenty-one with BACs in excess of 0.10 percent declined from 4.1 percent in 1973, to just 0.3 percent in 1996. For the sixteen-to-twenty age group, the number of alcohol-related traffic fatalities nationwide declined by over half between the mid-1980s and 2002, a time when the MLDAs were constant. So what would happen if the MLDA were lowered today? One RASPP study found that the reductions from twenty-one to eighteen during the early 1970s caused on average a 7 percent increase in traffic fatality deaths for youths age sixteen to twenty (Cook and Tauchen 1984). Now the effect would likely be considerably smaller.

Part of the credit for the reduction in DUI by youths goes to the zero-tolerance (ZT) laws. After several states imposed ZT with good results (Hingson, Heeran, and Winter 1994), in 1995 Congress made them a requirement for all states under threat of withdrawal of highway funds. The federal law required that states extend DUI laws to include youths driving after just one or two drinks (a BAC of 0.02 percent or greater), rather than the normal standard for adults of 0.08 percent. These laws have had some influence in persuading youths to separate drinking and driving, but have also had the unexpected additional benefit of reducing youthful drinking (Carpenter 2004a).

Currently, the bulk of the damage to public safety from underage drinking is the result of violent crime rather than impaired driving. Unfortunately, the direct evidence on whether and how a reduction in MLDA would affect youth violence is scant.

ENFORCING THE PROHIBITION ON YOUTHFUL DRINKING

Although minimum age prohibitions reduce youthful drinking, abuse, and injury rates, they are widely violated. As we have seen, half of high school seniors drink regularly, and the percentage is higher yet for college-aged youths. To put it more starkly, a majority of youths are made criminals by the minimum age laws, and so too are a large number of older people who are selling or furnishing the alcohol to them. In the face of so much criminal activity, few resources are devoted to enforcement, and the threat of punishment is dilute (Hafemeister and Jackson 2004). All this is a bit reminiscent of national Prohibition during the 1920s.

When high school students are asked about where they get their drinks, most indicate friends, parties, and family members as sources, or that they took them from someone's home. Relatively few actually purchase alcohol from commercial sources, either on-premise or off (Bonnie and O'Connell 2004; Harrison, Fulkerson, and Park 2000; Wagenaar et al. 1996). Social connections to older friends and relatives predominate. The source of that secondary transaction may be a friend doing a favor, the host of a party, or someone who is actually being paid something for his trouble. Or the transaction may be inadvertent, as in the case of a teenager taking a bottle from her parents' supply. These transactions, together with direct sales to minors, may be viewed as constituting a huge underground market. Notably this market, unlike markets for some illegal drugs, is free of violence or gang warfare. In fact, it is completely unorganized—precisely because there are so many adults ready to play the role of supplier.

It is interesting to imagine what would happen if law enforcement agencies decided to crack down on this market. Youths would be arrested for possession of alcohol and then grilled about their source under pressure of conviction and punishment. As a routine matter, sources would be tracked down, arrested, and prosecuted, with a real possibility of a prison sentence. This sort of enforcement does occur on occasion, but it is surely rare. Ordinarily the public would rather that the police devote their scarce resources to "real" crime. So arrests for underage drinking usually occur only as a result of disorderly conduct or neighbors' complaints about noisy parties, with minor legal consequence.

Most states do have enforcement efforts targeted on commercial sellers and servers, but these efforts also tend to be highly dilute. Purchase surveys, involving undercover buys by minors working with alcohol law enforcement, find that half or more of commercial outlets will sell alcohol to an underage buyer (Bonnie and O'Connell 2004, 168). Even the more conscientious establishments that do insist on the purchaser's showing identification may have trouble determining whether it is a forgery or real. For youths who are not enterprising enough to manufacture their own fake ID (with help from the Internet), there are professional forgers ready to provide them (Carnevale 2002; Leinwand 2001). States also mount other sorts of enforcement efforts. "Cops in shops" operations seek to create some deterrent to minors who attempt to buy directly from a commercial outlet, by having an officer pose as a clerk and cite any minor who attempts to buy alcohol. "Shoulder tap" undercover operations seek to deter store customers from accommodating minors who ask them to buy alcohol for them.

Whatever the cumulative damage done by underage drinking, any one instance of underage possession or of furnishing to a minor is hardly a serious offense. Underage drinking is simply too common, too much a part of our culture and tradition, to condemn the drinker or his social supplier. In the absence of public condemnation, criminal enforcement is hard to motivate.[11] Of course, enforcement operations and citizen complaints can also serve as a basis for civil penalties, including fines and ABC license suspension or revocation. Having the authorities treat the illegal sale of alcohol as a civil or regulatory violation rather than a crime seems like a promising approach, though in practice it is exceedingly rare for ABC boards to revoke a license or impose a fine large enough to make a difference. Keg registration laws have been adopted by some states, and may facilitate the effort to hold buyers accountable for serving minors (Bonnie and O'Connell 2004, 174).

Civil liability is a useful supplement to such enforcement efforts as do occur, and has the great advantage of potentially overcoming the problem of limited motivation and resources that burdens the public authorities. Most states allow third parties to sue a commercial establishment if they are injured as a result of a negligent sale to an underage buyer, with different provisos and limitations (Mosher and other contributors 2002). A lawsuit may well be viewed by proprietors as a more serious threat than the possibility of being cited for an illegal sale during an undercover operation. There is evidence that commercial liability may reduce highway fatalities involving underage drivers by a few percentage points (Chaloupka et al. 1993; Sloan et al. 2000).

The primary goal of enforcement efforts is to motivate licensed establishments to do their part in enforcing the MLDA, to wit, saying "no" to underage would-be buyers. Even if effective, the potential of such efforts is limited, given the predominance of social (rather than commercial) sources. A more comprehensive effort requires enlisting parents, older siblings, and other adults who have responsibility for youths. A majority of states have established liability for social hosts under some circumstances (Mosher and other contributors 2002), which may have some influence with parents who are inclined to be tolerant of drinking at their teenagers' parties. For older youths, colleges and the military have a role to play.

Colleges and Universities

College life is not necessarily "Animal House," but without a doubt there is a great deal of drinking on college campuses. This reality could engender at least three types of response by the relevant authorities: benign neglect, selective enforcement, or zero tolerance (Room 2004). Benign neglect, simply looking the other way, is the stance that was adopted in the "good old days" by many residential colleges, reflecting not only a sense of futility in enforcing a minimum age rule, but also a lack of concern on the part of the authorities. It has been replaced nationwide by zero tolerance, at least as the official stance—any instance of underage drinking is forbidden and actionable. In practice, college and university officials are not interested in meting out harsh punishments to large numbers of students, so enforcement tends to be selective.

The adoption of an official ban on underage drinking on campus has not been inspired by an objective increase in the prevalence of drinking or abuse—indeed, the trend since 1980 has generally been downward (O'Malley and Johnston 2002). Further, and contrary to the conventional wisdom, attending college does not appear to be a cause of increased drinking, at least on average. An analysis of data from the National Longitudinal Survey of Youth (introduced above) for the year 2000 demonstrates that while college students as a group drink somewhat more than their out-of-school age peers, that difference disappears when account is taken of personal characteristics (including aptitude and family background) and living arrangements. Youths who live in an apartment or house with other youths are more likely to drink (and drink more) than those living at home or in supervised group quarters (such as a dormitory)—regardless of whether they are in college or not.[12]

So saying, college students drink a great deal and are quite likely to experience alcohol-related problems. The extent of the problem has been documented by a series of College Alcohol Surveys conducted by Harvard Public Health Professor Henry Wechsler and associates (1994, 2002). About two in five undergraduates at 4-year schools reported binge drinking in the two weeks before the survey, and half of these had binged three or more times—statistics that didn't change much across the four surveys conducted during the period 1993–2001 (Wechsler et al. 2002). By their own report, frequent bingers were several times more likely to miss a class, fall behind in their schoolwork, experience a blackout, engage in unplanned or unprotected sex, argue with friends, get hurt or injured, damage property, and get into trouble with campus or local police. Abusers also tended to get lower grades and avoid the more challenging majors (Wolaver 2002). Unsurprisingly, other students did not escape from alcohol problems, but had to put up with noise, disruption, and property destruction.

Because colleges and universities have both an ethical and legal duty to protect the welfare of their students, alcohol abuse is recognized as an institutional problem as well as a personal one.[13] A tabulation of lawsuits involving alcohol-related injuries on campus documented evidence of a large increase in the 1980s and 1990s (Pierson and Helms 2000). Many of these lawsuits were brought against fraternities, where liability for serving underage or drunken students follows from the legal responsibilities of social hosts.[14] Faced with escalating insurance premiums and increased pressure from college administrators, the National Interfraternity Conference adopted a plan in 1997 calling for the adoption of an alcohol-free housing policy (Nuwer 1999)—a plan also adopted by the national sororities, even though they have had many fewer problems. A number of national fraternities have since complied and gone officially "dry," although the level of compliance with these policies may be less than 100 percent.

The case of Scott Krueger, an MIT freshman who died of alcohol over-dose in 1997, became an important turning point in persuading higher-education officials to take seriously the necessity of curtailing alcohol abuse by underage students. Krueger's parents brought suit on the grounds that MIT did not do enough to protect him. The case was settled out of court for $6 million (Busteed 2005). A series of other high-profile deaths of undergraduates that same year led to the Higher Education Amendments of 1998, which clarified rules governing confidentiality of student records: colleges are allowed but not required to notify parents if a student commits a disciplinary violation involving alcohol or drugs (Bonnie and O'Connell 2004, 204). The *in loco parentis* doctrine of the 1950s has not been fully reestablished, but the public surely holds colleges responsible for protecting students against their own inclination to drink too much.

Although the trend is toward tougher regulation, "softer" approaches are still the most pervasive. As of 2002, the vast majority of four-year colleges offered counseling and treatment services, as well as alcohol education for incoming freshmen, but only 43 percent required all dorms to be alcohol-free (Wechsler, Meoykens, and DeJong 2004). There is something of a split between schools that ban alcohol at campus events and in dorms, and those that emphasize an education approach to reducing student drinking. The bottom line is that these efforts, taken together, have apparently not reduced the prevalence of alcohol abuse—as noted, there is little trend in binge drinking from the Harvard College Alcohol Surveys through 2001. What's more, higher education officials are concerned about the perverse effects of efforts to ban alcohol at campus events, including displacement to off-campus locations and more "underground" consumption (Wechsler, Moeykens, and DeJong 1995).

Progress may await a more comprehensive approach of "environmental management" that includes a systematic effort to enlist the community in cutting off both commercial and social sources of alcohol (DeJong and Langford 2002). In fact, college drinking behavior is linked to the behavior of adults in the relevant community. One analysis of bingeing rates by college students found a high positive correlation with the prevalence of bingeing by adults in the same state, and evidence that state alcohol control measures also influenced the amount college students drank (Nelson et al. 2005).

Military Service

Another institution that has responsibility for a large group of college-age youths is the military. In 2003, 180,000 enlisted men and women were younger than twenty-one, about 15 percent of the total active-duty personnel.[15] Traditionally the military has been a "wet" environment: heavy drinking has been the custom (Bryant 1974). The drinking tradition is something more than what would be expected given the predominance of young men—even after adjusting for other demographic characteristics, military personnel age eighteen to twenty-five are twice as likely to engage in binge drinking (five or more drinks at least weekly) than their civilian counterparts (Bray et al. 2003). But just as with college campuses, the military has sought to implement policies to reduce excessive drinking (Bray et al. 1999).

Until the mid-1980s, legal drinking was a perk of enlistment, and anyone on active duty could consume alcohol on military installations.[16] But with the encouragement of MADD and other advocacy groups, Congress required military-installation commanders to adopt the same drinking age as the state in which the military base is located (U.S. Code Title 10, Section 2683)—which is to say, twenty-one. This rule was codified by the Pentagon (DoD Instruction 1015.10) to include several interesting exceptions. First, the minimum age in installations outside the United States is eighteen, subject to the judgment of the local commander. And even in the U.S., the commander of a military installation may allow minors to drink in special circumstances: "those infrequent, non-routine military occasions when an entire unit, as a group, marks at a military installation a uniquely military occasion such as the conclusion of arduous military duty or the anniversary of the establishment of a military service or organization."

The new minimum age restrictions have been part of a broad post-Vietnam effort by the military to combat drug and alcohol abuse in the ranks. Although highly successful with respect to illicit drugs, it is not clear that this effort has accomplished much with respect to the prevalence of alcohol abuse. Though the trend has indeed been downward since the early 1980s, that can be accounted for by the changing demographic makeup of the military—older, more women, more highly educated, and so forth (Bray and Marsden 2000).

CONCLUDING THOUGHTS

The prevalence of drinking and bingeing by high school students increased during the 1970s, peaked around 1981, and declined sharply during the next decade. It has plateaued since then. This pattern tracks adult drinking quite faithfully, and indeed, it is hard to find any other explanation for the large swings in youthful drinking than the tendency of youths to mimic their elders (Cook and Moore 2001). As a result, there are limits to what can be accomplished through an alcohol-control program focused only on youths. That is not to say that youth-oriented controls are useless.

The case for a minimum drinking age is compelling. Drinking exacerbates the all-too-pervasive risks associated with adolescence, including reckless driving and violence, and may establish a drinking habit that will be hard to shake. The scary possibility of brain damage can't be ignored. And the MLDA has demonstrated effectiveness in reducing youthful abuse and its consequences. The claims of "futility" and "perversity" in its effects are not groundless, but on balance the effects are salutary.

Still, the MLDA's success comes at substantial cost, starting with a loss of freedom. Most twenty-year-olds enjoy drinking, at least on occasion. Although older adults tend to side with John Stuart Mill in discounting youthful preferences, freedom from government coercion is a good thing at any age. Identifying the precise age at which the value of freedom should have weight in evaluating safety measures is always going to have an arbitrary quality. In most respects, eighteen-year-olds have the same rights and responsibilities as older people, with the logical implication that their preferences are to be accorded public respect. Twenty-one then has no more justification than, say, twenty-five, as a minimum drinking age. A large majority of college-age youths demonstrate their disrespect for the twenty-one minimum by drinking; the possibility that their disregard for this law may carry over to other laws is worth considering.

One alternative to the current approach draws on Zimring's notion of the generalized learner's permit. The goal would be to provide youths with licit opportunities to drink in an environment that offers some protection against abuse and its consequences. That idea used to be embodied in the laws of those states that allowed youths to drink beer (or at least weak beer) several years before they could drink liquor. And the same rationale may justify exemptions for homes, military bases, and residential households. The zero-tolerance laws that make it illegal to drive after any amount of drinking are somewhat effective, and there is some sense in preserving twenty-one as the zero-tolerance limit even if a limited drinking privilege were extended to eighteen- or nineteen-year-olds.

It would be nice if it were possible to change youthful preferences with respect to drinking through education and prevention programs. If more kids were inclined to say no to alcohol, minimum age laws would be less burdensome, and indeed, less necessary. But needless to say, persuading adolescents to lead more abstemious lives is not easy. Even though classroom instruction on drinking, smoking, and drug use is universal, the message from evaluation research has been discouraging: education appears to be of little avail when it comes to influencing actual choices, as opposed to answering questions on a test (Babor et al. 2003, chap 11). It might be helpful to restrict advertising of alcoholic beverages directed at youths, but current interpretations of the First Amendment bar legislation to that effect (Bonnie and O'Connell 2004, chap. 7). Efforts to persuade or educate youths through public media campaigns have uncertain consequences for behavior, and may even boomerang (Atkin 2004).

A more radical proposal is that policymakers accept the implications of the fact that youthful alcohol abuse occurs in the context of adult drinking. A panel commissioned by Congress (through the National Academy of Sciences) to develop a strategy to reduce underage drinking concluded: "underage drinking cannot be successfully addressed by focusing on youth alone. Youth drink within the context of a society in which alcohol use is normative behavior and images about alcohol are pervasive. They usually obtain alcohol—either directly or indirectly—from adults. Efforts to reduce underage drinking, therefore, need to focus on adults and must engage the society at large" (Bonnie and O'Connell 2004, 2). The truth in this conclusion (which I endorsed as a member of that panel) is demonstrated by the close statistical connection between underage drinking and per capita consumption. Indeed, the panel recommended a national campaign directed at adults rather than youths, with the goal of persuading parents of the seriousness of the problem and gaining adult support for alcohol-control measures and other effective measures.

CHAPTER 13

Alcohol-Control Policy for the Twenty-first Century

THERE IS NO CRISIS, NO EPIDEMIC, no dramatic upsurge of alcohol abuse that demands public attention. Average alcohol consumption is well below the peak years circa 1980, and the damage to public health and safety has declined as well. In particular, the DUI problem has dropped thanks not only to the reduction in overall alcohol consumption but also to tougher enforcement and the secular improvement in highway safety. Violent crime has dropped sharply since the peak in 1991, due to an easing of the crack-cocaine epidemic, increased incarceration, and other factors (Cook and Laub 2002; Levitt 2004; Blumstein and Wallman 2000). Progress in the treatment of alcohol dependence is indicated by FDA approval of anti-craving drugs (naltrexone, acomprosate) to support abstinence by alcoholics in recovery. Nonetheless, and despite all this good news, we are left with an endemic social and public health problem of considerable magnitude. Alcohol still accounts for something on the order of 100,000 deaths per year, not to mention a substantial share of sexually transmitted disease cases, birth defects, domestic and street violence, family breakdown, and the problems in making the transition from adolescence to adult responsibilities. Alcohol abuse remains our leading "drug" problem.

Alcohol control is an old remedy for problematic drinking, having been developed and implemented in its current form during the 1930s. But it is by means outmoded—as we have seen in previous chapters, during the last twenty-five years an extensive body of research has accumulated, documenting the efficacy and social benefits of alcohol-control measures. Unfortunately public confidence in this approach was lost long ago, and has not been restored. Perhaps the most important consequence in the post-War period has been the loss of a constituency strong enough to get the politicians' attention. Congress and the state legislatures have allowed the erosion of alcohol excise taxes, which are now at a fraction of the rates imposed in the 1950s and 1960s (after adjusting for inflation); the broad drift toward increased availability is also noteworthy. There is one exception to this trend: tougher controls on underage drinking, including a national minimum age law of twenty-one (adopted in 1984) and federal requirements that it be enforced on college campuses and military installations. That campaign has proven marginally effective, but the inescapable fact remains that most youths in their late teens drink and a large minority are frequent binge drinkers. There are real limits to the extent to which adolescents can be insulated from the alcohol environment created by adults. The case for broadening the agenda on alcohol control is strong.

The great challenge in controlling alcohol in the public interest is achieving the right balance. Neither prohibition nor laissez faire makes sense. The goal should be to preserve the benefits of drinking while reducing abuse, all without unwarranted government intrusion. It is less complicated in the case of tobacco: smoking has no known health benefits, and even "light" or "moderate" smoking carries substantial risks. In many circles smoking is offensive to others, and poses health risks to them as well. Even those who enjoy smoking are most often ambivalent about their habit. In contrast, a majority of adults enjoy drinking on occasion. For healthy people there are no known adverse health consequences from taking a drink or two each day, and there may even be some medical benefit in middle age—although that is far from proven. It is surely a welcome social "lubricant," a traditional accompaniment to many an occasion and ritual, a licit pleasure as straightforward as a beer on a hot day or as refined as a Napa Valley wine tasting. And yet alcohol is also a source in far too many cases of injury, loss, and despair.

The dual nature of alcohol was famously expressed by Mississippi Judge Noah Sweat in his 1948 satirical speech on fence-sitting politicians who avoid taking a stand on the issue of liquor control:

> If when you say 'whisky' you mean the devil's brew, the poison scourge, the bloody monster that defiles innocence, dethrones reason, destroys the home, creates misery and poverty . . . —then certainly I am against it.
>
> But, if when you say 'whisky' you mean the oil of conversation, the philosophic wine, the ale that is consumed when good fellows get together, that puts a song in their hearts and laughter on their lips, and the warm glow of contentment in their eyes . . . if you mean the drink that enables a man to magnify his joy, and his happiness, and to forget, if only for a little while, life's great tragedies, and heartaches, and sorrow . . . —then certainly I am for it (1997).

Fortunately it is not necessary to choose sides. Alcohol control is not all or nothing, but rather offers a continuum of possibilities. The question is not *whether* to subject alcohol to higher taxes or to impose a minimum age or to regulate outlets. The question is how high, what age, how stringent.

Evidence on Effectiveness

As we have seen, the evidence that alcohol-control measures are effective begins with the fact, amply documented in the scientific literature, that higher prices and restricted availability of alcoholic beverages reduce per capita consumption of ethanol. I am sometimes asked how *large* a price increase is needed to "make a difference." The answer is simple: a small increase will make a small difference, a large increase will make a greater difference. The decline in alcohol excise taxes since the 1950s means that alcoholic beverages are considerably cheaper now than in the previous generation—that change has been large.

These statements in no way contradict the common-sense view that individual drinking decisions are influenced by myriad factors. Individual consumption levels span a wide spectrum due to differences in personal preference and circumstance. In a sense, alcohol-control measures are relatively minor influences in comparison with, say, ethnic background, genetic makeup, sex, age, religion, and culture. But these factors, while important, are largely beyond the direct influence of public policy. The special importance of alcoholic beverage prices and availability in this array of factors is that they are under the direct control of legislatures and government agencies, and they have documented effectiveness.

Effective alcohol-control measures will reduce average sales and consumption of alcohol. Average consumption is closely linked to the prevalence of heavy drinking and binge drinking across communities, states, or countries, as documented particularly in chapter 6. As a result, when average drinking is observed to be on the rise for any reason, more alcohol-related problems are to be expected. Norman Giesbrecht, scientist with the Centre for Addiction and Mental Health in Toronto, developed this theme in connection with the observation that alcohol sales have been increasing in Canada since the mid-1990s; long experience in Canada and elsewhere suggests that this increase is a warning signal for higher mortality due to liver cirrhosis and motor vehicle crashes, as well as suicides and homicides (2003).

Ledermann's "Single Distribution Theory" would take the argument a large step farther, positing that a reduction in per capita consumption is both a necessary and sufficient condition for a reduction in the prevalence of heavy drinking and its consequences. But that theory remains just that, an intriguing generalization from the patterns observed in the data. Ledermann's theory is not necessary to establishing the case that alcohol-control saves lives. That alcohol-control measures are effective in reducing abuse rates and drinking-related consequences is based on direct evidence linking changes in taxes, MLDA, and other controls to changes in binge drinking prevalence, mortality rates, and other outcomes. The evidence from RASPP studies (chapter 6) has been particularly persuasive in this regard.

Per capita consumption, cultural norms, and the stringency of alcohol controls imposed by law and by the policies of schools, employers, and other institutions, all interact to form the relevant social environment in which drinking decisions are made—"wet" or "dry" or in between. Those decisions cumulate into habits over time. As Jellinek suggested long ago, a wet environment provides fertile ground for growing alcoholics and alcohol abusers (chapter 3). This is the context in which alcohol-control measures matter.

A PORTFOLIO OF POLICIES

As with financial investments, it is best to diversify the portfolio of policies implemented to reduce alcohol-related problems (Moore and Gerstein 1981; Bonnie and O'Connell 2004). Any one approach is likely to have diminishing returns and to miss some aspects of the problem. In addition to alcohol control, there are two other vital approaches for public intervention.

One category focuses on "time, place and circumstance" of drinking, including efforts to motivate people to refrain from drinking when it is likely to cause damage: driving, working on tasks requiring acuity or sound judgment, pregnancy and child care, periods of psychological distress or depression. To a large extent these matters are dealt with through counseling and private authority—for example, the employer's authority to require that workers be sober on the job, or physicians counseling women on the importance of refraining from drink during pregnancy. Government authority is needed for some interventions of this sort: deterring DUI, banning alcohol on Navy shipboard, removing children from a home endangered by the drunkenness of their parents.

A second category goes under the rubric of "harm reduction," or, with a smile, "making the world safe for drunks." The goal here is to ease some of the natural consequences of drinking too much. Building safer roads and more crashworthy vehicles makes everyone safer, but is of particular benefit to those who drive after drinking. The long-running campaign by the National Council on Alcoholism to educate the public that alcoholism is a disease rather than a choice was motivated partly by the hope of creating a more forgiving social environment; development of effective treatments for alcohol dependence also reduces the potential harm from years of heavy drinking. (The successful movement to decriminalize public drunkenness during the 1970s can be viewed as both harm reduction and the reverse—the old routine of jailing drunks at least provided them with some protection against the elements (Fagan and Mauss 1978; Jacobs 1989).[1]

These approaches are well targeted on alcohol-related problems and limit the domain of government coercion to behavior with obvious negative externalities. The freedom to drive drunk is not protected by

John Stuart Mill's "harm" principle. But there are clearly limits to what can be accomplished along these lines. Certainly under the current regime, which incorporates both approaches, the remaining external costs of alcohol abuse are substantial, much higher (on a per drink basis) than the excise tax rate. As argued in chapter 11, the case for higher taxes is strong whether considered through the goals of public health, fairness, or economic efficiency. Indeed, most anything that increased price, including the anticompetitive elements in the state regulations of the industry (such as the "three-tier system"), saves lives. But if the goal is raising prices in the public interest, then it is far preferable to do so through excise taxes than inefficient regulations. Taxes have the great advantage of benefiting the public twice—by curtailing alcohol abuse and also generating tax revenues.

In public opinion surveys, a large majority of the public indicate their support for raising alcohol taxes, with the proviso that the revenues be used for treatment and prevention programs or some other good use (Wagenaar et al. 2000).[2] The fact that tax serves as an effective prevention measure even without this sort of earmarking is a harder sell. Meanwhile, the alcohol industry, not content with allowing inflation to do the job over time, has been pushing hard for Congress to reduce alcohol tax rates. The beer distributors in particular have been a powerful force in Washington, and in 2005, 240 members of Congress (a majority of the House) signed on to a bill that would have cut beer tax rates in half. Convincing the public to pressure their representatives for higher alcohol prices is not easy.

The public also supports restricting alcohol to minors, and there Congress has enacted a series of regulations beginning in the first Reagan administration. At least in this arena, the objective evidence seems to have mattered. Research demonstrated that states which reduced their MLDA during the early 1970s experienced an increase in teen traffic fatality rates relative to those states that did not change their MLDA. The difference at that time amounted to something like 7 percent (Cook and Tauchen 1984). The federal requirement that all states raise their MLDA to twenty-one has saved many lives since then, despite the fact that most youths find a way to drink. The federal government has pushed for additional restrictions on youthful drinking, requiring campuses and military installations to enforce these laws, and states to adopt zero tolerance for teen drivers. States have also focused their regulation of licensed outlets to stop sales of alcohol to minors (Bonnie and O'Connell 2004).

Still, setting the MLDA so high—higher than any other developed nation—is costly. This age-based prohibition is a direct imposition on the liberty of college-age youths who are for most other purposes considered adult. It creates scofflaws out of the majority who choose to drink anyway. And it is bound to be of marginal effectiveness as long as the control measures are limited to youthful drinking. There is a case to be made for easing the MLDA restrictions, for example by giving certain institutions that house and have responsibility for eighteen- to twenty-year-olds the discretion to relax the prohibition: included in this list might be their families, residential colleges, and military bases. Another possibility is to give this age group a "learner's permit" to drink, to be revoked if it is misused, or perhaps to allow all of them the right to purchase weak beer. Any such change would probably result in some increase in alcohol-related problems if adopted in isolation. That risk could be forestalled if MLDA changes were accompanied by a policy to raise prices and strengthen alcohol-control measures for all adults.

The states all maintain systems for licensing and regulating on-premise and off-premise sales. The relevant agencies are typically underfunded, with meager capacity to enforce the regulations that are designed to protect patrons, the neighboring community, and the public at large. The evidence summarized in chapter 10 suggests considerable room for improvement. Regulatory enforcement capacity is supplemented in many states by dram-shop liability rules that create a sort of private enforcement mechanism, albeit one that leaves much to be desired with respect to consistency and reliability. More effective enforcement is just a matter of will, which is to say a greater claim on scarce public resources.

A Final Plea

The effort to limit alcohol abuse begins with the individual who has an excessive appetite for drinking, and may also engage her family, friends, physician, employer, church, the courts, social-service agencies, and others. That array of intervenors reflects the spectrum of consequences. Alcohol-control measures, if working well, complement and support their efforts. For the individual, self-control is strengthened and temptation eased by an environment that provides some control over price and availability. This statement is not just a matter of faith; it is well supported by modern scientific evidence. That we have allowed taxes and other controls to atrophy over time may have much to do with the lingering legacy of Prohibition. A reasonable goal at this point is not to bring back Prohibition, but simply to recapture some of the ground that has been lost in the last few decades. Although it is difficult to identify the optimum level of taxes and regulatory control, the right direction is clear. A selective strengthening of alcohol control, guided by the evidence and common sense, would ease the struggle to limit abuse, enhance the public health and safety, and ultimately increase our collective standard of living.

Methodological Appendix

Several variables used to compute the results in table 5.2 were constructed from available data on excise tax rates and prices. This appendix provides the details.

TAX RATES

The original data set included tax rates in dollars/gallon in real dollars (the year's tax rates divided by the year's CPI/100, with base years 1982–1984). The tax rates were in every case the sum of state and federal excises. The real tax rates were then converted to rates per ounce of ethanol first by multiplying the dollar figure by 100 (to change the rate to cents per gallon) and then dividing by the number of ounces of ethanol in each gallon of beer, wine, or liquor. The number of ounces of ethanol in turn was derived from taking the proportion of ethanol in each gallon of beer, wine, or liquor and multiplying it by 128. Thus, for beer, the percentage of ethanol is 4.5 percent or, for a 128-ounce gallon, 5.76 ounces of ethanol, so that the tax rate per gallon of beer was divided by 5.76. For wine, the alcohol percentage was assumed to be 12.0 percent, implying 15.35 ounces of ethanol per gallon, so the per gallon tax rate was divided by 15.35. For liquor, the excise tax is defined in proportion to ethanol content: the tax rate is per proof gallon (50 percent ethanol) and was hence divided by 64.

CALCULATING THE TAX INDEX

For tax rates, a weighted average index measure was calculated from the separate beer, wine, and liquor tax rates. Each state tax rate was multiplied by its percentage of ethanol consumed for that product by each state averaged over the period consumption data were available (1970–2000). The three rates were then summed to produce the index. An example of a tax index calculation for one state (Massachusetts) for the year 2000 is shown in the accompanying table.

	Tax Rate (Cents Per Ounce of Ethanol)	Average % Ethanol Consumed	Weighted Rate	Index
Beer	6.93	0.449	3.11	
Wine	6.12	0.161	0.99	
Liquor	15.92	0.389	6.19	
Totals	—	0.999	10.29	10.29

The tax index variable could only be calculated where beer, wine, and liquor tax rates were available, namely, the thirty-two license states and the District of Columbia. To create an index value for the control states, an imputed liquor tax rate was needed. First the net price, price minus tax, was calculated for 1988 for each license state except Alaska and Hawaii. These net prices were averaged and the average subtracted from the price for each of the monopoly states for each year. The result was an imputed liquor tax for each state for every year.

This imputed tax was then placed in the previously missing liquor tax observations for all the control states in the regression data set. The weighted tax index variable was then calculated as before and as described in detail above. The imputed spirits tax, the actual beer tax, and the actual wine tax, weighted by the state-specific fraction of ethanol, were summed to produce a tax index figure. The only states now missing an alcohol tax index number were New Hampshire and Utah that also control wine sales and have no wine tax rates available.

PRICES

Price data were from ACCRA, formerly known as the American Chamber of Commerce Researchers Association, for the period 1982–2000. The prices were for one leading brand of each beverage type, which have been adjusted for inflation (using the Consumer Price Index with base 1982–1984) and then converted to the price per ounce of ethanol. The ACCRA price figures were first sorted by state and the mean value for all cities in each state for each year (1982–2000) was derived. (The number of cities ranged across states from one to thirty-two.) Prices were converted to reflect ethanol content. For example, the price per ounce of ethanol in liquor was computed by dividing the price per 0.75 liter bottle of 86-proof scotch by 10.7 (the number of ounces of ethanol given ethanol content of 43 percent).

Price Elasticities

To compute estimated price elasticities, it was first necessary to estimate the effect of a change in the excise tax on the price. Markup rates were estimated by regressing the price data on the tax rate for the 1982–2000 panel of fifty states for each beverage type, including "year" fixed effects. The estimated coefficients are 1.938 (beer), 1.614 (wine), and 1.023 (liquor).

Notes

CHAPTER 1
INTRODUCTION

1. http://www.alcoholpolicymd.com/take_action/op_ed_1_ma.htm, accessed June 12, 2006.
2. "Cigarette tax increases by state per year 2000–2005 (as of September 1, 2005)" at http://www.tobaccofreekids.org, accessed June 9, 2006.
3. The changes are listed at *www.cspinet.org/booze/taxguide*, accessed June 12, 2006.
4. The estimate from the Centers for Disease Control and Prevention for the year 2000 was 140,000 alcohol-related deaths if the excess death rate among former drinkers is included, and 85,000 deaths if excluded (Mokdad et al. 2004, 1241).

CHAPTER 2
A BRIEF HISTORY OF THE SUPPLY SIDE

1. The U.S. Congress passed a law July 4, 1789, placing a tax on the importation of ale, beer, porter, cider, malt, molasses, spirits, and wines. "The purposes of the Congress in adopting this law were revenue, protection, and incidentally encouragement of temperance" (U.S. Congress 1931, 4).
2. Even though Jefferson opposed the liquor tax, he perceived a serious drinking problem. "The habit of using ardent spirits in public office, has often produced more injury to public service, and more trouble to me, than any other circumstance that has occurred in the internal concerns of the country during my administration" (Aaron and Musto, 1981, 138).
3. A "proof gallon" contains 64 ounces of pure ethanol. Hence, a gallon of 100 proof liquor is a proof gallon.
4. An income tax was imposed during the Civil War and again in 1894. The Supreme Court declared it unconstitutional in 1895. That obstacle was overcome by the Sixteenth Amendment, enacted in 1913.
5. New Jersey's legislature did not get around to ratifying the Eighteenth until 1922, while Connecticut and Rhode Island never did.
6. http://www.pbs.org/wgbh/amex/1900/peopleevents/pande4.html.
7. Norman H. Clark observes that "whatever else the 'Progressive temper' might have been, we know now that among almost any representative group of social activists who worked for child labor laws, for the regulation of industrial working conditions, for tax reform, for direct legislation, for women's suffrage, or even for honest government, most worked also for state dry laws and for the prohibition of the liquor traffic and the saloon" (Clark 1976, 11).
8. Modern-day advocates for reform of the marijuana laws often call for a similar set of distinctions. A policy which removes the criminal penalties from possession for own use, while continuing to outlaw production and sale, is called

"decriminalization." Note that Warburton (1934, 505) observes that the Supreme Court held that the purchaser of illicit liquor could not be prosecuted as such but that he could be prosecuted for the illegal possession of liquor.

9. The Volstead Act was unclear on this matter, and courts disagreed as to the proper interpretation of the language creating this loophole. But as a matter of practice, the federal government chose to allow home production (U.S. Congress 1931, 33).

10. Dana, et al., 1921; U.S. House Committee on the Judiciary 1921.

11. North and South Carolina.

12. For a discussion of the relationship between cirrhosis death rates and consumption, see the appendix to Cook and Tauchen (1982).

CHAPTER 3
THE ALCOHOLISM MOVEMENT

1. Jellinek noted: "We have termed as alcoholism any use of alcoholic beverages that causes any damage to the individual or society or both" (1960, 35), but was only willing to give the "disease" label to gamma and delta, for which "anomalous forms of drinking (loss of control and physical dependence) are caused by physiopathological processes" (1960, 40).

2. These data are not comprehensive, and apparently capture less than half of all episodes. In particular, TEDS does not include treatment supplied by federal agencies such as Veterans Affairs, the military, and the Bureau of Prisons, and in some states omits admissions to facilities that accept no public funding.

3. Forty-four percent of all admissions indicate alcohol as the primary substance of abuse, and in another 22 percent, alcohol is mentioned as a secondary substance. (It should be noted that some individuals were admitted more than once.)

4. *NYT*, December 7, 1948, p. 30, "Fifteen Years After."

5. The survey is NESARC (National Epidemiological Survey of Alcohol and Related Conditions), fielded in 2001–2002 by the National Institute on Alcohol Abuse and Alcoholism. Based on responses to this detailed survey, I have calculated that 7.2 million meet the criteria for current alcohol dependence, of whom 53 percent said they drove after three or more drinks; 29.1 million others had ever been dependent, of whom 22.5 percent had driven after drinking. Of the remainder, just 6.5 percent indicated that they had driven after drinking three or more drinks in the last year, but that group accounted for 52 percent of the total.

CHAPTER 4
DRINKING: A PRIMER

1. Since alcohol is somewhat lighter than water, the percentage of alcohol by volume slightly exceeds the percentage of alcohol by weight. It is standard to measure by volume.

2. Each state establishes its own procedures for collecting taxes, but in most cases it is the wholesaler or distributor who actually makes the payment.

3. These and other statistics in this paragraph are from http://pubs.niaaa.nih .gov/publications/surveillance73/tab1_03.htm, accessed June 13, 2006.

4. The volume of liquor declined less than the volume of ethanol; the average proof of bottles sold declined (Kling 1991).

5. New Hampshire, Nevada, and the District of Columbia all have higher per capita consumption than Delaware. However, they are excluded from this comparison because all three achieve such high levels of consumption through out-of-state resident purchases.

6. National Epidemiologic Survey on Alcohol and Related Conditions, a large survey conducted and sponsored by the National Institute on Alcohol Abuse and Alcoholism.

7. The most prominent are these two (Greenfield and Kerr 2003):

- The National Survey on Drug Use and Health (NSDUH), formerly known as the National Household Survey on Drug Abuse (NHSDA), which has collected information on alcohol use since 1974, and has included a fairly comprehensive list of questions on an annual basis since 1994.

- The National Alcohol Survey (NAS), which has been fielded approximately once every five years since 1959 to measure aspects of alcohol consumption, associated problems, and treatment utilization.

In contrast to these general-population surveys, the Monitoring the Future (MTF) Survey has focused on students. Samples of high school seniors have been interviewed every year since 1975 on their drinking, as well as smoking and drug use. In 1991, the survey was expanded to include samples of eighth and tenth graders (www.monitoringthefuture.org).

8. Based on NESARC data, the self-reported ethanol consumed in the past twelve months by respondents (who were age eighteen and over) averaged 141.3 ounces. The NIAAA reports that the annual per capita sales in 2000 was 2.18 gallons of ethanol or 277.76 ounces total consumed by the population age fifteen and older. Dividing the NESARC estimate by the NIAAA estimate gives the underreporting estimate of 49 percent.

9. The comparison was for 1982. Both surveys followed these high school seniors for a number of years after their graduation and continued to ask questions about their drinking. The prevalence estimates for the two samples converge, perhaps because the MTF's follow-up surveys, unlike the initial survey of seniors, were mailed to the respondents' homes. See also Hoyt and Chaloupka (1994).

10. These surveys were conducted over a four-year time span: the 1988 National Health Interview Survey, the 1990 National Alcohol Survey, and the 1992 National Longitudinal Alcohol Epidemiologic Survey.

11. Rare exceptions are Boland and Roizen (1973) and Popham and Schmidt (1981). Both studies compare self-reports to sales data. See also Cook and Moore (2000, 1640).

12. Ironically, Reagan borrowed this motto from an old Russian proverb, "Doveryai no Proveryai" (New York Times Staff 1987).

13. NESARC was sponsored by the National Institute on Alcohol Abuse and Alchoolism, and fielded in 2001–2002. The NESARC is a representative sample of the United States non-institutionalized population age eighteen and over, with a sample size of 43,093 (National Institute on Alcohol Abuse and Alcoholism 2003).

14. These figures were corrected for under-reporting by multiplying the survey estimate of drinks consumed during the previous year by 1.97 for each respondent. The result was to bring per capita consumption into line with national sales for 2000.

15. The evidence is not only from survey data. For example, Jan DeLint and Wolfgang Schmidt (1968) were able to confirm this general pattern based on administrative data in Ontario, at a time when sales from liquor stores were recorded.

16. Ledermann (1956) actually made a stronger claim, which has also stood the test of time. He asserted that any two populations with the same per capita alcohol consumption will have the same prevalence of heavy drinking (e.g., more than 50 liters per year), and that in any two populations with different consumption levels, the population with the higher per capita consumption will have a greater prevalence of heavy drinking (Cook and Skog 1995, 30; Skog 1985).

17. As reported in the 2003 Statistical Abstract of the United States, total personal expenditures in 2001 were $6,987 billion. Alcohol expenditures accounted for 1.85 percent of the total expenditures.

18. There doesn't appear to be a trend in off-/on-premise consumption. Since 1996, the shares of beer consumed on-premise has increase 1 percent, while wine and spirits have experienced fluctuations of less than 1 percent (Adams Business Media 2003).

CHAPTER 5
PRICES AND QUANTITIES

1. In thirty-one out of thirty-eight demand studies tabled in Edwards et al. (1994) that included estimated results for both beer and spirits, the former was less price elastic than the latter. A thorough review of econometric studies using data for the United States (Leung and Phelps 1993) provides additional information on results and methods.

2. On January 1, 1991, the excise tax on beer increased from $0.29 to $0.58 per gallon, the excise tax on wine increased from $0.17 to $1.07 per gallon, and the excise tax on liquor increased from $12.50 to $13.50 per proof gallon. During this period there were no other legislated changes in federal alcohol excises except for a small increase in the liquor tax in 1985.

3. The data are annual observations for the period 1970–2003. All variables except the trend are in first-difference form (represented by the Δ) to correct for serial correlation. Estimated standard errors are in parentheses.

$$\Delta \text{Ln Ethanol} = -.0067 \quad -.397 \; \Delta \text{Ln Price} \quad +.008 \; \Delta \text{Ln Income} \quad -.00002 \; \text{Trend}$$
$$\phantom{\Delta \text{Ln Ethanol} = } (.0078) \quad (.181) \qquad\qquad (.146) \qquad\qquad\quad (.00037)$$

where

- Ethanol: ethanol content of wholesale shipments in gallons per capita (adults age fourteen and older)

- Price: Consumer Price Index for alcoholic beverages divided by the overall CPI

- Income: median household income adjusted for inflation

- Trend: number of years since 1969

The coefficient estimates on Price and Income can be interpreted directly as elasticities because of the log-linear formulation.

4. Price data are available from ACCRA, formerly known as the American Chamber of Commerce Researchers Association, and these data have been used by some researchers. But the sampling of price data in this series is limited and inconsistent from year to year. The measurement errors in these data are sufficient to cause serious bias in the demand-equation estimation (Young and Bielinska-Kwapisz 2002, 2003).

5. NESARC was sponsored by the National Institute on Alcohol Abuse and Alcoholism, and fielded in 2001–2002. The NESARC is a representative sample of the United States non-institutionalized population age eighteen and over, with a sample size of 43,000.

6. Controlling for age, employment and/or student status, income, marital status, race, completed education, height, weight, and health status. For males, the logit regression coefficients on per capita sales are .36 (for being a drinker) and .17 (for bingeing); for females, the corresponding coefficients are .44 and .28. For those who do drink, the ln of daily consumption is related to per capita sales: the coefficients in the regression are .19 for males, and .24 for females. Separate regressions were also run for the following age groups: 18–20, 21–25, 26–34, 35–49, 50–64, and 65+.

7. Coefficient estimates on the tax variable are not much changed when per capita sales are excluded from the specifications.

8. But note that the most stringently regulated states tend to be the monopoly states, which are excluded from the analysis here due to data limitations.

9. This tendency has received less attention for drinking than smoking. One study found that a majority of youths who were smoking in high school predicted that they would not be smoking five years later, but only 31 percent had actually quit at that point, and the belief that they would was not predictive of whether they did (U.S. Department of Health and Human Services 1994).

10. The literature documenting inconsistencies in choice making over time is vast. See, for example, Ainslie (1992); Schelling (1980); Gruber and Köszegi (2001, 2004); and Vuchinich and Simpson (1999).

11. National Institute on Alcohol Abuse and Alcoholism 2003a.

12. The authors suggest that it is probably not the heaviest drinkers who are responsive to price, given other evidence on the subject (Manning, Blumberg, and Moulton 1995) indicating that the price elasticity declines at the highest consumption levels. But the penultimate group of drinkers is responsive and prone to alcohol-related problems.

13. The first results were reported in Grossman, Coate, and Arluck (1987) and Coate and Grossman (1988).

14. Dee 1999) reports results that confirm the efficacy of the MLDA, but raise some doubts about (without contradicting) the influence of the beer excise tax. One problem with his analysis is that he estimates the youthful drinking by state using a data set—Monitoring the Future—which is based on a sample that, while nationally representative, is not representative of each state, and changes from year to year.

15. Computed at the mean from coefficient estimates reported in table 8.7 of Cook and Moore (2001).

16. The per se limit was set at 0.02 of 1 percent blood alcohol concentration, which can be reached after just one beer.

17. Logit regressions were run for males and females using NESARC data. The coefficients on drinking status and average consumption per day are positive and estimated with considerable precision. Other things equal, a female who averages one drink per day has odds of smoking that are 2.5 times as high as an abstainer; for males, the factor is 2.0.

CHAPTER 6
ALCOHOL CONTROL AS INJURY PREVENTION

1. A sample calculation is as follows: Suppose that 50 percent of fatal crashes occurring on weekend evenings involve a driver with BAC in excess of 0.05 percent, while only 10 percent of all drivers on weekend evenings have a BAC that high. Then (with the help of a little algebra) drinkers with BAC in excess of 0.05 percent have nine times the chance of getting in a fatal accident as those who have drunk little or nothing.

2. A total of 6,298 drivers entered the Roadside Survey interview site. Blood alcohol content data are missing for 270 of the drivers. Seventy-four of these drivers agreed to the BAC test, but could not produce a valid measure; 196 of the drivers refused to take a BAC test. Thus, 196/6,298 = 0.031, giving a refusal rate of 3.1 percent (Voas et al. 1997).

3. No legal action was taken against the intoxicated drivers. The only time police were involved in the interview process was to flag down the randomly selected vehicles (Voas et al. 1997).

4. One problem with studies of this sort is that drivers have the right to refuse the breathalyzer test. It seems likely that those who refuse are more likely to be drinking than others, in which case the findings will be biased. In a *tour de force* of statistical reasoning, Steven D. Levitt and Jack Porter (2001) demonstrate that estimates of the prevalence of drunks and their relative crash risk can be made from data on fatal accidents alone. Their basic insight is that under reasonable assumptions, prevalence and relative risk are both indicated by the mix of drunk and sober drivers in two-car fatal crashes.

5. Low doses of alcohol have been demonstrated to impair performance in other complex mechanical tasks. In a series of experiments using simulators, Jonathan Howland and his associates have shown that the performance of maritime

cadets in operating a merchant-ship power plant are degraded by even a small amount of alcohol (Howland et al. 2000).

6. If 17 percent of the drivers account for 78 percent of the fatalities, then the remaining 83 percent of the drivers account for 22 percent of the fatalities. The ratio of relative contribution, (78/17)/(22/83), is 17.

7. 78.4 percent includes all drivers with positive BAC (BAC > 0). Breaking this down, 68.8 percent of all drivers in fatal crashes had BAC $\geq$ 0.08 percent. 9.6 percent of the drivers had BAC greater than 0 but less than 0.08 percent. The 61.4 percent was calculated by taking the actual percentage of alcohol-related fatalities minus the expectation that 17 percent of drivers had been drinking.

8. This term is used because it is conventional. A more accurate term would be minimum legal purchase age, since a number of states allow underage youths to drink under some circumstances.

9. The most influential study at the time was prepared by researchers at the Insurance Institute of Highway Safety (Williams et al. 1983), the results of which were greatly exaggerated in subsequent Congressional testimony (Males 1986).

10. Saffer and Grossman (1987b) note the possibility that states which chose to raise their MLDA in the late 1970s tended to differ from those that did not, and use an estimation method that treats MLDA as endogenous. Although it is true, as illustrated above, that states which chose to change their MLDA may be unrepresentative, there is evidence that they were not unrepresentative with respect to trends.

11. It should be noted that several studies have utilized survey data on risk-taking behaviors to provide some insight into the mechanisms by which alcohol-control measures affect fatality rates. Donald Kenkel (1993) analyzed the Health Promotion and Disease Supplement to the 1985 Health Interview Survey, which contained information on drinking and driving practices. He incorporated alcohol-control measures, measures of the legal threat to drunk driving, and an indicator of health knowledge based on individual awareness of connections between drinking and health risks. Binge drinking is defined as the number of days in the past year with five or more drinks, and drunk driving by responses to a survey question asking how many times in the past year the sample member drove after having too much to drink.

Kenkel concluded that increases in price and health knowledge reduce the prevalence of binge drinking, while a state monopoly in liquor sales is associated with an *increase* in heavy drinking. Binge drinking in turn increases the prevalence of drunk driving. Interestingly, the legal-threat variables tend to reduce drunk driving as well, and by the same mechanism—the threat of punishment reduces binge drinking rather than persuading people to separate their drinking and driving.

Sloan et al. (1995) also analyzed microdata, in this case from the Behavioral Risk Factor Surveys. In addition to the alcohol-control and deterrence effects, they incorporate indicators of the tort-liability rules to the binge drinking and drunk driving models. Whereas some effects of the criminal and legal variables have the expected effects on the two outcome variables, most are not statistically significant. The price and MLDA variables exert a strong effect on drunk driving, primarily through their effect on binge drinking. Also interesting are the results on the incentive effects of compulsory-insurance laws and experience rating. It appears that these policies, which tend to raise the price of careless behavior, lead to significant declines in binge drinking.

12. A number of analysts have attempted to further increase sensitivity by focusing just on night time fatal crashes, when alcohol involvement is highest. But this increase in sensitivity comes at a cost—we want to know the overall effect of the MLDA change, not just the effect during the night time. When the added sensitivity is not required for statistical reasons, the more comprehensive measure is to be preferred (Cook and Tauchen 1984).

13. See, for example, Donovan and McEwan (1995); Fergusson and Lynskey (1996); Rees, Argys, and Averett (2001); and the references in Chesson, Harrison, and Kassler (2000).

14. The tax index is something new, and needs explanation. It is meant to represent the average excise tax per ounce of ethanol sold in the state. More precisely, it is the weighted average of the combined federal and state excise taxes over the three types of alcoholic beverage, in each case converted to pennies per ounce of ethanol. The weights used in computing this average are based on the average share of total ethanol consumption in that state from each beverage type. In control states, where a meaningful liquor tax is not defined, an imputed liquor tax is used. The details of the tax index are given in an NBER working paper (Cook and Peters 2005), and in the appendix to this book.

CHAPTER 7
LONG-TERM EFFECTS: HEARTS AND MINDS

1. For one partially successful attempt to show how past controls influence current drinking, see Cook and Moore (2001).

2. To be precise, the statistical distribution of the differences between the two groups can be computed and taken into account if the groups are created through random assignment.

3. See the Alcohol-related Disease Impact (ARDI) estimates, http://apps.nccd.cdc.gov/ardi/HomePage.aspx. For 2001, the estimate is 2.28 million years of potential life lost, of which 1.49 million were the result of acute effects. This source estimates total deaths at 75,766, of which 54 percent were due to acute effects.

4. Actually there is a small literature that reports findings suggesting that those who drink while young tend to have fewer risk factors for cardiovascular disease (Donahue et al. 1986; Twisk et al. 2001). These studies are purely correlational, and there is reason to be dubious in the absence of a known causal process.

CHAPTER 8
THE DRINKER'S BONUS

1. Much of what follows in this chapter is taken from my article with Bethany Peters (Cook and Peters 2005).

2. Several other studies have analyzed the effect of drinking on absenteeism. Manning et al. (1991) report results from two data sets, the Rand Health Insur-

ance Experiment (HIE) and the National Health Interview Study for 1983. In neither do they find a relationship between quantity consumed by current drinkers and absenteeism. (Using the HIE they find that "former drinkers" have 38 percent higher absentee rates than others.) On the other hand, French and Zarkin (1995), using survey data for workers at four large work sites, find that both overall drinking and frequency of drunkenness are positively related to absenteeism.

3. They defined "drinker" as someone who reported drinking at least once or twice per week. Those who drank less often were lumped in with the abstainers.

4. This interpretation is developed by MacDonald and Shields (2001) and others. The importance of a social network in job finding is documented by Granovetter (1975, 2nd ed. 1995). The economic interpretation of social capital is developed by Glaeser, Laibson, and Sacerdote (2002) and by Durlauf and Fafchamps (2004).

5. The local labor market is characterized by the county unemployment rate and on MSA-level wage index. The overall list of covariates is quite full in this specification, and it could be argued that a sparser list of covariates would be preferable. An alternative specification with a much shorter list of covariates produces qualitatively similar results, although the "drinker's bonus" estimate is somewhat larger (Cook and Peters 2005).

6. Further, there is some danger of *over*-controlling. For example, married men earn more than unmarried men, and it is standard practice to include marital status in an explanation of earnings. But since there is good evidence that alcohol abuse affects the likelihood of being married (Kenkel and Ribar 1994), controlling for marital status actually absorbs one of the mechanisms by which drinking may influence earnings.

7. An alternative possibility for reverse causation is that higher earnings cause drinking initiation because more lucrative jobs tend to have greater stress associated with them, or have other attributes that induce drinking (Trice and Sonnenstuhl 1988).

8. Instrumental-variables estimates may also eliminate omitted-variables bias and bias due to errors in the measurement of self-reported current drinking. The challenge is to find good instruments, which is to say, variables that satisfy two conditions: (1) they have a strong statistical association with individual drinking; and (2) they have no direct effect on the individual's earnings. A long list of instruments has been utilized by economists working on this problem (Cook and Peters 2005). State-level measures of alcohol availability, such as excise taxes or even per capita consumption, are plausible candidates to satisfy the requirements of a good instrument, although in some data sets they may not have enough variation to generate the statistical power needed. Some analysts have used certain individual characteristics as instruments, including whether the individual suffers from any of several chronic diseases, characterizations of his or her religious practices, attitudes toward the risk of alcohol and drugs, parents' smoking, and whether the respondent reports having close relatives who are alcoholic. Although all of these variables are correlated with drinking, it is quite likely in each case that they also have a direct effect on work and earnings. For example, people who attend church frequently drink less than others, but their religion may also influence their career choices and performance on the job, and hence earnings. Therefore, using some

quantitative characterization of religious practice as an instrument does not identify the effect of drinking per se on earnings.

9. One challenge to our interpretation of these results is that the state-level
policy variables we used are correlated with other state policies that may also
affect schooling (Dee and Evans 2003).

CHAPTER 9
EVALUATING INTERVENTIONS

1. See, for example, the contributions and reviews by Ainslie (1992);
Loewenstein (1996); Laibson (1997); Vuchinich and Simpson (1999); Gruber and
Köszegi (2004); and Bernheim and Rangel (2004).

2. The contrary view has been developed by Gary Becker and Kevin Murphy
(Becker and Murphy 1988; Becker et al. 1991), who assert that much of what
we observe in connection with the consumption of addictive commodities can be
explained in terms of a rational choice framework, and does not require an assertion of behavior inconsistent with rational preferences. This analysis is of considerable interest, but it does not account for costly efforts at self-management.

3. This approach to assessing the costs of illness and other social burdens has
a long history (Hu and Sandifer 1981). The first formal COI study was published
as early as 1950. In 1967, Dorothy Rice codified this approach, and later, as head
of the National Center for Health Statistics, she chaired a task force that issued
Guidelines for Cost of Illness Studies in the Public Health Services (Hodgson and
Meiners 1979). By 1980, over 200 such studies had been performed (Hu and
Sandifer 1981).

4. A great advantage of using market-price data, rather than data from surveys
and other hypothetical exercises, is that market data are based on real choices
made by people who have to reckon with a real possibility of injury or death.

5. Note that what is relevant here includes only real resources. Money is just
a means of keeping score. For example, someone with inherited wealth may be a
net drain on the economy even though she lives within her (substantial) means,
simply because she is consuming more than she is producing.

CHAPTER 10
REGULATING SUPPLY

1. In 2001, Phillip Morris sold Miller to South African Breweries.

2. In 1977, the federal tax rate on the first 60,000 barrels from brewers producing less than 2 million barrels per year was reduced from $9 to $7. In 1991, the
federal tax doubled to $18, but small brewers continued to enjoy the $7 rate on
their first 60,000 barrels.

3. *Adam's Beer Handbook 2004*, p. 22.

4. E. & J. Gallo Winery accounted for 23 percent of domestic sales by volume
in 2003. Together, the top four producers accounted for 55 percent. *Adam's Wine
Handbook 2004*, p. 101.

5. See "Analysis and Implications of the Costco Decision" at http://www
.retailassociation.org/ , accessed June 19, 2006.

6. Distilled spirits are sold only in ABC stores in Alabama, Idaho, North Carolina, Oregon, and Virginia. Distilled spirits are sold by both ABC stores and licensed stores in Iowa, Maine, Michigan, Montana, New Hampshire, Ohio, Pennsylvania, Utah, Vermont, Washington, and West Virginia. Mississippi and
Wyoming have a public monopoly on wholesale distribution but do not operate
any retail stores.

7. The data are collected by ACCRA.

8. In 1982, the median price among control states was just 2.5 percent higher
than the median of license states. Control states actually had *lower* prices circa
1960 than the license states (Simon 1966).

9. The top four suppliers by volume in 2003 were Diageo (20.3%), Constella-
tion Brands (9.5%), Jim Beam Brands (9.1%), and Schieffelin & Somerset (8.1%).
Adams Liquor Handbook 2004, p. 208.

10. South Carolina has had an interesting variation on this regulation. Before
1973, it did not allow liquor to be sold by the drink. In 1972, a constitutional
amendment was adopted to allow liquor by the drink in containers of 2 ounces or
less, and the 1.7-ounce mini-bottles became standard. That limitation was finally
abolished in 2005.

11. As of 1998, the four states were Florida, New Jersey, Vermont, and
Wyoming.

12. The British Licensing Act of 2003 swept away fixed closing times for pubs
beginning in November 2005, making it easier for them to stay open later. One
newspaper opined that "The impulse to excess among young Britons remains as
powerful as ever, but the force that used to keep the impulse in check has all but
disappeared" (*The Economist*, Nov. 26, 2005, p. 73). But others argued that there
would be less last-minute guzzling when "last call" was done away with.

CHAPTER 11
TAXING THE ALCOHOL INDUSTRY

1. An odd feature of the federal wine tax is that sparkling wine is taxed much
more heavily than still wine. The tax per gallon of sparkling wine is $3.40 as of
2006.

2. Since the taxes on beer are proportional to the overall volume of liquid
rather than the volume of ethanol contained in that liquid, there is considerable
variation in the tax per ounce of ethanol among different styles of beer.

3. See the studies by Pacula (1998) and by Williams and her colleagues (2001).
But there is some disagreement with this conclusion in the literature (DiNardo
and Lemieux 1992; Saffer and Chaloupka 1999).

4. See my NBER Working Paper with Jan Ostermann and Frank Sloan (2005).
The estimate reported in table 1, column 2 implies that a one penny increase per
ounce of ethanol (1982–1984 prices) would result in a 0.68 percent reduction in
mortality rates. With the Consumer Price Index in 2006 twice as high as in 1982–

1984, that implies a best guess of 3.4 percent reduction associated with a 10 cent increase (2006 prices).

5. The violator may be judgment-proof, in the sense of not being able to pay a fine as large as the cost to the victim and society (Shavell 1986). Imposing other forms of punishment is socially costly. And if the probability of being apprehended is less than one, the punishment must be greater than the harm to preserve an appropriate deterrent. For a similar argument about gun control, see my article with Jim Leitzel (1996).

CHAPTER 12
YOUTH AS A SPECIAL CASE

1. http://www.monitoringthefuture.org/pubs/monographs/vol1_2003.pdf, p. 48, accessed July 14, 2005.

2. Estimates of the fraction of total ethanol consumed by underage drinkers range from 11 percent to 20 percent (Bonnie and O'Connell 2004, 54; Foster et al. 2003). Ted Miller and his associates (2005) offer a best estimate of 16 percent. Estimates differ depending on which survey results are used to estimate prevalence and intensity of drinking for youths and adults.

3. The Miller et al. estimates do not include injuries and deaths sustained by people who become victims of violent crime as a result of their imprudent behavior while drinking.

4. Its efficiency is enhanced through increased myelination and synaptic "pruning."

5. Respondents who were old for their grade, and in particular too old to graduate from high school by age nineteen, were excluded, leaving a total of 3,915 in the sample.

6. All regressions controlled for indicators of respondent's race, mother's and father's education, household size, indicator of whether the family was intact, household income, urban residence, and geographic region. The measure of aptitude was the math score from the Armed Services Vocational Aptitude Battery.

7. The reported regression results control for ability as measured by the math portion of the Armed Services Vocational Aptitude Battery. One mechanism by which youthful drinking may affect school continuation is by degrading cognitive ability, as measured, for example, by this test. The possible effects through this mechanism cannot be estimated from this regression.

8. *New York Times*, July 24, 1971, p. 29, "Michigan to give 18-year-olds adults' legal rights and duties."

9. *South Dakota v. Doles*, 483 U.S. 203 (1987).

10. The National Institute of Alcohol Abuse and Alcoholism tabulates state laws at http://alcoholpolicy.niaaa.nih.gov.

11. An exception that helps prove the rule: A woman in Charlotte, North Carolina, was convicted of involuntary manslaughter and sentenced to a jail term for the overdose death of a sixteen-year-old that resulted from a party at her home where she allowed teenagers to drink beer and vodka (*News & Observer*, July 31, 2005, p. 2B, "Woman sentenced in teen's alcohol death.").

12. These results are taken from an analysis by Rebecca Hutchinson (2003). It should be noted that if smoking is controlled for, then private (but not public) college students do drink more than their noncollege age peers. Among college students, those attending private colleges drink more than those in public colleges and universities.

13. In 1989, Congress amended Title 12 of the Higher Education Act of 1965. This amendment, known as the "Drug-Free Schools and Communities Act of 1989," requires that every educational institution receiving federal funding certify its adoption and implementation of programs designed to prevent use of illegal drugs and abuse of alcohol by students and employees. Prior federal law applicable to the College regulated only criminal drug activity of federally grant-funded employees and recipients of federal aid.

14. About thirty states have social-host liability in place, which establishes that social hosts, like commercial ones, may be liable when injury results from serving alcohol to an underage or drunken guest (Bonnie and O'Connell 2004, 177; Mosher and other contributors 2002).

15. http://www.dior.whs.mil/mmid/M01/fy03/m01fy03.pdf, accessed July 27, 2005.

16. See Rod Powers, "Military Drinking Age," http://usmilitary.about.com/od/justicelawlegislation/a/drinkingage.htm, accessed September 19, 2006.

CHAPTER 13
ALCOHOL-CONTROL POLICY FOR THE TWENTY-FIRST CENTURY

1. In general harm-reduction measures, like other insurance schemes, create a moral hazard, which in this case might cause more alcohol abuse. For that reason, drunkenness is usually no defense to criminal behavior, and alcoholism no legal excuse for DUI.

2. A 2005 survey of a nationally representative sample of American adults found overwhelming support (79%) for raising alcohol taxes rather than cutting social programs as a means for reducing the budget deficit. http://www.cspinet.org/new/200512071.html, accessed June 21, 2006.

References

Aaron, Paul, and David Musto. (1981). "Temperance and prohibition in America: A historical overview." In Mark H. Moore and Dean R. Gerstein (eds.), *Alcohol and Public Policy: Beyond the Shadow of Prohibition*. Washington, D.C.: National Academy Press.

Adams Beverage Group. (2004). *Adams Beer Handbook 2004*. New York: Adams Media.

Adams Beverage Group. (2004). *Adams Liquor Handbook 2004*. New York: Adams Media.

Adams Beverage Group. (2004). *Adams Wine Handbook 2004*. New York: Adams Media.

Ainslie, George. (1992). *Picoeconomics*. Cambridge: Cambridge University Press.

Anthony, James C., and Fernando Echeagaray-Wagner. (2000). "Epidemiologic analysis of alcohol and tobacco use." *Alcohol Research & Health* 24 (4): 201–8.

Armstrong, Elizabeth. (2003). *Conceiving Risk, Bearing Responsibility*. Baltimore: Johns Hopkins University Press.

Arnett, Jeffrey. (1992). "Reckless behavior in adolescence: A developmental perspective." *Developmental Review* 12 (4): 339–73.

Arthur, Brian W. (1981). "The economics of risks to life." *American Economic Review* 71 (1): 54–64.

Ashenfelter, Orley, and Michael Greenstone. (2004). "Estimating the value of a statistical life: The importance of omitted variables and publication bias." Working Paper 10401. Cambridge, MA: National Bureau of Economic Research, March.

Atkin, Charles. (2004). "Media intervention impact: Evidence and promising strategies." In Richard J. Bonnie and Mary Ellen O'Connell (eds.), *Reducing Underage Drinking: A Collective Responsibility*, 565–96. Washington, DC: National Academies Press.

Atkinson, Anthony B., and T. W. Meade. (1974). "Methods and preliminary findings in assessing the economic and health consequences of smoking with particular reference to lung cancer." *Journal of Royal Statistical Society Series* 137: 297–312.

Avorn, Jerry. (2004). *Powerful Medicines: The Benefits, Risks, and Costs of Prescription Drugs*. New York: Knopf.

Babor, Thomas F. (1985). "Alcohol, economics and the ecological fallacy: Toward an integration of experimental and quasi-experimental research." In Eric Single and T. Storm (eds.), *Public Drinking and Public Policy*, 161–89. Toronto: Addiction Research Foundation.

Babor, Thomas F., Wilson Acuda, Carlos Campillo, et al. (1996). "A cross-national trial of brief interventions with heavy drinkers." *American Journal of Public Health* 86 (7): 948–55.

Babor, Thomas F., Raul Caetano, Sally Casswell, et al. (2003). *Alcohol: No Ordinary Commodity—Research and Public Policy*. Oxford: Oxford University Press.

Babor, Thomas F., Jack H. Mendelson, Isaac Greenberg, and John Kuehnle. (1978). "Experimental analysis of the 'happy hour': Effects of purchase price on alcohol consumption." *Psychopharmacology* 58 (Spring): 35–41.

Baumann, Karl E., and Susan T. Ennett. (1996). "On the importance of peer influence for adolescent drug use: commonly neglected considerations." *Addiction* 91 (2): 185–98.

Beauchamp, Dan E. (1980). *Beyond Alcoholism*. Philadelphia: Temple University Press.

Becker, Gary S. (1968). "Crime and punishment: An economic approach." *Journal of Political Economy* 78 (2): 526–36.

Becker, Gary S., Michael Grossman, and Kevin M. Murphy. (1991). "Rational addiction and the effect of price on consumption." *American Economic Review* 81 (2): 237–41.

Becker, Gary S., and Kevin M. Murphy. (1988). "A theory of rational addiction." *Journal of Political Economy* 96 (4): 675–700.

Berger, Dale E., and John R. Snortum. (1985). "Alcoholic beverage preferences of drinking-driving violators." *Journal of Studies on Alcohol* 46 (3): 232–39.

Berger, Mark C., and J. Paul Leigh. (1988). "The effect of alcohol use on wages." *Applied Economics* 20: 1343–51.

Bernheim, B. Douglas, and Antonio Rangel. (2004). "Addiction and cue-triggered decision processes." *American Economic Review* 94 (5): 1558–90.

Binkley, Robert C. (1930). *Responsible Drinking, a Discreet Inquiry and a Modest Proposal*. New York: Vanguard Press.

Birckmayer, Jo, and David Hemenway. (1999). "Minimum-age drinking laws and youth suicide, 1970–1990." *American Journal of Public Health* 89: 1365–8.

Blose, James O., and Harold D. Holder. (1987). "Liquor-by-the-drink and alcohol-related traffic crashes: A natural experiment using time-series analysis." *Journal of Studies on Alcohol* 48 (1): 52–60.

Blumstein, Alfred, and Joel Wallman. (2000). *The Crime Drop in America*. New York: Cambridge University Press.

Bobo, Janet Kay, and Corinne Husten. (2000). "Sociocultural influences on smoking and drinking." *Alcohol Research & Health* 24 (4): 225–32.

Boland, Bradley, and Ron Roizen. (1973). "Sales slips and survey responses: New data on the reliability of survey consumption measures." *Drinking and Drug Practices Surveyor* 8: 5–10.

Bonnie, Richard J. (1978). "Discouraging unhealthy personal choices: Reflections on new directions in substance abuse policy." *Journal of Drug Issues* 8: 199.

Bonnie, Richard J., and Mary Ellen O'Connell. (2004). *Reducing Underage Drinking: A Collective Responsibility*. Washington, DC: National Academies Press.

Borkenstein, Robert F., R. F. Crowther, R. P. Shumate, W. B. Ziel, and R. Zylman. (1964). *The Role of the Drinking Driver in Traffic Accidents*, ed. Allen Dale. Indiana University: Department of Police Administration.

Bowles, Samuel, Herbert Gintis, and Melissa Osborne. (2001). "The determinants of earnings: A behavioral approach." *Journal of Economic Literature* 39 (4): 1137–76.

Boyd, Roy, and Barry J. Seldon. (1991). "Revenue and land-use effects of proposed changes in sin taxes: A general equilibrium perspective." *Land Economics* 67 (3): 365–74.

Boyd, Steven R. (1985). *The Whiskey Rebellion: Past and Present Perspectives.* Westport, CT: Greenwood Press.

Bray, Jeremy W. (2005). "Alcohol use, human capital, and wages." *Journal of Labor Economics* 23 (2): 279–312.

Bray, Robert M., Laurel L. Hourani, Kristine L. Rae, et al. (2003). *2002 Department of Defense Survey of Health Related Behaviors Among Military Personnel.* Report prepared for the U.S. Department of Defense (Cooperative Agreement No. DAMD17–00–2-0057), RTI Report 7841–006-FR. Research Triangle Park, NC: Research Triangle Institute.

Bray, Robert M., and Mary Ellen Marsden. (2000). "Trends in Substance Use among U.S. military personnel: the impact of changing demographic composition." *Substance Use and Misuse* 35 (6–8): 949–69.

Bray, Robert M., Mary Ellen Marsden, John F. Mazzuchi, and Roger W. Hartman. (1999). "Prevention in the military." In Ralph E. Tarter, Robert T. Ammerman, and Peggy J. Ott (eds.), *Prevention and Societal Impact of Drug and Alcohol Abuse*, 345–67. Mahwah, NJ: Lawrence Erlbaum Associates.

Brent, David A. (1995). "Risk factors for adolescent suicide and suicidal behavior: mental and substance abuse disorders, family environmental factors, and life stress." *Suicide Life Threat Behav* 25 (Supp.): 52–63.

Brewer, Robert D., and Monica H. Swahn. (2005). "Binge drinking and violence." *Journal of the American Medical Association* 294 (5): 616–18.

Brown, Sandra A., and Susan F. Tapert. (2004). "Health consequences of adolescent alcohol involvement." In Richard J. Bonnie and Mary Ellen O'Connell (eds.), *Reducing Underage Drinking: A Collective Responsibility*, 383–401. Washington, DC: National Academies Press.

Bruere, Martha Bensley. (1927). *Does Prohibition Work? A Study of the Operation of the Eighteenth Amendment Made by the National Federation of Settlements, Assisted by Social Workers in Different Parts of the United States.* New York: Harper & Brothers.

Bruun, Kettil, Griffith Edwards, Martti Lumio, et al. (1975). *Alcohol Control Policies in Public Health Perspective.* Helsinki, Finland: The Finnish Foundation for Alcohol Studies.

Bryant, Clifton D. (1974). "Olive-drab drunks and GI junkies: Alcohol and narcotic addiction in the U.S. Military." In C. D. Bryant (ed.), *Deviant Behavior*, 129–45. Chicago: Rand McNally.

Bullers, Susan, M. Lynne Cooper, and Marcia Russell. (2001). "Social network drinking and adult alcohol involvement: A longitudinal exploration of the direction of influence." *Addictive Behaviors* 26: 181–99.

Burnham, John C. (1968). "New perspectives on the prohibition 'experiment' of the 1920's." *Journal of Social History* 2: 51–68.

Busteed, Brandon. (2005). "Confronting the threat of high-risk drinking." *Association of Governing Boards of Universities and Colleges Priorities* 25 (Winter): 1–16.

Cabot, Richard C. (1904). "The relation of alcohol to arteriosclerosis." *Journal of the American Medical Association* 43: 774–75.

Carnevale, Dan. (2002). "With the latest technology, students find that creating fake ID's is easy." *Chronicle of Higher Education* 48 (32): A34.

Carpenter, Christopher. (2003). "Does heavy alcohol use cause crime? Evidence from underage drunk driving laws." Working Paper. University of California, Irvine: Economics, November 1.

Carpenter, Christopher. (2004a). "How do zero tolerance drunk driving laws work?" *Journal of Health Economics* 23 (1): 61–83.

Carpenter, Christopher. (2004b). "Heavy alcohol use and youth suicide: Evidence from tougher drunk driving laws." *Journal of Policy Analysis and Management* 23 (4): 831–42.

Carpenter, Christopher, and Philip J. Cook. (2006). "Effects of tobacco price increases on drinking." Working Paper. Durham, NC: Duke University, Sanford Institute of Public Policy.

Centers for Disease Control and Prevention. (2004a). *Preventing Heart Disease and Stroke: Addressing the Nation's Leading Killers 2004*. Atlanta, GA: Center for Disease Control and Prevention.

Centers for Disease Control and Prevention. (2004b). http://webappa.cdc.gov/sasweb/ncipc/mortrate.html. In *WISQARS Fatal Injuries: Mortality Reports*.

Center for Science in the Public Interest. (1990). *State alcohol taxes: Case studies of the impact of higher excise taxes in 14 states and the District of Columbia*. Washington, DC: Center for Science in the Public Interest.

Chafetz, Morris E., and Harold W. Demone Jr. (1962). *Alcoholism and Society*. New York: Oxford University Press.

Chaloupka, Frank J., Michael Grossman, Gary S. Becker, and Kevin M. Murphy. (1993). "Alcohol addiction: An econometric analysis." American Economic Association, Anaheim, CA, January.

Chaloupka, Frank J., Michael Grossman, and Henry Saffer. (2002). "The effects of prices on alcohol consumption and alcohol related problems." *Alcohol Research & Health* 26 (1): 22–34.

Chaloupka, Frank J., Henry Saffer, and Michael Grossman. (1993). "Alcohol control policies and motor vehicle fatalities." *Journal of Legal Studies* 22 (1): 161–86.

Chesson, Harrell W., Paul Harrison, and William J. Kassler. (2000). "Sex Under the influence: The effect of alcohol policy on sexually transmitted disease rates in the United States." *Journal of Law and Economics* 43 (1): 215–38.

Cho, Young Ik, Timothy P. Johnson, and Michael Fendrich. (2001). "Monthly variations in self-reports of alcohol consumption." *Journal of Studies on Alcohol* 62 (2): 268–80.

Clark, Norman H. (1976). *Deliver Us From Evil: An Interpretation of American Prohibition*. New York: Norton.

Clements, Kenneth W., Wang Yang, and Simon W. Zheng. (1997). "Is utility additive? The case of alcohol." *Applied Economics* 29: 1163–67.

Coate, Douglas, and Michael Grossman. (1988). "Effects of alcoholic beverage prices and legal drinking ages on youth alcohol use," *Journal of Law and Economics* 31 (1): 145–71.

Cohen, Mark A. (1988). "Pain, suffering, and jury awards: a study of the costs of crime to victims." *Law and Society Review* 22 (3): 537–55.

Collins, James J., Jr. (1986). "The relationship of problem drinking to individual offending sequences." In Alfred Blumstein, Jacqueline Cohen, Jeffrey A. Roth, and Christy A. Visher (eds.), *Criminal Careers and "Career Criminals,"* 89–120. Washington, DC: National Academy Press.

Collins, James J. Jr. (1989). "Alcohol and interpersonal violence: Less than meets the eye." In Neil A. Weiner and Marvin E. Wolfgang (eds.), *Pathways to Criminal Violence*, 49–67. Newbury Park, CA: Sage Publications.

Commodity Board for the Distilled Spirits Industry. (1999). *World Drink Trends 1999: International Beverage Consumption and Production Trends*. Henley-on-Thames, UK: NTC Publications.

Cook, Philip J. (1981). "The effect of liquor taxes on drinking, cirrhosis, and auto fatalities." In Michael Moore and Dean R. Gerstein (eds.), *Alcohol and Public Policy: Beyond the Shadow of Prohibition*, 255–85. Washington, DC: National Academy of Sciences.

Cook, Philip J. (1988). "Increasing the federal excise taxes on alcoholic beverages." *Journal of Health Economics* 7 (1): 89–91.

Cook, Philip J. (1991). "The social cost of drinking." In Olaf G. Aasland (ed.), *The Expert Meeting on the Negative Social Consequences of Alcohol Abuse*, 49–81. Oslo, Norway: Norwegian Ministry of Health and Social Affairs.

Cook, Philip J., and Rebecca Hutchinson. (2005). "Smoke Signals: Adolescent smoking and school continuation." Durham, NC: Duke University, Sanford Institute of Public Policy, March 15.

Cook, Philip J., and John H. Laub. (2002). "After the epidemic: Recent trends in youth violence in the United States." In Michael Tonry (ed.), *Crime and Justice: A Review of Research, Vol. 29*, 1–37. Chicago: University of Chicago Press.

Cook, Philip J., and James Leitzel. (1996). "Perversity, futility, jeopardy: An economic analysis of the attack on gun control." *Law and Contemporary Problems* 59 (1): 91–118.

Cook, Philip J., and Jens Ludwig. (2000). *Gun Violence: The Real Costs*. New York: Oxford University Press.

Cook, Philip J., and Michael J. Moore. (1993a). "Taxation of alcoholic beverages." In Michael E. Hilton, and Gregory Bloss (eds.), *Economic Research on the Prevention of Alcohol-Related Problems*. National Institute on Alcohol Abuse and Alcoholism: NIH Publication No. 93–3513, 33–58.

Cook, Philip J., and Michael J. Moore. (1993b). "Drinking and schooling." *Journal of Health Economics* 12 (4): 411–29.

Cook, Philip J., and Michael J. Moore. (1993c). "Economic perspectives on reducing alcohol-related violence." In Susan E. Martin (ed.), *Alcohol and Interpersonal Violence: Fostering Multidisciplinary Perspectives*, 193–212. NIH Publication No. 93–3496.

Cook, Philip J., and Michael J. Moore. (1993d). "Violence reduction through restrictions on alcohol availability." *Alcohol Health & Research World* 17 (2): 151–56.

Cook, Philip J., and Michael J. Moore. (2000). "Alcohol." In A. J. Culyer and Joseph P. Newhouse (eds.), *Handbook of Health Economics*, 1630–73. North Holland Press.

Cook, Philip J., and Michael J. Moore. (2001). "Environment and persistence in youthful drinking patterns." In Jonathan Gruber (ed.), *Risky Behavior Among Youths: An Economic Analysis*, 375–437. Chicago: University of Chicago Press.

Cook, Philip J., Michael J. Moore, and Roaslie Liccardo Pacula. (1993). "Drinking by young adults, Part 1: Demographics." Durham, NC: Duke University, Sanford Institute Working Paper.

Cook, Philip J., Jan Ostermann, and Frank A. Sloan. (2005a). "Are alcohol excise taxes good for us? Short- and long-term effects on mortality rates." Working Paper, Cambridge, MA: National Bureau of Economic Research.

Cook, Philip J., Jan Ostermann, and Frank A. Sloan. (2005b). "The net effect of an alcohol tax increase on death rates in middle age." *American Economic Review* 95 (2) 278–81.

Cook, Philip J., and Bethany Peters. (2005). "The myth of the drinkers' bonus." Working Paper 11902, Cambridge, MA: National Bureau of Economic Research.

Cook, Philip J., and Ole-Jørgen Skog. (1995). "Alcool, alcoolisme, alcoolisation." *Alcohol Health & Research World* 19 (1): 30–32.

Cook, Philip J., and George Tauchen. (1982). "The effect of liquor taxes on heavy drinking." *Bell Journal of Economics* 13 (2): 379–90.

Cook, Philip J., and George Tauchen. (1984). "The effect of minimum drinking age legislation on youthful auto fatalities, 1970–77." *Journal of Legal Studies* 13 (January): 169–90.

Corlett, Wilfred J., and Douglas C. Hague. (1953). "Complementarity and the excess burden of taxation." *Review of Economic Studies* 21 (1): 21–30.

Corrao, Giovanni, Luca Rubbiati, Vincenzo Bagnardi, Antonella Zambon, and Kari Poikolainen. (2000). "Alcohol and coronary heart disease: a meta-analysis." *Addiction* 95 (10): 1505–23.

Criqui, Michael H., and Brenda L. Ringel. (1994). "Does diet or alcohol explain the French paradox?" *The Lancet* 344 (8939–40): 1719–23.

Currie, Candace., Klaus Hurrelmann, Wolfgang Settertobulte, Rebecca Smith, and Joanna Todd. (2000). *Health and Health Behaviour among Young People*. Copenhagen: World Health Organization, Regional Office for Europe.

Cutler, David, Edward L. Glaeser, and Karen E. Norberg. (2001). "The economic approach to teenage suicide." In Jonathan Gruber (ed.), *Risky Behavior Among Youths*, 219–69. Chicago: University of Chicago Press.

Dana, Charles L., Samuel A. Brown, Samuel W. Lambert, et al. (1921). "Medical profession's response to the Volstead Act." *Journal of the American Medical Association* 76 (23): 1592–3.

Dawson, Deborah A. (2003). "Methodological issues in measuring alcohol use." *Alcohol Research & Health* 27 (1): 18–29.

Dee, Thomas S. (1999). "State alcohol policies, teen drinking, and traffic accidents." *Journal of Public Economics* 72 (2): 289–315.

Dee, Thomas S. (2001). "The effects of minimum legal drinking ages on teen childbearing." *Journal of Human Resources* 36 (4): 823–8.

Dee, Thomas S., and William N. Evans. (2003). "Teen drinking and educational attainment: Evidence from two-sample instrumental variables estimates." *Journal of Labor Economics* 21 (1): 178–209.

DeJong, William, and Linda M. Langford. (2002). "A typology for campus-based alcohol prevention: Moving toward environmental management strategies." *Journal of Studies on Alcohol* (Supp. 14): 140–47.

De Lint, Jan, and Wolfgang Schmidt. (1968). "The distribution of alcohol consumption in Ontario." *Quarterly Journal of Studies in Alcohol* 29: 968–73.

Dexter, Edwin G. (1900). "Drunkenness and the weather." *Annals of the American Academy of Political and Social Science* 41 (July–December): 77–90.

Diamond, Peter. (1974). "Consumption externalities and imperfect corrective pricing." *Bell Journal of Economics* 5: 526–38.

Dietary Guidelines Advisory Committee, Agricultural Research Service. (1995). *Report of the Dietary Guidelines Advisory Committee on the Dietary Guidelines for Americans, 1995, to the Secretary of Health and Human Services and the Secretary of Agriculture.* NTIS Publication No: PB 96 104 344. Washington, DC: National Technical Information Service.

Dills, Angela K., and Jeffrey A. Miron. (2003). "Alcohol prohibition and cirrhosis." National Bureau of Economic Research Working Paper No. 9681, May.

DiNardo, John, and Thomas Lemieux. (1992). "Alcohol, marijuana, and American youth: The unintended effects of government regulation." National Bureau of Economic Research Working Paper No. 4212, November.

Donahue, Richard P., Trevor J. Orchard, Evan A. Stein, and Lewis H. Kuller. (1986). "Apolipoproteins AI, AII and B in young adults: associations with CHD risk factors." *Journal of Chronic Diseases* 39 (10): 823–30.

Donovan, Catherine, and Robert McEwan. (1995). "A review of the literature examining the relationship between alcohol use and HIV-related sexual risk-taking in young people." *Addiction* 90 (3): 319.

Donovan, Dennis M., G. Alan Marlatt, and Philip M. Salzberg. (1983). "Drinking behavior personality factors and high risk driving: A review and theoretical formulation." *Journal of Studies on Alcohol* 44 (3): 395–428.

Douglass, Duncan Baird. (2000). "Constitutional crossroads: Reconciling the Twenty-First Amendment and the Commerce Clause to evaluate state regulation of interstate commerce in alcoholic beverages." *Duke Law Journal* 49: 1619–62.

Draper, Brian. (1994). "Suicidal behavior in the elderly." *Journal of Geriatric Psychiatry* 9:655–61.

DuMouchel, William A., Allan F. Williams, and Paul L. Zador (1987). "Raising the alcohol purchase age: Its effect on fatal motor crashes in 26 states." *Journal of Legal Studies* 16: 249–66.

Durlauf, Steven N., and Marcel Fafchamps. (2004). "Social capital." Cambridge, MA: National Bureau of Economic Research, May.

Dworkin, Gerald. (1971). "Paternalism." In Richard A. Wasserstrom (ed.), *Morality and the Law*, 107–26. Belmont, CA: Wadsworth.

Edwards, Griffith, Peter Anderson, Thomas F. Babor, et al. (1994). *Alcohol Policy and the Public Good*. New York: Oxford University Press.

Eisenberg, Daniel. (2003). "Evaluating the effectiveness of policies related to drunk driving." *Journal of Policy Analysis and Management* 22 (2): 249–74.

Elster, Jon. (1984). *Ulysses and the Sirens: Studies in Rationality and Irrationality*. New York: Cambridge University Press.

Evans, Leonard. (2004). *Traffic Safety*. Bloomfield Hills, MI: Science Serving Society.

Evans, William N., Doreen Neville, and John D. Graham. (1991). "General deterrence of drunk driving: Evaluation of recent American policies." *Risk Analysis* 11 (2): 279–89.

Ewing, John A. (1984). "Detecting alcoholism: The CAGE questionnaire." *Journal of the American Medical Association* 252: 1905–7.

Exum, M. Lyn. (2002). "The application and robustness of the rational choice perspective in the study of intoxicated and angry intentions to aggress." *Criminology* 40(4): 933–66.

"Factbook on $State Beer Taxe$." (2004). www.cspinet.org/booze/taxguide/040802BeerReport.pdf, accessed January 2, 2006.

Fagan, Jeffrey. (1990). "Intoxication and aggression." In Michael Tonry and James Q. Wilson (eds.), *Crime and Justice*, 241–320. Chicago: University of Chicago Press.

Fagan, Ronald W., Jr., and Armand L. Mauss. (1978). "Padding the revolving door: An initial assessment of the Uniform Alcoholism and Intoxication Treatment Act in practice." *Social Problems* 26 (2): 232–46.

Farrell, Susan, Willard G. Manning, and Michael D. Finch. (2003). "Alcohol dependence and the price of alcoholic beverages." *Journal of Health Economics* 22 (1): 117–47.

Farrelly, Matthew C., Jeremy W. Bray, Gary A. Zarkin, Brett W. Wendling, and Rosalie L. Pacula. (1999). "Effects of prices and policies on the demand for marijuana: Evidence from the National Household Surveys on Drug Abuse." NBER Working Paper No. 6940.

Fergusson, David M., and Michael T. Lynskey. (1996). "Alcohol misuse and adolescent sexual behaviors and risk taking." *Archives of Pediatric and Adolescent Medicine* 98(1): 91–96.

Fingarette, Herbert. (1988). *Heavy Drinking: The Myth of Alcoholism as a Disease*. Berkeley: University of California Press.

Finkelstein, Eric A., Ian C. Fiebelkorn, and Guijing Wang. (2003). "National medical spending attributable to overweight and obesity; How much and who's paying?" *Health Affairs* W3: 219–26.

Finney, John W., Annette C. Hahn, and Rudolph B. Moos. (1996). "The effectiveness of inpatient and outpatient treatment for alcohol abuse: The need to focus on mediators and moderators of setting effects." *Addiction* 91: 1773–96.

Fisher, Irving. (1926). *Prohibition At Its Worst*. New York: MacMillan.

Fisher, Irving. (1927). *Prohibition At Its Worst, Revised*. New York: Alcohol Information Committee.

Fisher, Irving. (1928). *Prohibition Still At Its Worst*. New York: Alcohol Information Committee.

Fisher, Irving. (1930). *The "Noble Experiment."* New York. N.Y.: Alcohol Information Committee.

Foege, William H. (1987). "Highway violence and public policy." *New England Journal of Medicine* 316 (22): 1407–08.

Fosdick, Raymond B., and Albert L. Scott. (1933). *Toward Liquor Control*. New York: Harper & Brothers.

Foster, Susan E., Roger D. Vaughan, William H. Foster, and Joseph A. Califano. (2003). "Alcohol consumption and expenditures for underage drinking and adult excessive drinking." *Journal of the American Medical Association* 289 (8): 989–95.

Freedman, Alix M., and John R. Emshwiller. (1999). "Vintage system: Big liquor wholesaler finds change stalking its very private world—Southern Wine & Spirits is a mandated middleman under increasing attack—a vineyard breaks the mold." *Wall Street Journal*, A, October 4, 1.

French, Michael T., and Gary A. Zarkin. (1995). "Is moderate alcohol use related to wages? Evidence from four worksites." *Journal of Health Economics* 14 (3): 319–44.

Friedman, Milton. (1962). *Capitalism and Freedom*. Chicago: University of Chicago Press.

Fuller, Richard K., and Susanne Hiller-Sturmhöfel. (1999). "Alcoholism treatment in the United States: An overview." *Alcohol Research & Health* 23 (2): 69–77.

Gaviria, Alejandro, and Steven Raphael. (2001). "School-based peer effects and juvenile behavior." *Review of Economics & Statistics* 83: 257–68.

Gayer, Theodore, James T. Hamilton, and W. Kip Viscusi. (2000). "Private values of risk tradeoffs at Superfund sites: Housing market evidence on learning about risk." *Review of Economics and Statistics* 82 (3): 439–51.

Gerstein, Dean R. (1981). "Alcohol use and consequences." In Mark H. Moore and Dean R. Gerstein (eds.), *Alcohol and Public Policy: Beyond the Shadow of Prohibition*, 182–224. Washington, DC: National Academy of Sciences.

Giacopassi, David and Russell Winn. (1995). "Alcohol availability and alcohol-related crashes: Does distance make a difference?" *American Journal of Drug and Alcohol Abuse* 21 (3): 407–16.

Giancola, Peter R. (2004) "Executive functioning and alcohol-related aggression" *Journal of Abnormal Psychology* 113(4): 541–55.

Giesbrecht, Norman. (2003). "Rising per capita alcohol consumption and drinking-related harm: Suggestions for meeting the challenge." *The Globe* 4, 7–12.

Glaeser, Edward L., Bruce Sacerdote, and Jose Scheinkman. (2003). "The social multiplier." *Journal of the European Economic Association* 1 (2): 345–53.

Glaeser, Edward, David Laibson, and Bruce Sacerdote. (2002). "An economic approach to social capital." *Economic Journal* 112: 437–58.

Gmel, Gerhard, Elisabeth Gutjahr, and Jürgen Rehm. (2003). "How stable is the risk curve between alcohol and all-cause mortality and what factors influence the shape? A precision-weighted hierarchical meta-analysis." *European Journal of Epidemiology* 18 (7): 631–42.

Godfrey, Christine. (1989). "Factors influencing the consumption of alcohol and tobacco: the use and abuse of economic models." *British Journal of Addiction* 84 (10): 1123–38.

Godfrey, Christine, and Larry Harrison. (1990). "Preventive health objectives and tax policy options." In Alan Maynard and Philip Tether (eds.), *Preventing Alcohol and Tobacco Problems*, 54–74. Hants, UK: Gower Publishing.

Granovetter, Mark. 1975, 2nd ed., 1995. *Getting a Job: A Study of Contacts and Careers*. Chicago: University of Chicago Press.

Grant, Bridget, F., and Deborah A. Dawson. (1997). "Age at onset of alcohol use and its association with DSM-IV alcohol abuse and dependence: Results from the National Longitudinal Alcohol Epidemiologic Survey." *Journal of Substance Abuse* 9: 103–10.

Greenfield, Lawrence A., and Maureen A. Henneberg. (2001). "Victim and offender self-reports of alcohol involvement in crime." *Alcohol Research & Health* 25 (1): 20–31.

Greenfield, Thomas K., and William C. Kerr. (2003). "Tracking alcohol consumption over time." *Alcohol Research & Health* 27 (1): 30–38.

Gronbaek, Morton. (2001). "Factors influencing the relation between alcohol and mortality—with focus on wine." *Journal of Internal Medicine* 250: 291–308.

Grossman, Michael. (1972). "On the concept of health capital and the demand for health." *Journal of Political Economy* 80: 223–55.

Grossman, Michael. (2000). "The human capital model." In A. J. Culyer and J. P. Newhouse (eds.), *Handbook of Health Economics, Vol. 1A*, 347–408. New York: Elsevier.

Grossman, Michael, Frank J. Chaloupka, Henry Saffer, and Adit Laixuthai. (1994). "Effects of alcohol price policy on youth: A summary of economic research." *Journal of Research on Adolescence* 4: 437–64.

Grossman, Michael, Douglas Coate, and Gregory M. Arluck. (1987). "Price sensitivity of alcoholic beverages in the United States: Youth alcohol consumption." In Mark H. Moore, and Dean R. Gerstein (eds.), *Control Issues in Alcohol Abuse Prevention: Strategies for States and Communities*, 169–98. Greenwich, CT: JAI Press.

Grossman, Michael, and Sara Markowitz. (2001). "Alcohol regulation and violence on college campuses." In Michael Grossman and Chee-Ruey Hsieh (eds.), *Economic Analysis of Substance Use and Abuse: The Experience of Developed Countries and Lessons for Developing Countries*, 257–89. Cheltenham, UK: Edward Elgar.

Grossman, Michael, Jody L. Sindelar, John Mullahy, and Richard Anderson. (1993). "Alcohol and cigarette taxes." *Journal of Economic Perspectives* 7 (4): 211–22.

Grube, Joel W. (1997). "Preventing sales of alcohol to minors: Results from a community trial." *Addiction* 92 (2): S251–60.

Gruber, Jonathan. (2002–2003). "Smoking's 'internalities,' " *Regulation* (Winter): 52–57.

Gruber, Jonathan, and Botond Köszegi. (2001). "Is addiction 'rational?' " *Theory and evidence*." *Quarterly Journal of Economics* 116 (4): 1261–1305.

Gruber, Jonathan, and Botond Köszegi. (2004). "Tax incidence when individuals are time-inconsistent: the case of cigarette excise taxes." *Journal of Public Economics* 88: 1959–87.

Gruenewald, Paul J., and William R. Ponicki. (1995). "The relationship of the retail availability and alcohol sales to alcohol-related traffic crashes." *Accident Analysis and Prevention* 27 (2): 249–59.

Gusfield, J. (1963). *Symbolic Crusade: Status Politics and the American Temperance Movement.* Urbana: University of Illinois Press.

Hafemeister, Thomas L., and Shelly L. Jackson. (2004). "Effectiveness of sanctions and law enforcement practices targeted at underage drinking not involving operation of a motor vehicle." In Richard Bonnie and Mary Ellen O'Connell (eds.), *Reducing Underage Drinking: A Collective Responsibility, Background Papers* [CD-ROM]. Washington, DC: National Academies Press.

Hamill, Pete. (1995). *Drinking Life: A Memoir.* Boston: Little, Brown.

Hamilton, Vivian, and Barton H. Hamilton. (1997). "Alcohol and earnings: does drinking yield a wage premium?" *Canadian Journal of Economics* 30 (1): 135–51.

Harrison, Leonard, and Elizabeth Laine. (1936). *After Repeal: A Study of Liquor Control Administration.* New York: Harper & Brothers Publishers.

Harrison, Patricia A., Jayne A. Fulkerson, and Eunkyung Park. (2000). "The relative importance of social versus commercial sources in youth access to tobacco, alcohol, and other drugs." *Preventive Medicine* 31 (1): 39–48.

Harwood, Henrick D., Douglas Fountain, and Gina Livermore. (1998). *The Economic Costs of Alcohol and Drug Abuse in the United States 1992.* Washington, DC: U.S. Government Printing Office.

Harwood, Henrick. (2000). *Updating Estimates of the Economic Costs of Alcohol Abuse in the United States: Estimates, Update Methods, and Data.* National Institute on Alcohol Abuse and Alcoholism.

Hasin, Deborah. (2003). "Classification of alcohol use disorders." *Alcohol Research & Health* 27 (1): 5–17.

Hayward, Linda, Stephen R. Zubrick, and Sven R. Silburn. (1992). "Blood alcohol levels in suicide cases." *Journal of Epidemiology and Community* 46: 256–60.

Heien, Dale M. (1995). "The economic case against higher alcohol taxes." *Journal of Economic Perspectives* 9 (1): 207–9.

Heien, Dale M. (1996). "Do drinkers earn less?" *Southern Economic Journal* 63 (1): 60–68.

Heien, Dale M., and David J. Pittman. (1993). "The external costs of alcohol abuse." *Journal of Studies on Alcohol* 54 (3): 302–7.

Higley, J. Dee. (2001). "Individual differences in alcohol-induced aggression." *Alcohol Research & Health* 25 (1): 12–19.

Hilton, Michael E., and Walter Clark, E. (1987). "Changes in American drinking patterns and problems, 1967–1984." *Journal of Studies on Alcohol* 48 (6): 515–22.

Hingson, Ralph, Timothy Heeren, and Michael Winter. (1994). "Lower blood alcohol limits for young drivers." *Public Health Reports* 109 (6): 738–44.

Hingson, Ralph, Daniel Merrigan, and Timothy Heeren. (1985). "Effects of Massachusetts raising its legal drinking age from 18 to 20 on death from teenage homicide, suicide, and nontraffic accidents." *Pediatric Clinics of North America* 32 (1): 221–32.

Hingson, Ralph, and Michael Winter. (2003). "Epidemiology and consequences of drinking and driving." *Alcohol Research & Health* 27 (1): 63–78.

Hirschman, Albert O. (1991). *The Rhetoric of Reaction: Perversity, Futility, Jeopardy*. Cambridge, MA: Harvard University Press.

Hodgson, Thomas A., and Mark Meiners. (1979). *Guidelines for Cost-of-Illness Studies in the Public Health Service*. Bethesda, MD: Public Health Service Task Force on Cost-of-Illness Studies.

Holder, Harold D., and James O. Blose. (1985). "Impact of changes in distilled spirits availability on alcohol distribution." *Alcohol* 2: 541–44.

Holder, Harold D., Paul J. Gruenewald, William R. Ponicki, et al. (2000). "Effect of community-based interventions on high-risk drinking and alcohol-related injuries." *Journal of the American Medical Association* 284 (18): 2341–7.

Holder, Harold D., Kathleen Janes, James Mosher, Robert F. Saltz, S. Spurr, and Alexander C. Wagenaar. (1993). "Alcoholic beverage server liability and the reduction of alcohol-involved problems." *Journal of Studies on Alcohol* 54 (2): 23–26.

Holder, Harold D., and Alexander C. Wagenaar. (1994). "Mandated server training and reduced alcohol-involved traffic crashes: A time series analysis of the Oregon experience." *Accident and Prevention* 26: 89–97.

Holder, Harold D., and Alexander C. Wagenaar. (1995). "Changes in alcohol consumption resulting from the elimination of retail wine monopolies: Results from five U.S. states." *Journal of Studies on Alcohol* 56 (5): 566–73.

Howland, Jonathan, Damaris J. Rohsenow, Jennifer Cote, Michael Siegel, and Thomas W. Mangione. (2000). "Effects of low-dose alcohol exposure on simulated merchant ship handling power plant operation by maritime cadets." *Addiction* 95 (5): 719–26.

Hoyt, Gail M., and Frank J. Chaloupka. (1994). "Effect of survey conditions of self-reported substance use." *Contemporary Economic Policy* 12 (3): 109–21.

Hu, Teh Wei, and Frank Sandifer. (1981). "Synthesis of cost of illness methodology—final report." Unpublished Report. Washington, DC: National Center for Health Statistics.

Hu, Tun Yuan. (1950). *The Liquor Tax in the United States 1791–1947*. New York: Columbia University, Graduate School of Business.

Hurst, Paul M., David Harte, and William J. Firth. (1994). "The Grand Rapids dip revisited." *Accident Analysis & Prevention* 26:, 647–54.

Hutchinson, Rebecca. (2003). "College-aged youth and drinking: How do high school drinking behaviors affect the likelihood of college enrollment?" thesis. Duke University: Economics Department, December.

Institute of Medicine. (1981). *Cost of Environment-Related Health Effects: A Plan for Continuing Study*. Washington, DC: National Academy Press.

Jacobs, James B. (1989). *Drunk Driving: An American Dilemma*. Chicago: University of Chicago Press.

James, William. (1900). *Talks with Teachers About Psychology, and to Students about Some of Life's Ideals.* New York: H. Holt.

Jellinek, Elvin Morton. (1952). "Phases of alcohol addiction." *Quarterly Journal of Studies in Alcohol* 13: 673–84.

Jellinek, Elvin Morton. (1960). *The Disease Concept of Alcoholism.* New Haven, CT: Hillhouse Press.

Joint Committee of the States to Study Alcoholic Beverage Laws. (1950). *The 1950 Alcoholic Beverage Control: An Official Study. First Edition.* New York: Joint Committee of the States to Study Alcoholic Beverage Laws.

Kansas State Government. (Legislative Council). (1949). *Liquor Control: License & Taxes in 45 States.* In *158.* Ed. F. H. Guild. Research Department, Kansas Legislative Council.

Kaplow, Louis. (2006). "Taxation." Working Paper 12061. Cambridge, MA: National Bureau of Economic Research, February.

Kay, John, and Michael Keen. (1986). "Alcohol and tobacco taxes: Criteria for harmonisation." In Sijbren Cnossen (ed.), *Tax Coordination in the European Community,* 85–111. Amsterdam: Kluwer Academic.

Keller, Mark (1978). *The New Encyclopaedia Britannica in 30 Volumes: Macropaedia.* Vol. 1, Alcohol Consumption, 15. Chicago: Encyclopedia Britannica.

Kenkel, Donald. (1993). "Drinking, driving, and deterrence: The effectiveness and social costs of alternative policies." *Journal of Law and Economics* 36: 877–913.

Kenkel, Donald S. (1996). "New estimates of the optimal tax on alcohol." *Economic Inquiry* 34: 296–319.

Kenkel, Donald S., and Willard G. Manning. (1996). "Perspectives on alcohol taxation." *Alcohol Health & Research World* 20 (4): 230–38.

Kenkel, Donald S., and David C. Ribar. (1994). "Alcohol consumption and young adults' socioeconomic status." *Brookings Papers on Economic Activity Micro,* June, 119–61.

Kenkel, Donald S., and Ping Wang. (1999). "Are alcoholics in bad jobs?" In Frank J. Chaloupka, Michael Grossman, and Warren K. Bickel (eds.), *The Economic Analysis of Substance Use and Abuse,* 251–78. Chicago: University of Chicago Press.

Kerr, William C., and Thomas K. Greenfield. (2003). "The average ethanol content of beer in the U.S. and individual states: estimates for use in aggregate consumption statistics." *Journal of Studies on Alcohol* 64 (1): 70–74.

Kiefer, Falk, Holger Jahn, Timo Tarnaske, et al. (2003). "Comparing and combining naltrexone and acamprosate in relapse prevention of alcoholism: A double-blind, placebo-controlled study." *Archives of General Psychiatry* 60: 92–9.

Klatsky, Arthur L. (2002). "Alcohol and cardiovascular diseases: A historical overview." *Annals of the New York Academy of Sciences* 957: 7–15.

Klatsky, Arthur L., Gary D. Friedman, Mary Anne Armstrong, and Harald Kipp. (2003). "Wine, liquor, beer, and mortality." *American Journal of Epidemiology* 158 (6): 585–95.

Klatsky, Arthur L., Gary D. Friedman, and Abraham B. Siegelaub. (1974). "Alcohol consumption before myocardial infarction: Results from the Kaiser-Permanente Epidemiologic Study of Myocardial Infarction." *Annals of Internal Medicine* 81: 294–301.

Kleiman, Mark A. R. (1992). *Against Excess: Drug Policy for Results*. New York: Basic Books.

Kling, William. (1991). "Measurement of ethanol consumed in distilled spirits [Revision]." *Journal of Studies on Alcohol* 52: 503–4.

Klingemann, Harald, and Gerhard Gmel. (2001). *Mapping the Social Consequences of Alcohol Consumption*. Boston, MA: Kluwer Academic.

Krauss, Ronald M., Richard J. Deckelbaum, Nancy Ernst, et al. (1996). "Dietary guidelines for healthy American adults. A statement for health professionals from the Nutrition Committee, American Heart Association." *Circulation* 94: 1795–1800.

Kuhn, Cynthia, Scott Swartzwelder, and Wilkie Wilson. (1998). *Buzzed: The Straight Facts about the Most Used and Abused Drugs from Alcohol to Ecstasy*. New York: Norton.

Kurtz, Ernest. (1980). *NOT-GOD: A History of Alcoholics Anonymous*. Center City, MN: Hazelden Educational Services.

Kyvig, David. (2000). *Repealing National Prohibition*. Kent, OH: Kent State University Press.

Laibson, David. (1997). "Golden eggs and hyperbolic discounting." *Quarterly Journal of Economics* 112: 443–77.

Landefeld, J. Steven, and Eugene P. Seskin. (1982). "The economic value of life: linking theory to practice." *American Journal of Public Health* 76 (6): 555–66.

Ledermann, Sully. (1956). *Alcool, alcoolisme, alcoolisation. Vol. 1. Données scientifiques de caractère physiologique, économique et social. (Institute Nationale d'Ètudes Demographique, Travaux et Documents, Cahier. No. 29.)* Paris Presses Universitaires de France.

Leinwand, Donna. (2001). "Tech-savvy teens swamp police with fake IDs." *ULA Today*, July 2.

Leung, Siu, and Charles E. Phelps. (1993). "My kingdom for a drink? A review of estimates of the price sensitivity of demand for alcoholic beverages." In Michael E. Hilton and Gregory Bloss (eds.), *Economics and the Prevention of Alcohol-Related Problems: National Institute on Alcohol Abuse and Alcoholism Research Monograph No. 25*, 1–31. Bethesda, MD: NIH Pub. No. 93–3513.

Levitt, Steven D. (2004). "Understanding why crime fell in the 1990s: Four factors that explain the decline and six that do not." *Journal of Economic Perspectives* 18 (1): 163–90.

Levitt, Steven D., and Jack Porter. (2001). "How dangerous are drinking drivers?" *Journal of Political Economy* 109 (6): 1198–1237.

Liang, Lan, Frank A. Sloan, and Emily M. Stout. (2004). "Precaution, compensation, and threats of sanction: the case of alcohol servers." *International Review of Law and Economics* 24: 49–70.

Little, Hilary J. (2000). "Behavioral mechanisms underlying the link between." *Alcohol Research & Health World* 24 (2): 215–24.

Loewenstein, George. (1996). "Out of control: Visceral influences on behavior." *Organization Behavior and Human Decision Processes* 65: 272–92.

Loewenstein, George. (1999). "A visceral account of addiction." In Jon Elster and Skog Ole-Jörgen (eds.), *Getting Hooked: Rationality and Addiction*, 235–64. Cambridge: Cambridge University Press.

Ludwig, Jens, and Philip J. Cook. (2001). "The benefits of reducing gun violence: Evidence from Contingent-Valuation Survey Data." *Journal of Risk and Uncertainty* 22 (3): 207–26.

Lyon, Andrew B., and Robert M. Schwab. (1995). "Consumption taxes in a life-cycle framework: are sin taxes regressive?" *Review of Economics and Statistics* 77 (3): 389–406.

MacAndrew, Craig, and Robert B. Edgerton. (1969). *Drunken Comportment: A Social Explanation*. Chicago: Aldine.

MacClintock, S. S. (1901). "The Kentucky mountains and their feuds I: the people and their country." *American Journal of Sociology* July 7(1): 1–28.

MacCoun, Robert J., and Peter Reuter. (2001). *Drug War Heresies*. New York: Cambridge University Press.

MacDonald, Ziggy, and Michael A. Shields. (2001). "The impact of alcohol consumption on occupational attainment in England." *Economica* 68: 427–53.

Maher, Jacquelyn J. (1997). "Exploring alcohol's effects on liver function." *Alcohol Health & Research World* 21 (1): 5–12.

Mäkelä, Klaus. (1969). *Alkoholinkulutuksen Jakautuma*. Helsinki: Social Research Institute of Alcohol Studies.

Males, Mike A. (1986). "The minimum purchase age for alcohol and young-driver fatal crashes: A long-term view." *Journal of Legal Studies* 15: 181–217.

Mangione, Thomas W., Jonathan Howland, Benjamin Amick, Jennifer Cote, Marianne Lee, Nicole Bell, and Sol Levine. (1999). "Employee drinking practices and work performance." *Journal of Studies on Alcohol* 60 (2): 261–74.

Manning, Willard G., Linda Blumberg, and Lawrence Moulton. (1995). "The demand for alcohol: The differential response to price." *Journal of Health Economics* 14 (2): 123–48.

Manning, Willard G., Emmett B. Keeler, Joseph P. Newhouse, Elizabeth M. Sloss, and Jeffrey Wasserman. (1989). "The taxes of sin: Do smokers and drinkers pay their way?" *Journal of the American Medical Association* 261, 1604–09.

Manning, Willard G., Emmett B. Keeler, Joseph P. Newhouse, Elizabeth M. Sloss, and Jeffrey Wasserman. (1991). *The Costs of Poor Health Habits*. Cambridge, MA: Harvard University Press.

Markowitz, Sara. (2000). "The price of alcohol, wife abuse, and husband abuse." *Southern Economic Journal* 67 (2): 279–303.

Markowitz, Sara, Pinka Chatterji, and Robert Kaestner. (2003). "Estimating the impact of alcohol policies on youth suicides." *Journal of Mental Health Policy and Economics* 6: 37–46.

Markowitz, Sara, and Michael Grossman. (1998). "Alcohol regulation and domestic violence towards children." *Contemporary Economic Policy* 16 (3): 309–20.

Markowitz, Sara, and Michael Grossman. (2000). "The effects of beer taxes on physical child abuse." *Journal of Health Economics* 19 (2): 271–82.

236 • References

Mason, W. Alex, and Michael Windle. (2001). "Family, religious, school and peer influences on adolescent alcohol use: a longitudinal study." *Journal of Studies on Alcohol* 62 (1): 44–53.

McElduff, Patrick, and Annette J. Dobson. (1997). "How much alcohol and how often? Population based case-control study of alcohol consumption and risk of a major coronary event." *British Medical Journal* 314 (7089): 1159–64.

Medicine in the Public Interest. (1979). *The Effects of Alcoholic-Beverage-Control Laws.* Washington, DC: Medicine in the Public Interest.

Mello, Nancy K. (1972). "Behavioral studies of alcoholism." In Benjamin Kissin and Henri Begleiter (eds.), *The Biology of Alcoholism, Vol. 2.* New York: Plenum Publishing.

Mello, Nancy K., H. Brian McNamee, and Jack H. Mendelson. (1968). "Drinking patterns of chronic alcoholics: gambling and motivation for alcohol." In J. O. Cole (ed.), *Clinical Research in Alcoholism.* Washington, DC: American Psychiatric Association.

Miczek, Klaus A., Elise M. Weerts, and Joseph F. DeBold. (1993). "Alcohol, benzodiazepine-GABA(A) receptor complex and aggression: Ethological analysis of individual differences in rodents and primates." *Journal of Studies on Alcohol* 54 (Special Suppl.) 170–79.

Midanik, Lorraine. (1982). "The validity of self reported alcohol consumption and alcohol problems: A literature review." *British Journal of Addiction* 77: 357–82.

Midanik, Lorraine T., Frank J. Chaloupka, Richard Saitz, et al. (2004). "Alcohol-attributable deaths and years of potential life lost—United States, 2001." *Morbidity and Mortality Weekly Report* (September 24): 866–70.

Miller, Ted R., and Lawrence J. Blincoe. (1994). "Incidence and costs of alcohol involved crashes in the United States." *Accident Analysis & Prevention* 26 (5): 583–92.

Miller, Ted R., Daniel R. Lestina, and Rebecca S. Spicer. (1998). "Highway crash costs in the United States by driver age, blood alcohol level, victim age, and restraint use." *Analysis and Prevention* 30 (2): 137–50.

Miller, Ted R., David T. Levy, Rebecca S. Spicer, and Dexter Taylor. (2005). "Underage drinking: Societal costs and seller profits." Calverton, MD: Pacific Institute for Research and Evaluation.

Miller, William R., Janice M. Brown, T. L. Simpson, et al. (1995). "What works? A methodological analysis of the alcohol treatment outcome literature." In R. K. Hester, and W. R. Miller (eds.), *Handbook of Alcoholism Treatment Approaches: Effective Alternatives, 2nd Edition,* 12–44. Needham Heights, MA: Allyn & Bacon.

Miller-Tutzauer, Carol, Kenneth E. Leonard, and Michael Windle. (1991). "Marriage and alcohol use: A longitudinal study of 'maturing out.'" *Journal of Studies on Alcohol* 52 (2): 434–40.

Miron, Jeffrey A., and Jeffrey Zwiebel. (1991). "Alcohol consumption during prohibition." *American Economic Review* 81 (2): 242–47.

Mishan, E. J. (1971). "Evaluation of life and limb: A theoretical approach." *Journal of Political Economy* 79 (July–August), 687–705.

Moeller, F. Gerard, and Donald M. Dougherty. (2001). "Antisocial personality disorder, alcohol, and aggression." *Alcohol Research & Health* 25 (1): 5–11.

Mokdad, Ali H., James S. Marks, Donna F. Stroup, and Julie L. Gerberding. (2004). "Actual causes of death in the United States, 2000." *Journal of the American Medical Association* 291 (10): 10, 1238–45.

Moore, Mark H. (1990). "What sort of ideas become public ideas?" In Robert B. Reich (ed.), *The Power of Public Ideas*, 55–83. Cambridge: Harvard University Press.

Moore, Mark H., and Dean R. Gerstein. eds. (1981). *Alcohol & Public Policy: Beyond the Shadow of Prohibition.* Washington, DC: National Academy Press.

Moore, Michael, and W. Kip Viscusi. (1990). *Compensation Mechanisms for Job Risks.* Princeton, N.J.: Princeton University Press.

Morone, James A. (2002). "Moralism, politics, and health policy." *Investigator Awards in Health Policy Research, The Robert Woods Johnson Foundation Research in Profile Series,* issue 5.

Mosher, James F. (1980). "The history of youthful-drinking laws: Implications for current policy." In Henry Wechsler (ed.), *Minimum-Drinking-Age Laws: An Evaluation,* 11–38. Lexington, MA: Lexington Books.

Mosher, James F. (1988). *Liquor Liability Law.* New York: Matthew Bender.

Mosher, James F., and Joseph R. Mottl. (1981). "The role of nonalcohol agencies in federal regulation of drinking behavior and consequences." In Mark H. Moore and Dean R Gerstein (eds.), *Alcohol and Public Policy: Beyond the Shadow of Prohibition,* 388–458. Washington, D.C.: National Academy Press.

Mosher, James, and other contributors. (2002). *Liquor Liability Law.* Newark, NJ: Lexis Nexis.

Mukamal, Kenneth J., Katherine M. Conigrave, Murray A. Mittleman, Carlos A. Camargo Jr., Meir J. Stampfer, Walter C. Willett, and Eric B. Rimm. (2003). "Roles of drinking pattern and type of alcohol consumed in coronary heart disease in men." *New England Journal of Medicine* 348 (2): 109–18.

Mulford, Harold A., and J. L. Fitzgerald. (1999). "Alcohol consumption and Iowa's control policy shift." *Journal of Studies on Alcohol* 60 (11): 139–40.

Mulford, Harold A., Johannes Ledolter, and J. L. Fitzgerald. (1993). "Alcohol availability and consumption: Iowa sales data revisited." *Journal of Studies on Alcohol* 53: 487–94.

Mullahy, John. (1993). "Alcohol and the labor market." In Michael E. Hilton and Gregory Bloss (eds.), *Economics and the Prevention of Alcohol-Related Problems.* Washington, DC: National Institute on Alcohol Abuse and Alcoholism.

Mullahy, John, and Jody L. Sindelar. (1989). "Life cycle effects of alcoholism on education, earnings, and occupation." *Inquiry* 26: 272–82.

Mullahy, John, and Jody L. Sindelar. (1991). "Gender differences in labor market effects of alcoholism." *American Economic Review* 81 (2): 161–5.

Mullahy, John, and Jody L. Sindelar. (1993). "Alcoholism, work, and income." *Journal of Labor Economics* 11(3): 494–520.

Mullahy, John, and Jody L. Sindelar. (1996). "Employment, unemployment, and problem drinking." *Journal of Health Economics* 15 (4): 409–34.

Murray, Christopher J. L., and Alan D. Lopez. (1997). "Global mortality, disability, and the contribution of risk factors: Global Burden of Disease Study." *Lancet* 349 (9063): 1436–42.

Myrdal, Gunnar. (1930). "Alkoholens vinst-och forlustkonto." *Tirfling* 24 (4): 106–9.

Naimi, Timothy S., David W. Brown, Robert D. Brewer, et al. (2005). "Cardiovascular risk factors and confounders among nondrinking and moderate-drinking U.S. adults." *American Journal of Preventive Medicine* 28 (4): 369–73.

National Council on Alcoholism. (1984). *National Council on Alcoholism 40th Anniversary Commemorative Journal 1944–1984.* Englewood, NJ: Enterprise Press.

National Highway Traffic Safety Administration. (1992). *Fatal Accident Reporting System.* Washington, DC: Department of Transportation, National Highway Traffic Safety Administration.

National Institute of Diabetes and Digestive and Kidney Diseases. (National Institute of Health). (2004). *National Diabetes Statistics Fact Sheet: General Information and National Estimates on Diabetes in the United States, Revised edition 2004.* Bethesda, MD: Department of Health and Human Services, National Institutes of Health.

National Institute on Alcohol Abuse and Alcoholism. (2003a). "2001–2002 National Epidemiologic Survey on Alcohol and Related Conditions (NESARC)." Bethesda, MD.

National Institute on Alcohol Abuse and Alcoholism. (2003b). "The genetics of alcoholism." http://www.niaaa.nih.gov/publications/aa60.htm. *Alcohol Alert* 60: (July).

Nelson, Toben F., Timothy S. Naimi, Robert D. Brewer, and Henry Wechsler. (2005). "The state sets the rate: The relationship of college binge drinking to state binge drinking rates and selected state alcohol control policies." *American Journal of Public Heath* 95 (3): 441–6.

Nephew, Thomas M., Gerald D. Williams, Hsiao-ye Yi, Allison K. Hoy, Fredrick S. Stinson, and Mary C. Dufour. (2003). *Apparent per capita alcohol consumption: National, state, and regional trends, 1977–2000.* Surveillance Report, 62. National Institute on Alcohol Abuse and Alcoholism: Division of Biometry and Epidemiology.

New York Times Staff. (1987). "Excerpts From the Reagan Interview with 4 Correspondents." *New York Times*, A, December 4, A16.

Norström, Thor. (1987). "The abolition of the Swedish alcohol rationing system: effects on consumption distribution and cirrhosis mortality." *British Journal of Addiction* 82: 633–41.

Norton, Edward C., Richard C. Lindrooth, and Susan T. Ennett. (1998). "Controlling for the endogeneity of peer substance abuse on adolescent alcohol and tobacco use." *Health Economics* 7: 439–53.

Nuwer, H. (1999). "Eliminating the frat rats: Why Greeks need to expel hazers in their midst." http://www.stophazing.org/nuwer/exterminating.htm, accessed March 29, 2005.

Nycander, Svante. (1998). "Ivan Bratt: the man who saved Sweden from prohibition." *Addiction* 93 (1): 17–25.

O'Donoghue, Ted, and Matthew Rabin. (1999). "Addiction and self control." In Jon Elster (ed.), *Addiction: Entries and Exits*, 169–206. New York: Russel Sage Foundation.

O'Malley, Patrick M., and Lloyd D. Johnston. (2002). "Epidemiology of alcohol and other drug use among American college students." *Journal of Studies on Alcohol* (Supp. 14): 23–39.

Office of National Drug Control Policy. (2001). *The Economic Costs of Drug Abuse in the United States, 1992–1998*, Publication No. NCJ-190636. Washington, DC: Executive Office of the President.

Orford, Jim, and Griffith Edwards. (1977). *Alcoholism: A Comparison of Treatment and Advice, with a Study of the Influence of Marriage*. Oxford: Oxford University Press.

Oscar-Berman, Marlene, and Ksenija Marinkovic. (2003). "Alcoholism and the brain: An overview." *Alcohol Health & Research World* 27 (2): 125–33.

Österberg, Esa. (1983). "Calculating the costs of alcohol: The Scandinavian experience." In Marcus Grant, Martin Plant, and Alan Williams (eds.), *Economics and Alcohol*, 82–96. New York: Gardner Press, Inc..

Pacula, Rosalie Liccardo. (1998). "Can increasing the beer tax reduce marijuana consumption." *Journal of Health Economics* 17 (5): 557–86.

Pattison, E. Mansell, Mark B. Sobell, and Linda C. Sobell, eds. (1977). *Emerging Concepts of Alcohol Dependence*. New York: Springer.

Pearl, Raymond. (1926). *Alcohol and Longevity*. New York: Knopf.

Peele, Stanton, and Archie Brodsky. (2000). "Exploring psychological benefits associated with moderate alcohol use: a necessary corrective to assessments of drinking outcomes?" *Drug and Alcohol Dependence* 60: 221–47.

Pernanen, Kai. (1981). "Theoretical aspects of the relationship between alcohol abuse and crime." In James J. Collins Jr., (ed.), *Drinking and Crime: Perspectives on the Relationship Between Alcohol Consumption and Criminal Behavior*, 1–69. New York: Guilford Press.

Pernanen, Kai. (1991). *Alcohol in Human Violence*. New York: Guilford Press.

Petersilia, Joan, Peter W. Greenwood, and Marvin Lavin. (1978). *Criminal Careers of Habitual Felons*. U.S. Department of Justice: National Institute of Law Enforcement and Criminal Justice.

Phelps, Charles E. (1988). "Death and taxes: an opportunity for substitution." *Journal of Health Economics* 7 (1): 1–24.

Picone, Gabriel A., Frank A. Sloan, and Justin G. Trogdon. (2004). "The effect of the tobacco settlement and smoking bans on alcohol consumption." *Health Economics* 13 (10): 1063–80.

Pierson, Christopher T., and Lelia B. Helms. (2000). "Liquor and lawsuits: Forty years of litigation over alcohol on campus." *West's Education Law Reporter* 142: 609–25.

Pigou, Arthur C. (1962). *A Study in Public Finance*, 3rd. ed. London: Macmillan.

Pogue, Thomas F., and Larry G. Sgontz. (1989). "Taxing to control social costs: The case of alcohol." *American Economic Review* 79 (1): 235–43.

Polich, J. Michael, and Bruce R. Orvis. (A Project Air Force report prepared for the United States Air Force). (1979). *Alcohol Problems: Patterns and Prevalence in the U.S. Air Force*. Rand Corporation, R-2308-AF. Rand Corporation, June.

Popham, Robert E., and Wolfgang Schmidt. (1981). "Words and deeds: The validity of self report data on alcohol consumption." *Journal of Studies on Alcohol* 42 (3): 355–58.

Portney, Paul R. (1981). "Housing prices, health effects, and valuing reductions in the risk of death." *Journal of Environmental Economics and Management* 8 (1): 72–8.

Poterba, James M. (1989). "Lifetime incidence and the distributional burden of excise taxes." *American Economic Review* 79 (2): 325–33.

Prendergast, Michael L. (1987). "A history of alcohol problem prevention efforts in the United States." In Harold Holder (ed.), *Advances in Substance Abuse: Behavioral and Biological Research*, 25–52. Greenwich, CT: JAI Press.

Rees, Daniel I., Laura Argys, and Susan Averett. (2001). "New evidence on the relationship between substance use and adolescent sexual behavior," *Journal of Health Economics* 20 (5): 835–45.

Rehm, Jürgen. (1998). "Measuring quantity, frequency, and volume of drinking." *Alcoholism: Clinical and Experimental Research* 22 (2): 4S–14S.

Rehm, Jürgen, Gerhard Gmel, Christopher T. Sempos, and Maurizio Trevisan. (2003). "Alcohol-related morbidity and mortality." *Alcohol Research & Health* 27 (1): 39–51.

Rehm, Jürgen, Thomas K. Greenfield, and John D. Rogers. (2001). "Average volume of alcohol consumption, patterns of drinking, and all-cause mortality: results from the U.S. National Alcohol Survey." *American Journal of Epidemiology* 153 (1): 64–71.

Rehm, Jürgen, Elisabeth Gutjahr, and Gerhard Gmel. (2001). "Alcohol and all-cause mortality: a pooled analysis." *Contemporary Drug Problems* 28 (3): 337–62.

Rice, Dorothy P., Sander Kelman, Leonard S. Miller, and Sarah Dunmeyer. (1990). *The Economic Costs of Alcohol and Drug Abuse and Mental Illness: 1985.* Office of Financing and Coverage Policy of the Alcohol, Drug Abuse, and Mental Health Administration. University of California, San Francisco: U.S. Department of Health and Human Services, Institute for Health & Aging.

Roberts, James S. (1984). *Temperance and the Working Class in Nineteenth Century Germany.* Boston: Allen & Unwin.

Room, Robin. (1983). "Alcohol and crime: behavioral aspects." In Sanford H. Kadish (ed.), *Encyclopedia of crime and justice*, vol. 1., 35 New York: The Free Press.

Room, Robin. (1984). "Alcohol control and public health." *American Review of Public Health* 5: 293–317.

Room, Robin. (1989). "The U.S. general population's experiences of responding to alcohol problems." *British Journal of Addiction* 84, 1291–1304.

Room, Robin. (2004). "Drinking and coming of age in a cross-cultural perspective." In Richard J. Bonnie and Mary Ellen O'Connell (eds.), *Reducing Underage Drinking: A Collective Responsibility*, 654–77. Washington, DC: National Academies Press.

Rosen, Harvey S. (1980). "What is labor supply and do taxes affect it?" *American Economic Review* 70 (2): 171–76.

Ross, H. Laurence. (1973). "Law, science, and accidents: The British Road Safety Act of 1967." *Journal of Legal Studies* 2: 1–78.

Ruhm, Christopher J. (1995). "Economic conditions and alcohol problems." *Journal of Health Economics* 14 (5): 583–603.

Ruhm, Christopher J. (1996). "Alcohol policies and highway vehicle fatalities." *Journal of Health Economics* 15, 435–54.

Rumbarger, John J. (1989). *Profits, Power, and Prohibition: Alcohol Reform and the Industrializing of America 1800–1930*. Albany: University of New York Press.

Saffer, Henry, and Frank J. Chaloupka. (1994). "Alcohol tax equalization and social costs." *Eastern Economic Journal* 20 (1): 33–43.

Saffer, Henry, and Frank J. Chaloupka. (1999). "Demographic differentials in the demand for alcohol and illicit drugs." In Frank J. Chaloupka, Michael Grossman, Warren K. Bickel, and Henry Saffer (eds.), *The Economic Analysis of Substance Use and Abuse: An Integration of Econometric and Behavioral Economic Research*, 187–211. Chicago: University of Chicago Press.

Saffer, Henry, and Michael Grossman. (1987a). "Beer taxes, the legal drinking age, and youth motor vehicle fatalities." *Journal of Legal Studies* 16: 351–74.

Saffer, Henry, and Michael Grossman. (1987b). "Drinking age laws and highway mortality rates: Cause and effect." *Economic Inquiry* 25 (3): 403–17.

Saffer, Henry, Michael Grossman, and Frank Chaloupka. (1998). "Alcohol control." In Peter Newman (ed.), *The New Palgrave Dictionary of Economics and the Law*. London: Macmillan Reference, 1: 44–48.

Sammartino, Frank. (1990). *Federal Taxation of Tobacco, Alcoholic Beverages, and Motor Fuels*. Washington, DC: Congressional Budget Office.

Sass, Tim R. (2005). "The competitive effects of exclusive dealing: evidence from the US beer industry." *International Journal of Industrial Organization* 23 (3–4): 203–25.

Sass, Tim R., and David S. Saurman. (1995). "Advertising restrictions and concentration: the case of malt beverages." *Review of Economics and Statistics* 77 (1):, 66–81.

Schelling, Thomas C. (1968). "The life you save may be your own." In Samuel B. Chase (ed.), *Problems in Public Expenditure and Analysis*, 127–62. Washington, DC: Brookings Institution.

Schelling, Thomas C. (1980). "The intimate contest for self-command." *The Public Interest* 60: 94–118.

Schmidt, Wolfgang, and Robert E. Popham. (1978). "The single distribution theory of alcohol consumption: A rejoinder to the critique of Parker and Harman." *Journal of Studies on Alcohol* 39 (3): 400–19.

Scribner, Richard A., David P. MacKinnon, and James H. Dwyer. (1994). "Alcohol outlet density and motor vehicle crashes in Los Angeles County cities." *Journal of Studies on Alcohol* 55 (4): 47–53.

Scrivo, Karen Lee. (1998). "Drinking on campus." *CQ Researcher* 8 (11): 243–63.

Seeley, John R. (1960). "Death by liver cirrhosis and the price of beverage alcohol." *Canadian Medical Association Journal* 83: 1361.

Shavell, Steven. (1986). "The judgment-proof problem." *International Review of Law and Economics* 6 (1): 45–58.

Shenon, Philip. (1991). "War in the Gulf: Troops; Some G.I.'s in Gulf vanquish an old foe: Drink or drugs." *New York Times*, 1, February 18, 1.

Simon, Julian. (1966). "The economic effects of state monopoly on packaged-liquor retailing." *Journal of Political Economy* 74 (2): 188–94.

Sindelar, Jody L. (1993). "Measurement issues in alcohol survey data." In Michael E. Hilton and Gregory Bloss (eds.), *Economics and the Prevention of Alcohol-Related Problems, NIH Pub. No. 93–3513*, 201–28. Rockville, MD: National Institute on Alcohol Abuse and Alcoholism.

Single, Eric, Lynda Robson, Jrgen Rehm, and Xiaodi Xie. (1999). "Morbidity and mortality attributable to alcohol, tobacco, and illicit drug use in Canada." *American Journal of Public Health* 89 (3): 385–90.

Skog, Ole-Jørgen. (1971). *Alkoholkonsumets Fordeling I Befolkningen*. Mimeo. Oslo, Norway: Statens Institutt for Alkoholforskning.

Skog, Ole-Jørgen. (1980). "Is alcohol consumption lognormally distributed?" *British Journal of Addiction* 75: 169–73.

Skog, Ole-Jørgen. (1985). "The collectivity of drinking cultures: A theory of the distribution of alcohol consumption." *British Journal of Addiction* 80: 83–99.

Slemrod, Joel. (1990). "Optimal taxation and optimal tax systems." *Journal of Economic Perspectives* 4 (1): 157–78.

Sloan, Frank A., and Penny B. Githens. (1994). "Drinking, driving, and the price of automobile insurance." *Journal of Risk and Insurance* 61 (1): 33–58.

Sloan, Frank A., Bridget A. Reilly, and Christopher Schenzler. (1995). "Effects of tort liability and insurance on heavy drinking and drinking and driving." *Journal of Law and Economics* 38: 49–77.

Sloan, Frank A., Bridget A. Reilly, and Christopher Schenzler (1994). "Effects of prices, civil and criminal sanctions, and law enforcement on alcohol-related mortality." *Journal of Studies on Alcohol* 55: 454–65.

Sloan, Frank A., Emily Stout, Kathryn Whetten-Goldstein, and L. Liang. (2000). *Drinkers, Drivers, and Bartenders: Balancing Private Choices and Public Accountability*. Chicago: University of Chicago Press.

Smith, Gordon S., Charles C. Branas, and Ted R. Miller. (1999). "Fatal nontraffic injuries involving alcohol: A meta-analysis." *Annals of Emergency Medicine* 33 (6): 659–68.

Smith, Suzanne M., Richard A. Goodman, Stephen B. Thacker, Anthony H. Burton, John E. Parsons, and Page Hudson. (1989). "Alcohol and fatal injuries: Temporal patterns." *American Journal of Preventive Medicine* 5 (5): 296–302.

Sobell, Linda C., John A. Cunningham, and Mark B. Sobell. (1996). "Recovery from alcohol problems with and without treatment: Prevalence in two population surveys." *American Journal of Public Health* 86: 966–72.

Steele, Claude M., and Robert A. Josephs. (1990). "Alcohol myopia: Its prized and dangerous effects." *American Psychologist* 45 (8): 921–33.

Stinson, Fredrick S., Sainer F. DeBakey, and Rebecca A. Steffens. (1992). "Prevalence of DSM-III-R alcohol abuse and/or dependence among selected occupations." *Alcohol Health & Research World* 16 (2): 165–72.

Stout, David. (2005). "Supreme Court strikes down bans on wine shipments." *New York Times*, May 16.

Strumpf, Koleman S., and Felix Oberholzer-Gee. (2000). "Local liquor control from 1934 to 1970." In Jack C. Heckelman, John C. Moorhouse, and Robert M. Whaples (eds.), *Public Choice Interpretations of American Economic History*, 1–20. Boston: Kluwer.

Strumpf, Koleman S., and Felix Oberholzer-Gee. (2002). "Endogenous policy decentralization: Testing the central tenet of economic federalism." *Journal of Political Economy* 110 (1): 1–36.

Substance Abuse and Mental Health Administration. (2003). *Alcohol and Drug Services Study (ADSS): The National Substance Abuse Treatment System: Facilities, Clients, Services, and Staffing*. Rockville, MD: Office of Applied Studies.

Substance Abuse and Mental Health Services Administration. (2003). *DASIS Series: S-20 Treatment Episode Data Set (TEDS): 1992–2001. National Admissions to Substance Abuse Treatment Services*. In DHHS Publication No. (SMA) 03–3778. Rockville, MD: Office of Applied Studies.

Sulkunen, Pekka. (1983). "Alcohol consumption and the transformation of living conditions: A comparative study." In Reginald G. Smart, Fredrick B. Glaser, Yedy Israel, Harold Kalant, Robert E. Popham, and Wolfgang Schmidt (eds.), *Research Advances in Alcohol and Drug Problems, Vol. 7*, 247–97. New York: Plenum Publishing.

Sweat, Noah. (1948). (1997). "Speech." In William Safire (ed.), *Lend Me Your Ears: Great Speeches in History*, 877. New York: Norton.

Tachau, Mary K. Bonsteel. (1985). "A new look at the Whiskey Rebellion." In Steven R. Boyd (ed.), *The Whiskey Rebellion: Past and Present Perspectives*, 97–118. Westport, CT: Greenwood Press.

Terris, Milton. (1967). "Epidemiology of cirrhosis of the liver: national mortality data." *American Journal of Public Health* 57, 2076–88.

Thaler, Richard H., and Hersh M. Shefrin. (1981). "An economic theory of self-control." *Journal of Political Economy* 89 (June): 643–60.

Thaler, Richard H., and Cass R. Sunstein. (2003). "Libertarian paternalism." *American Economic Review* 93 (2): 175–9.

Thaler, Richard, and Sherwin Rosen. (1975). "The value of saving a life: Evidence from the labor market." In N. E. Terleckyj (ed.), *Household Production and Consumption*, 265–300. New York: Columbia University Press.

Thomasson, Richard. (1998). "Alcohol and alcohol control in Sweden." *Scandinavian Studies* 70 (4): 477–508.

Thun, Michael J., Richard Peto, Alan D. Lopez, Jane H. Monaco, S. Jane Henley, Clark W. Heath Jr., and Richard Doll. (1997). "Alcohol consumption and mortality among middle-aged and elderly U.S. adults." *New England Journal of Medicine* 337 (24): 1705–14.

Timberlake, James H. (1963). *Prohibition and the Progressive Movement, 1900–1920*. Cambridge, MA: Harvard University Press.

Todd, J. E. (1882). Drunkenness as a vice, not as a disease. Read at the General Association at Middletown, June 21.

Tremblay, Victor J., and Carol Horton Tremblay. (2005). *The U.S. Brewing Industry: Data and Economic Analysis*. Cambridge, MA: MIT Press.

Trice, Harrison M., and William J. Sonnenstuhl. (1988). "Drinking behavior and risk factors related to the work place: Implications for research and prevention." *Journal of Applied Behavioral Science* 24 (4): 327–46.

Twisk, Jos W. R, Han C. G. Kemper, William Van Mechelen, and G. Bertheke Post. (2001). "Clustering of risk factors for coronary heart disease: the longitudinal relationship with lifestyle." *Annals of Epidemiology* 11 (3): 157–65.

U.S. Census Bureau. (2003). *Statistical Abstract of the United States: 2003*. http://www.census.gov/prod/www/statistical-abstract-03.html. U.S. Census Bureau, March 2, 2004.

U.S. Congress. (National Commission on Law Observance and Enforcement). (1931). "Wickersham Commission." *House Document Report on the Enforcement of the Prohibition Laws of the United States*. In 722. Washington, DC: Government Printing Office, 162.

U.S. Department of Commerce. (1934). *Statistical Abstract of the United States 1934*. Washington, DC: U.S. Government Printing Office.

U.S. Department of Health and Human Services. (National Center for Chronic Disease Prevention and Health Promotion). (1994). "Office on Smoking and Health." In *Preventing Tobacco Use among Young People: A Report of the Surgeon General*. Washington, DC.

U.S. Department of Labor. (As prepared by the Center for Human Resource Research). (2002). *The National Longitudinal Survey: NLSY97 User's Guide 2002*.

U.S. Deptartment of Health and Human Services. (National Institute of Health). (2000). "National Institute on Alcohol Abuse and Alcoholism." In *10th Special Report to the U.S. Congress on Alcohol and Health*. Washington, DC: Government Printing Office.

U.S. House Committee on the Judiciary. (1921). "Prohibition Legislation." In *Hearings of the 67th Congress, 1st session*, vol. serial 2.

Vaillant, George E. (1983). *The Natural History of Alcoholism*. Cambridge, MA: Harvard University Press.

Vallee, Bert L. (1998). "Alcohol in the Western World." *Scientific American* 278 (6): 80–85.

van Ours, Jan C. (2004). "A pint a day raises a man's pay; but smoking blows that gain away." *Journal of Health Economics* 23, 863–86.

Vaupel, James W., and Philip J. Cook. (1978). "Life, liberty and the pursuit of self-hazardous behavior." Working paper. Durham, NC: Duke University, Institute of Policy Sciences and Public Affairs.

Viscusi, W. Kip. (1993). "The value of risks to life and health." *Journal of Economic Literature* 31 (4): 1912–46.

Viscusi, W. Kip. (2004). "The value of life: Estimates with risks by occupation and industry." *Economic Inquiry* 42 (1): 29–48.

Voas, Robert B., and Deborah A. Fisher. (2001). "Court procedures for handling intoxicated drivers." *Alcohol Research & Health* 25 (1): 32–42.

Voas, Robert B., JoAnn Wells, Diane Lestina, Alan Williams, and Michael Greene. (1997). "Drinking and driving in the U.S.: 1996 National Roadside Survey." *Accident Analysis & Prevention* 30 (2): 1159–66.

Vuchinich, Rudy E., and Cathy E. Simpson. (1999). "Delayed reward discounting in alcohol abuse." In Frank J. Chaloupka, Michael Grossman, Warren K. Bickel, and Henry Saffer (eds.), *The Economic Analysis of Substance Use and Abuse: An Integration of Econometric and Behavioral Economic Research*, 103–22. Chicago: University of Chicago Press.

Wagenaar, Alexander C. (1993). "Research affects public policy: The case of the legal drinking age in the United States." *Addiction* 88 (Suppl.): 75S–81S.

Wagenaar, Alexander C., Traci L. Toomey, David M. Murray, Brian J. Short, Mark Wolfson, and Rhonda Jones-Webb. (1996). "Sources of alcohol for underage drinkers." *Journal of Studies on Alcohol* 57: 325–33.

Wagenaar, Alexander C., Eileen M. Harwood, Traci L. Toomey, Charles E. Denk, and Kay M. Zander. (2000). "Public opinion on alcohol policies in the United States: results from a national survey." *Journal of Public Health Policy* 21 (3): 303–27.

Wagenaar, Alexander C., and Harold D. Holder. (1991). "Effects of alcoholic beverage server liability on traffic crash injuries." *Alcoholism: Clinical and Experimental Research* 15 (6): 942–7.

Wagenaar, Alexander C., and Traci L. Toomey. (2002). "Effects of minimum drinking age laws: Review and analyses of the literature from 1960 to 2000." *Journal of Studies on Alcohol* (Suppl. 14): 206–25.

Walsh, Dana C. (1982). "Employee Assistance Programs." *Milbank Memorial Fund Quarterly/Health and Society* 60 (3): 492–517.

Warburton, Clark. (1932). *The Economic Results of Prohibition*. New York: Columbia University Press.

Warburton, Clark. (1934). "Prohibition." In Edwin R. Seligman (ed.), *Encyclopedia of the Social Sciences*, vol. 12, 499–510. New York: MacMillan.

Wasserman, Danuta, Airi Värnik, and Gunnar Eklund. (1994). "Male suicides and alcohol consumption in the former USSR." *Acta Psychiatrica Scandinavica* 89: 306–13.

Watts, Ronald K., and Jerome Rabow. (1983). "Alcohol availability and alcohol-related problems in 213 California cities." *Alcoholism: Clinical and Experimental Research* 7: 47–58.

Wechsler, Henry, Andrea Davenport, George Dowdall, Barbara Moeykens, and Sonia Castillo. (1994). "Health and behavioral consequences of binge drinking in college." *Journal of the American Medical Association* 272 (21): 1672–77.

Wechsler, Henry, Jae Eun Lee, Meichun Kuo, Mark Seibering, and Toben F. Nelson. (2002). "Trends in college binge drinking during a period of increased prevention efforts; findings from 4 Harvard School of Public Health College Alcohol Study Surveys: 1993–2001." *Journal of American College Health* 50 (5): 203–17.

Wechsler, Henry, Barbara A. Moeykens, and William DeJong. (1995). *Enforcing the Minimum Age Drinking Law: A Survey of College Administrators and Security Chiefs*. Newton, MA: Education Development Center. http://www.edc.org/hec/.

Wechsler, Henry, Mark Seibring, I-Chao Liu, and Marilyn Ahl. (2004). "Colleges respond to student binge drinking: Reducing student demand or limiting access." *Journal of American College Health* 52 (4): 159–68.

Weed, Frank J. (1987). "Grass-roots activism and the drunk driving issue." *Law and Policy* 9: 259–78.

Whitlock, Evelyn P., Michael R. Polen, Carla A. Green, C. Tracy Orleans, and Jonathan Klein. (2004). "Behavioral counseling interventions in primary care to reduce risky/harmful alcohol use by adults: a summary of the evidence for the U.S. Preventive Services Task Force." *Annals of Internal Medicine* 140 (7): 557–68.

Whitman, Douglas Glen. (2003). *Strange Brew: Alcohol and Government Monopoly.* Oakland, CA: The Independent Institute.

Williams, Allan F., Paul L. Zador, Sandra S. Harris, and Ronald S. Karpf. (1983). "The effect of raising the legal minimum drinking age on involvement in fatal crashes." *Journal of Legal Studies* 12: 169–79.

Williams, Jenny, Roaslie Liccardo Pacula, Frank J. Chaloupka, and Henry Wechsler. (2001). "Alcohol and marijuana use among college students: Economic complements or substitutes?" National Bureau of Economic Research Working Paper No. 8401. National Bureau of Economic Research, July.

Wilson, R. J. (1992). "Convicted impaired drivers and high-risk drivers: How similar are they?" *Journal of Studies on Alcohol* 46 (6): 531–7.

Windle, Michael. (2003). "Alcohol use among adolescents and young adults." *Alcohol Research & Health* 27 (1): 79–86.

Wiseman, Alan E., and Jerry Ellig. (2004). "Market and nonmarket barriers to Internet wine sales: The case of Virginia." *Business and Politics* 6 (2): Article 4.

Wolaver, Amy M. (2002). "Effects of heavy drinking in college on study effort, grade point average, and major choice." *Contemporary Economic Policy* 20 (4): 415–28.

Wolkenberg, R. C., C. Gold, and E. R. Tichauer. (1975). "Delayed effects of acute alcohol intoxication on performance with reference to work safety." *Journal of Safety Research* 7 (3): 104–18.

Yoon, Young-Hee, Hsiao-ye Yi, Bridget F. Grant, Fredrick S. Stinson, and Mary C. Dufour. (2003). *Liver cirrhosis mortality in the United States, 1970–2000.* National Institute on Alcohol Abuse and Alcoholism, Surveillance Report #63. Arlington, VA: CSR, August.

Yoshimoto, K., M. Hori, Y. Sorimachi, T. Watanabe, T. Tano, and M. Yasuhara. (2002). "Increase of rat alcohol drinking behavior depends on the age of drinking onset." *Alcoholism: Clinical and Experimental Research* 26 (8): 63S–65S.

Young, Douglas J., and Agnieszka Bielinska-Kwapisz. (2002). "Alcohol taxes and beverage prices." *National Tax Journal* 55 (1): 57–74.

Young, Douglas J., and Agnieszka Bielinska-Kwapisz. (2003). "Alcohol consumption, beverage prices and measurement error." *Journal of Studies on Alcohol* 64 (2): 235–8.

Zador, Paul L., Sheila A. Krawchuk, and Robert B. Voas. (2000). "Alcohol related relative risk of driver fatalities and driver involvement in fatal crashes in relation to driver age and gender: An update using 1996 data." *Journal of Studies on Alcohol* 61 (3): 387–95.

Zarkin, Gary A., Michael T. French, Thomas A. Mroz, and Jeremy W. Bray. (1998). "Alcohol use and wages: New results from the National Household Survey on Drug Abuse." *Journal of Health Economics* 17 (1): 53–68.

Zeigler, Donald W., Claire C. Wang, Richard A. Yoast, Barry D. Dickinson, Mary Anne McCaffree, Carolyn B. Robinowitz, and Melvyn L. Sterling. (2005). "The neurocognitive effects of alcohol on adolescents and college students." *Preventive Medicine* 40 (1): 23–32.

Zimring, Franklin E. (1982). *The Changing Legal World of Adolescence*. New York: Free Press.

Index

Aaron, Paul, 13, 16, 19–20AARP, 27
abstinence, 58, 76; income and, 122; price and, 77; reasons for, 66–67. *See also* Alcoholics Anonymous (AA); temperance movements
Adams Beverage Group, 155
Adams Business Media, 63
Addiction Research Foundation, 110
Air Force Qualification Test, 124
Alabama, 53, 72
alcohol: absorption rates and, 84; attributable portion and, 86–91; availability issues and, 157–64; black market and, 19, 26–27, 29–32; blood alcohol concentration (BAC) and, 84–89, 91–92, 100, 188; bootleggers and, 26; consumption measurement of, 50–64; as drug, 83–85, 168–69, 196; ethyl, 49–50; habit formation and, 75–78, 182–83; home production and, 18–19; industrial use of, 19; interstate shipments and, 18; as luxury item, 26; medical use of, 19; metabolization of, 84; as poison, 17; price of, 1–2 (*see also* price); production of, 49–50; productivity effects of, 120–30; proof number and, 50; pure, 50; as sedative, 84; supply regulation and, 148–64; taxes for, 4–5 (*see also* taxes)
alcohol abuse, xii; community-oriented approach and, 3–4; defined, 40; denial and, 55; drunk driving and, 85–89, 96–101; evidence assessment and, 6–7; habit formation and, 75–78, 182–83; health issues and, 2 (*see also* health issues); individual responsibility and, 201; mortality curves and, 112–13, 116, 169–70; national cost of, 145–47; public response to, xi, 1
Alcohol and Drug Service Study, 41
Alcohol and Longevity (Pearl), 107
Alcohol and Public Policy (National Academy of Sciences), 3
Alcohol and Tobacco Tax and Trade Bureau, 152

alcohol beverage control (ABC) systems, 29, 156, 158, 160–64, 189–90, 217n6
alcohol-breath analyzers, 150
alcohol control: ABC systems and, 29, 156, 158, 160–64, 189–90, 217n6; Alcoholics Anonymous (AA) and, 34–36, 40–41; blacklisting and, 18; cops-in-shops operations and, 189; effectiveness of, 197–99; Food Control Law and, 18; as injury prevention, 82–106; interventions and, 133–47; keg registration and, 190; learner's permits and, 183–84, 194; licensing and, 28–29, 150, 157–61; post-Repeal era and, 27–33; Prohibition and, 2–3, 5, 7, 13, 16–33, 65, 157–58, 188; rationing and, 149–64; Reed "bone-dry" Amendment and, 18; Russia and, 92, 117–18; sexually transmitted diseases (STDs) and, 101–2; supply regulation and, 148–64; targeted policies and, 148–51; taxes and, 13–15, 165–78 (*see also* taxes); Twenty-first Amendment and, 13, 27, 29, 92; twenty-first-century policies and, 196–201; voluntary self-control and, 29–30; Webb-Kenyon Act of 1913 and, 18; youths and, 179–95
Alcohol Control Policies in Public Health Perspective (Bruun), 65
alcohol-free drinks, 60
Alcoholics Anonymous (AA), 8, 139; alcoholism movement and, 35–45; core ideas of, 35; origins of, 34–35
alcohol industry: aggregate sales evidence and, 69–73; blacklisting and, 18; Commerce Clause and, 155; commerce restriction and, 133–37, 144–45; *Costco v. Hoen* and, 148; French paradox and, 110–11; home consumption and, 63; industry structure and, 151–57; licensing and, 150, 157–61; market research and, 153; multiple determinants of demand and, 66–69; office parties and, 64; Pareto Law and, 56; price and, 151–57 (*see also* price); privatized package sales and,

Cabot, Richard C., 111
CAGE protocol, 43, 122
Canada, xi, 3–4, 69, 119; Addiction Research Foundation and, 110; Centre for Addiction and Mental Health and, 198; cirrhosis and, 109; consumption rates in, 52; suicide and, 118; supply side economics and, 19, 27–28; youths and, 185
cancer, 112
Capitalism and Freedom (Friedman), 136
cardiovascular disease (CVD). *See* heart disease
Carnevale, Dan, 189
Carpenter, Christopher, 79, 91, 100, 102, 188
Center for Science in the Public Interest, 173, 177
Centers for Disease Control and Prevention, 85, 108, 118
Centre for Addiction and Mental Health, 198
Chafetz, Morris, 184
Chaloupka, Frank J., 158, 177–78, 190
Changing Legal World of Adolescence, The (Zamring), 179
Chatterji, Pinka, 102
Chesson, Harrell W., 101
Cho, Young Ik, 68
cholesterol, 110–11, 115
cirrhosis, 25, 107, 112, 118; alcohol control and, 103–4; deaths from, 108–9; gender and, 109; RASPP method and, 109; single distribution theory and, 109–10, 198
civil liability, 176
Clark, Norman H., 17, 207n7
Clements, Kenneth W., 69
Cohen, Mark A., 142
Collins, James J., Jr., 90–91
Commerce Clause, 155
complement effect, 79–81
consumption. *See* drinking
Cook, Philip J., 56; alcohol control and, 90–91, 96–97, 102, 196; drinker's bonus and, 126–27, 129; health issues and, 109–10, intervention evaluation and, 140, 142–43, 147; price and, 69, 71, 76, 78; supply regulation and, 151; taxes and, 165, 169–70, 172, 178; youths and, 182, 184, 188, 193
Coolidge administration, 19
Cooper, Daniel, 68, 186
Coors, 152–53

Corlett, Wilfred J., 176
Corrao, Giovanni, 111, 113, 117
Costco, 148, 156
cost-of-illness (COI) method, 141–47
crack-cocaine, 196
Criqui, Michael H., 110
Currie, Candace, 184
Cutler, David, 91

Dawson, Deborah A., 51, 56, 181
DeBakey, Sainer F., 67
DeBold, Joseph F., 90
Deckelbaum, Richard J., 111
Declaration of Independence, 133
Dee, Thomas, 80, 101, 182
DeJong, William, 192
Delaware, 53
De Lint, Jan, 110
Democratic National Convention of 1932, 20–21
Demone, Harold W., Jr., 184
Denmark, 27
detox, 41
Dexter, Edwin G., 68
Diagnostic and Statistical Manual of Mental Disorders (DSM) (American Psychiatric Association), 40, 128
Diamond, Peter, 175
Dills, Angela K., 18, 24
Disease Concept of Alcoholism, The (Jellinek), 35
District of Columbia, 4, 156–57, 204
disulfiram, 42–43
Dobson, Annette, 113–14
Donovan, Catharine, 88
Dougherty, Donald M., 90
Douglass, Duncan Baird, 155
dram-shop liability, 161–63
Draper, Brian, 91
drinker's bonus: income and, 122–30; other variables and, 124–26; productivity effects and, 120–30; reverse causation and, 126–30
drinking, 49; absorption rates and, 84; age and, 59, 75–79 (*see also* youths); aggregate data for, 50–51; alcohol content and, 50; Anstie's Rule and, 113; attributable portion and, 86–91; availability issues and, 157–64; benefits of moderate, 110–19; binge, 59, 180, 193–94; blood alcohol concentration (BAC) and, 84–89, 91–92, 100, 188; cirrhosis and, 25, 103–

Strumpf, Koleman S., 158
Substance Abuse and Mental Health Services Administration, 41
suicide, 91–92, 102–3, 118, 181
Sunstein, Cass, 139
surveys, 53–55; campus environment and, 190–91; distributional analysis and, 56–64; drunk driving and, 87–88; Epidemiological Catchment Area and, 128; group patterns and, 58–60; mortality curves and, 112–13, 116, 169–70; multivariate logit regressions and, 58–63; National Alcohol Survey and, 56, 209n7; National Longitudinal Survey of Youth (NLSY) and, 56, 122, 125–26, 181–82, 191; productivity studies and, 120–30
Swahn, Monica H., 90
Swartzwelder, Scott, 84
Sweat, Noah, 197
Sweden, 27, 69, 149

Tapert, Susan F., 181
Tauchen, George, xii, 71, 96–97, 109, 188
taxes, xi, 1, 6, 8, 82, 130, 178, 200; ad valorem, 174; aggregate drinking data and, 50–53, 91; Appalachian farmers and, 14; beer and, 155; black market and, 169; case for uniform, 176–77; Civil War era and, 15; corruption and, 15; decreasing of, 165; drunk driving and, 99–101; efficiency and, 174–76; excise, 14–15, 51, 165–67, 210n2, 214n14; fairness and, 170–74; First Law of Economics and, 66; historical perspective on, 13–15, 165–67; incidence and, 173–74; income and, 176; liquor industry and, 144–45, 165–78; low collection rates and, 30–31; methodology for, 203; minimum-legal-drinking-age (MLDA) and, 99–101; Pigovian, 175; price and, 69–75; Prohibition and, 21, 23; proof gallon, 51, 203; public safety and, 167–70; raising of, 15; RASPP method and, 168–69; regulatory variety and, 9–10; revenue from, 15; state legislatures and, 4–5; sumptuary role of, 13–14; tobacco and, 4, 166–67; U.S. Bureau of Internal Revenue and, 31–32; vertical equity and, 173–74; voluntary self-control and, 29–30; whiskey, 2, 7, 14–15, 165
Taylor, Frederick W., 18

technology, 22; alcohol-breath analyzers and, 150; Fatal Accident Reporting System (FARS) and, 87–88
teetotalers, 19
Temperance and Prohibition in America (Aaron and Musto), 13
temperance movements, 32, 35, 49, 157; Anti-Saloon League and, 2, 16–17, 20; blacklisting and, 18; business community and, 17–18; family and, 17; political clout of, 17; rationing and, 149; Women's Christian Temperance Union, 2, 17
Terris, Milton, 3, 24, 109
Thaler, Richard, 139, 143
Theory of Moral Sentiments, The (Smith), 134
Thomasson, Richard, 149
Thun, Michael J., 111–13
Thurber, James, 34
Tichauer, E. R., 121
Timberlake, James H., 17
tobacco, 5, 110; complement effect and, 79–81; drinking and, 79–81; gender and, 112; interventions and, 137–38, 140; Master Settlement Agreement and, 80–81; persona of, 79; taxes and, 4, 166–67; youths and, 183–84
Todd, J. E., 36
Toomey, Traci L., 97, 187
Toward Liquor Control (Fosdick and Scott), 27, 165
treatment, 1, 8, 45; Alcoholics Anonymous (AA) and, 40–41; detox and, 41; evaluation of, 41–42; medical interventions and, 40, 43–44; professional, 40; variety of approaches to, 41–42
Treatment Episode Data Set (TEDS), 41, 208n2
Tremblay, Carol Horton, 152–54
Tremblay, Victor J., 152–54
Trogdon, Justin G. 80
Twenty-first Amendment, 13, 27, 29, 92, 152, 155
Twenty-sixth Amendment, 92, 186
twins, 39

Ulysses, 138
United Kingdom, xi, 27; British Stamp Act and, 14; consumption rates in, 52; New South Wales study and, 113–14; price